NICKELODEON CITY

NICKELODEON

UNIVERSITY OF PITTSBURGH PRESS

CITY

Pittsburgh at the Movies, 1905–1929

MICHAEL ARONSON

Published by the University of Pittsburgh Press, Pittsburgh, Pa., 15260

Copyright © 2008, University of Pittsburgh Press

All rights reserved

Manufactured in the United States of America

Printed on acid-free paper

10 9 8 7 6 5 4 3 2 1

Library of Congress Cataloging-in-Publication Data

Aronson, Michael (Michael G.)
  Nickelodeon city : Pittsburgh at the movies, 1905–1929 / Michael Aronson.
    p. cm.
  Includes bibliographical references and index.
  ISBN-13: 978-0-8229-4322-8 (cloth : alk. paper)
  ISBN-10: 0-8229-4322-0 (cloth : alk. paper)
  1. Motion pictures—Pennsylvania—Pittsburgh—History. I. Title.
  PN1993.5.U775A76 2008
  791.4309748'86—dc22

                    2008020101

The material in chapter 2 was first published as: "The Wrong Kind of Nickel Madness: Pricing Problems for Pittsburgh Nickelodeons," *Cinema Journal* 42, no. 1: 71–96. Copyright © 2002 by the University of Texas Press. All rights reserved.

The material in chapter 5 was first published as "Charlie Silveus Makes a Quotidian Spectacle: An Exhibitor-Filmmaker and His Local View," *Moving Image* 5, no. 2 (Fall 2005): 1–25, and is reprinted here with the permission of the University of Minnesota Press.

All figures taken from the *Pittsburgh Moving Picture Bulletin* are courtesy of the Library and Archives Division of the Western Pennsylvania Historical Society, Pittsburgh, Pa.

This book belongs to Keri, Eliza, & Ruby

CONTENTS

List of Illustrations — ix
Preface — xi
Acknowledgments — xv

1 NICKELS AND STEEL: An Introduction — 1

2 THE EPONYMOUS NICKELODEON — 16

3 THE WRONG KIND OF NICKEL MADNESS — 50

4 SWATTING FLIES AND WINNING CHICKENS — 104

5 THE MORALS OF THE MOVIES — 154

6 THE LOCAL VIEW — 208

EPILOGUE — 248

Notes — 255
Index — 289

LIST OF ILLUSTRATIONS

	George Callahan on the cover of *Pittsburgh Moving Picture Bulletin*, December 18, 1914	xiii
Fig. 1.1.	Theatorium, circa 1914	2
Fig. 1.2.	"Penn Ave., looking East, East Liberty, Pittsburg, Pa.," postcard, circa 1914	10
Fig. 1.3.	View of the Strip District, circa 1925	14
Fig. 2.1.	Thomas L. Tally, circa 1900	24
Fig. 2.2.	Bijou Theatre interior, circa 1900	30
Fig. 2.3.	Grand Opera House, circa 1900	32
Fig. 2.4.	Map of downtown Pittsburgh, circa 1905	38
Fig. 2.5.	Exterior of the Nickelodeon opened by Harris and Davis	45
Fig. 2.6.	Interior of the Nickelodeon opened by Harris and Davis	45
Fig. 2.7.	Pittsburgh's Bijou Dream, circa 1906	47
Fig. 2.8.	Harris and Davis's Nickelodeon from across Smithfield Street	48
Fig. 3.1.	The cover of the inaugural *Pittsburgh Moving Picture Bulletin*, April 15, 1914	55
Fig. 3.2.	"The Fourth Avenue Section of Film Row"	58
Fig. 3.3.	"Directory of the Seltzer Building"	58
Fig. 3.4.	Richard A. Rowland, portrait by W. S. Wasburn	60
Fig. 3.5.	Calcium Light and Film advertisement, 1906	61
Fig. 3.6.	Western Film Company advertisement, 1914	71
Fig. 3.7.	*The Lure of New York* advertisement, 1914	75
Fig. 3.8.	A "demonstration banquet" held by Mayer Silverman, October 28, 1914	77
Fig. 3.9.	Map of Pittsburgh, circa 1914	79
Fig. 3.10.	Regent Theater, exterior, circa 1915	81
Fig. 3.11.	Regent Theater, interior lobby, circa 1915	82
Fig. 3.12.	Regent Theater, interior, circa 1915	83
Fig. 3.13.	C. A. Graninger, caricature by George S. Applegarth	84
Fig. 3.14.	P. J. Demas, caricature by George S. Applegarth	101

Fig. 4.1.	"Swat the Fly" booklet illustration by Ernest Hamlin Baker, circa 1910	108
Fig. 4.2.	Feature on Mike Ray of Warner Brothers, 1914	117
Fig. 4.3.	*The Three of Us* advertisement, 1914	123
Fig. 4.4.	Famous Players Film Service advertisement, 1914	125
Fig. 4.5.	"Stars, Stars, Nothing But Stars" advertisement, 1915	126
Fig. 4.6.	Mayer Publishing and Printing advertisement for "Chaplin Cuts," 1915	127
Fig. 4.7.	Liberty Film Renting Company advertisement for Pincus, the Chaplin imitator, 1915	129
Fig. 4.8.	*The Shielding Shadow* serial advertisement with images of Pittsburgh exhibitors, 1916	134
Fig. 4.9.	S. Van Lewen advertisement for movie poster paper, 1914	143
Fig. 4.10.	"Local ballyhoo artist" Tex Arthur, 1923	147
Fig. 4.11.	Major William H. McCloskey as "the original drummer boy of Winchester," 1914	148
Fig. 4.12.	Universal Moviegame advertisement, 1915	152
Fig. 5.1.	*John Barleycorn* at the Garrick Theatre, Philadelphia, 1914	179
Fig. 5.2.	Application for examination, Pennsylvania State Board of Censors, circa 1915	183
Fig. 5.3.	Seal of approval, Pennsylvania State Board of Censors, circa 1915	185
Fig. 5.4.	Savoy Theater advertisement for *Three Weeks*, 1915	188
Fig. 5.5.	Specialty Film Company advertisement for *Three Weeks*, 1915	189
Fig. 5.6.	Selznick Pictures advertisement for *War Brides*, 1916	192
Fig. 5.7.	Telegram from H. J. Ruthven to Dr. Ellis Oberholtzer of the State Board of Censors, 1916	195
Fig. 5.8.	Anti-censorship banners, Pittsburgh Screen Club, 1916	200
Fig. 6.1.	Roadmen for Pittsburgh's Universal Exchange, 1920	210
Fig. 6.2.	Eclipse Theatre advertisement, 1919	219
Fig. 6.3.	Pittsburgh Commercial Motion Picture Company advertisement, 1914	219
Fig. 6.4.	Bass Camera Company advertisement, 1917	224

PREFACE

MY WIFE AND I arrived in Pittsburgh in 1995. It was a place neither of us really knew. While we were both raised in Pennsylvania, I in its rural middle and she in Philadelphia, we both found our new city at once familiar and strange, unknown in its details and possibilities. My wife worked for a trucking company, selling their shipping services in and around the city. As a new graduate student, my fresh occupational challenge was to somehow reimagine myself as a potential film historian. My former working life as an assistant cameraman on television commercials had given me few opportunities to learn about Foucault or even Edison; so without a doubt, my wife felt more at ease with her job description. In many ways, her daily tour of this working city was an ideal introduction to Pittsburgh's present, to a region whose visible surface continues to tender its contested history of capital and labor, a showing made partly out of civic pride but mostly out of an inability to fully erase the paroxysmal traces of the city's lost industrial supremacy. Increasingly, I too spent my days moving through Pittsburgh, but my travels took me across the terrain of its archived past, involving movement in time rather than space. At the end of the day, my wife and I would often compare notes about the city we each saw. Perhaps it is not surprising then, that before too long our Pittsburghs would draw near and touch. During one of my wife's cold-calling excursions into nearby McKees Rocks she met Jack Callahan, a chain-smoking businessman, who would award her a major account and give me a critical lesson in writing history.

Jack's company is located in the "Bottoms," the flat part of the "Rocks," four miles west of Pittsburgh across the Ohio River. His company is one of a number of still-operating businesses encircled by the empty mesh of train tracks once belonging to the town's long gone industries. Jack distributed magazines. A family business, it is the type of almost invisible concern that fills generic warehouses and industrial parks around the world, a small but profitable link in the logistical chain required to connect us to the endless things we consume. My wife was good at her job, in large part because she truly enjoys listening to people tell their stories, and so it was not too long before she heard the tale of Jack Callahan, his family, and what they had delivered before their warehouse was full of *Vogue* and *Cosmo*. What came before the magazines was the movies.

Sometime around 1910, George Callahan, Jack's grandfather, had an idea. George was out late one evening when he saw four boys standing together waiting for a streetcar, all carrying metal boxes of similar size and style. An inquiry brought forth that each of the young men was employed by different picture houses, their jobs to nightly transport new films to the theater and return the previously shown ones to the various local film exchanges. In a period when movie production companies were collectively making dozens of films every week and most theaters were changing their shows every day, it was immediately clear to George there were a lot of other boys out traversing the city on very similar missions. Identifying this waste of manpower as a potential business opportunity, Callahan immediately started the Exhibitors' Service Company, soon becoming *the* delivery service for Pittsburgh's growing movie business. In only a few years, Jack's grandfather had more than sixty employees moving movies around the clock, seven days a week, by trolley, train, and horse-drawn truck, to picture houses throughout western Pennsylvania, Ohio, West Virginia, and even in far-flung parts of Maryland and Kentucky.

I originally met Jack one night at a fancy restaurant during one of the recurring company-financed steak dinners that were an odd if regular part of my existence as a grad student wedded to a businesswoman. That first time I heard about George and the history of his familial business, I smiled and nodded, asked a few inane questions, and generally feigned interest. Initially, I hate to admit, both Jack and my wife found his grandfather's story more important than I did. In my defense, in the history of film that I knew of then, people like George and companies like Exhibitors' Service were largely absent. So at first, Jack's story of George seemed to me at once too small and too personal, more family history than film history. But over time that changed, or rather I changed. I began to listen, like my wife, to

George Callahan on the cover of *Pittsburgh Moving Picture Bulletin*, December 18, 1914.

the stories that I was being told, even when most of my storytellers happened to be as dead as the region's steel industry. And as my research continued further into Pittsburgh and its movie culture, I kept returning to George, not because he became increasingly critical to the history—his role as it reveals itself in the archive is common if constant throughout the 1910s and 1920s—but because he came to individually represent an invisible collective of singularities that often elude historical definition but that shape this particular past and my telling of it. Simply put, George was a real man who lived a real life, but to me he is a symbol. He is a reminder of the vast ensemble of people and practices involved in the movies at any one place and time that often fall beyond the borders of history. How exactly the past gets remembered or forgotten, whom it embraces and whom it excludes, what images it creates and explanations it offers all have a tremendous impact on the kind of stories that can be told by history. The history I propose and hope to reveal in the pages ahead is neither founded upon the inspired genius of "great men" (or even great women) nor based on broad, impenetrable forces. Rather, I draw upon George, and many others unknown and lesser known, not simply as Pittsburgh's witnesses to film history but as active and often resourceful contributors to the formation of a community and institution. Some idiosyncratic, some inventive, some lucky, some failures—all are producers of Pittsburgh's movie culture, and all are also its products, shaped by both larger structures and the host of social relations that my history and their stories describe.

ACKNOWLEDGMENTS

THIS PROJECT INITIALLY BEGAN while I was at the University of Pittsburgh and I want to first express my thanks to Jane Feuer as well as Marcia Landy, Jonathan Arac, and the late Carol Kay who all went out of their way to make me feel at home there. My biggest debts and deepest gratitude in this particular regard go to Lucy Fischer, whose kind patience helped transform me from an assistant cameraman to a film historian. Less directly, but no less significantly, Carol Stabile played a central role in my understanding of how history works. While the focus of my work does not explicitly follow in the footsteps of these two feminist scholars, I truly hope they find their efforts on my behalf worthwhile. Along with Lucy and Jane, Moya Luckett was an enthusiastic reader for this project's earliest stages and her insights into the importance of local history helped transform abstract ideas into chapters. No one does the local like Greg Waller, and I am particularly thankful to him for his wise reading and gracious mentorship throughout the process of writing this book. Jane told me, on my departure from Pittsburgh, that I would never have it so good again, and, at least in terms of my cohorts there, she was grumpily prescient: thanks to Andrew Miller, Hugh Manon, Daniel Wild, Kirsten Strayer, Allen Larson, Mark Harrison, and Dawn Schmitz for their friendship, good humor and shared sense of purpose.

The research for this study could not have been done without the professional enthusiasm and energetic cooperation of numerous librarians and archivists at the University of Pittsburgh, the Western Pennsylvania Historical Society at the Heinz History Center, the Pennsylvania State Archives in Harrisburg, the State Library in Philadelphia, Northeast Historic Film, UCLA's Art Library, and the Margaret Herrick Library of the Center for Motion Picture Academy in Los Angeles. At the University of Pittsburgh library I would particularly like to thank Ann Ronchetti and William Daw for their willingness to seek out a seemingly neverending necessary stream of materials and microfilms. The Historic Pittsburgh Web site run by the ULS Digital Research Library at the University of Pittsburgh has been a critical and much appreciated resource for this project; all historians should be so lucky to have this kind of information at their online disposal. Librarians are cool, and Elizabeth Peterson at the University of Oregon proves the point, and for that and more I thank her. Not all archives are kept by institutions, and I owe a great deal of gratitude to a cadre of collectors and self-trained historians whose willingness to share their knowledges, images, and objects with me have deeply enriched the stories this book has to offer. Thanks to Ron Keller, who generously shared his passion for Pittsburgh theaters, and who, without a second thought, lent me his personal collection of local theater ephemera. Similarly, Q. David Bowers considerately offered local images from his stunning collection of American theater postcards, a number of which are reproduced in this book with his gracious permission. John G. Arch kindly lent me the history of his family, the Gorseks, and their nickelodeon, the Theatorium, an image of which is reproduced with his permission. And in Waynesburg, Bill Molzon and Miles Davin were more than thoughtful enough to introduce me to Charlie Silveus and the magic of his movies.

Much of what follows has been shaped by colleagues who have read or heard portions of this book in its various stages and I thank them all for their questions, answers, and encouragement. Among them I am especially grateful to Kathy Fuller-Seeley, Richard Abel, Chris Horak, Charlie Musser, Matthew Bernstein, Vanessa Schwartz, Tom Gunning, Mark Lynn Anderson, Adam Lowenstein, Danae Clark, Paul Moore, Robert Allen, and Karen Sheldon. As far as I know, Brady Lewis, the director of education at Pittsburgh Filmmakers, never read a page of my work, but just as good, and maybe even better, he gave me a job (and a paycheck) teaching the joys of Super-8 filmmaking.

This project, as a whole, was supported at the University of Pittsburgh with an Andrew Mellon Dissertation Fellowship and at the University of Oregon with a variety of timely research awards and teaching releases. It rains in Oregon, a lot. But it only makes the hot coffee and pinot noir taste better, and I've been lucky to share quite a bit of it with an excellent set of colleagues, especially Kathleen Karlyn-Rowe, Julia Lesage, Priscilla Peña Ovalle, Sangita Gopal, Bish Sen, Diasuke Miyao, Janet Wasko, Lesli Larson, and Paul Peppis.

Special thanks go to Cynthia Miller, my editor at the University of Pittsburgh Press, who from day one consistently conveyed her enthusiasm for the project. Deborah Meade managed the tough task of overseeing the multiple phases of editing with grace and humor. I am greatly indebted to the three readers for the press who selflessly gave their time and offered invaluable ideas for organizing and completing the manuscript, as well as suggestions for a number of productive sources and ideas that have made their way into this book.

Writing a history book requires perseverance, perhaps least of all from its author. Recognition must go to my close friends who remained close over the years, even when I disappeared into the archives, particularly, Noel and Holly Heitmann, Leigh and Andy Gustine, and, more recently, Jo Larcombe, Damien North, Devorah Signer-Hill, Jerry Hill, Aimee Varnon, and Dustin Welch. Thanks, of course, goes to my parents, Judy and Nick, two people who have given me their unconditional support from the start. But my family's assistance to this project has not just been emotional, and I want to acknowledge the real help they have given me with any number of arduous archival tasks over the years. Archivists are just as cool as librarians, and in this category none can top my youngest sister, Jen Sellar. Finally, I would like to thank Keri Aronson, without whom this book would not exist. Keri's unwavering love and support has made everything possible. I know the debt I owe her, and it's not just a good meal. Both our daughters, Eliza and Ruby, were born in the midst of this project. Despite the resulting sleep deprivation, the energy of their lives has enriched this project in ways both big and small. This book is dedicated to them, the three great loves of my life; it is as much theirs as mine.

NICKELODEON CITY

1

NICKELS AND STEEL

An Introduction

IN THE SPRING OF 1914, one quiet Sunday morning, they posed for the photograph. Oscar stood self-assuredly, hand on hip, while Stephanie, neatly dressed, was shadowed in the booth. The neighborhood boy's blurred attendance at the photo's edge was likely accidental, unnoticed until the photographer made his print. The Gorseks were pleased with their theater—the grandly named Theatorium—as well as its new display. The draped American flags did double duty, announcing their proud patriotism while colorfully promoting their newest offering, Pathé's two-reel Civil War photoplay, *In The Days of War*. "Feature" films like this one were a recent addition to the regular program for their moving picture show, and they were worriedly hopeful that its spectacle of exploding bridges and "gripping sequences . . . in the lives of two families bound by love and divided by war" would allow for a profit, even at their usual five-cent admission price.[1]

FIG. 1.1.
Theatorium, circa 1914. *Courtesy of John G. Arch.*

The oldest Gorsek son, Oscar, was the theater's manager, Stephanie sold the tickets, Marian played the piano, and their three other brothers, Joseph Jr., William, and Frank, served as ushers and did chores.[2] Their parents, Joseph and Johanna, had immigrated to the United States in the late 1890s from Slovenia, which was then part of the Austro-Hungarian Empire, and initially settled the family in San Francisco, where Joseph worked as a baker. The family chose San Francisco based on the fantastic tales they had heard in their mother country of the California gold rush, but the reality was, of course, far removed from the myths. A long way from home and finding few other Slovenes that far west, within a few years they moved east to Pittsburgh, where multiple waves of eastern and central European immigrants had created comfortably familiar, if overlapping, ethnic communities. On arrival, the Gorseks established themselves in Lawrenceville, a neighborhood along the Allegheny River that originally had been populated by "first wave" English, German, and Irish mill workers, but which by the turn of the century was primarily inhabited by Russians, Poles, and Slovaks. Although Joseph died of an unknown illness just a few years after arriving in Pittsburgh, the family survived otherwise largely intact. On a busy part of Lawrenceville's Butler Street, they opened and operated the Theatorium, a two-hundred-seat nickelodeon.

OVER THE LAST few decades, the history of the silent era has become one of the most dynamic and contested areas of inquiry within film studies. This history would be incomplete without the nickelodeon, a site and sign of cinema's modern emergence in America. And the history of the nickelodeon cannot be written without Pittsburgh. If the movies were once chiefly believed to offer audiences an experience unvaried by space, place, person, or time, this literal snapshot of the Theatorium, a theater started by immigrants and run by their American-born children in a neighborhood of mill workers and their families, is a visible reminder of a history of the motion pictures as much determined by exhibition and consumption as by production, as much by Pittsburgh as by Hollywood.

This book is, as must be clear by now, about Pittsburgh and the movies. It's about a city and its exhibitors, distributors, and audiences, about their desires, investments, and actions—some collective, many competing—to define what the movies were and what they might become in this place and time. While written from this very local perspective, this study aims to provide an intimate view not only of a city but also of film history itself, from the nickelodeon era to the late 1920s, focusing in particular on the transformative middle period in the 1910s. My emphasis on the local—on neighborhoods like Lawrenceville, places like the Theatorium, and families like the Gorseks—signifies not only a belief in the importance of geographic and biographic specificity, of real places and the real people that lived there, but also a critical perspective, a resistance to broader histories that are determined and overdetermined by studios, producers, and their Hollywood films.

It has often been said that history begins with a question. But this particular history actually began with a footnote: precisely, footnote number 6 in chapter 13 of Charles Musser's 1990 book, *The Emergence of Cinema: The American Screen to 1907*.[3] The chapter, entitled "Nickels Count," is devoted to the origination of the five-cent movie theater. A rigorous scholar of film's earliest years, Musser journeyed to Pittsburgh to research the long-standing but empirically underscrutinized belief that the "official birthplace of the nickelodeon was Pittsburgh," that the nickelodeon was in fact a "Pittsburgh Idea."[4] His canvass of archival materials related to the nickelodeon in this city led Musser to the local historical society and eventually to an unusual trade journal entitled the *Pittsburgh Moving Picture Bulletin* (1914–1923). The end result of his Pittsburgh research was a productive reassertion of this city's significant historical place in the emergence of the movies as mass entertainment. However, within the scope of Musser's much larger national project—whose chronological endpoint predates the *Bulletin*'s arrival by seven years—the Pittsburgh story plays a fairly minor role. It is not surprising that after extracting a brief quote from a single issue of the journal, Musser left Pittsburgh and its weekly *Bulletin* behind. While this city's trade journal afforded Musser with a limited if useful source of information, from the moment I opened the first issue of the *Bulletin*, it provided me with an abundant source of wonder.

This book significantly draws on the *Pittsburgh Moving Picture Bulletin*, the first known regional trade journal for the movies, as both a body of evidence and an object of study. The *Bulletin* is a rare survivor, for while there is some evidence of several similar journals from other parts of the country, few are extant and none appear to have begun as early. National trade journals from the same approximate time period and even earlier, including *Variety, Motography, Motion Picture News,* and *Moving Picture World*, are widely available, at least on microfilm, and these have, over the last twenty years, become one of the primary shared resources for historians of American cinema. However, the significant role that regional trade papers like the *Bulletin* had in shaping the movies as an institution and a culture at both the local and national level has been largely unknown.

Published weekly, the *Bulletin* was wholly devoted to the movie business in the Pittsburgh region. It focused on issues specific to its local audience, the formation of a community of exhibitors and distributors, and the cultural, economic, and institutional challenges that such a community faced in its city and beyond. The journal's editorials, articles, ads, and images make visible an intricate set of alliances and conflicts, both local and national, among constituencies whose (often blurred) borders are often arranged along social, economic, religious, ethnic, and political lines.

One of the primary reasons for my strong sense of pleasure on initial contact with the *Bulletin* is that it allows us to see and hear the city's varied populace of moving picture workers, entrepreneurs, and impresarios not simply as abstract categories but as embodied individuals. We learn about Pete Antonopolis, the first-generation Greek American who used a one-armed violinist and other "old-style museum stuff" to attract an audience to his downtown theater. We also discover Mrs. C. C. Emmel, widow-owner of the Broadway Theatre in McKees Rocks, and her promotion of an elaborate street parade heralding the arrival of a new Pathé serial. We come to know Mayer Silverman, the rebellious manager of the Liberty Film Renting Company, and his brief arrest for "neglecting" to submit the films he distributed to the Pennsylvania State Board of Censors for approval. It is often impossible to locate figures like Antonopolis, Emmel, and Silverman, the practices they evolved, and the work they performed within the existing history of the movies, but these local men and women, along with thousands of others much like them, were central to the movie business of their era.

Of course, Pittsburgh was not alone, and the history of other communities has considerable value, too. People of every place and time deserve to be measured, deserve to have a history. Local history offers an invaluable potential to reconstruct the everyday lives of our ancestors, whether long or recently gone. At its best, it can provide a powerful link between experience and history, provoking in us an awareness of how those of the past might have experienced the world. This book hopes to offer a few of those resulting moments by joining a small but significant body of work by scholars devoted to local history of a very specific kind, the history of exhibition and moviegoing as practiced in individual towns and cities across the country.[5] While film historians now collectively agree that locale matters, there remains a deep lacuna of knowledge regarding the potent variations between and within communities small and large, rural and urban. Local film history, in its narrow empirical vision and fine attention to detail, reveals the complex dynamics of everyday life in relation to the encompassing social and economic forces within which it is embedded.

In regard to these broad and determinative forces, Pittsburgh often appears as much a symbol as a city; a steel-fired, smoke-belching metonym for the stunning advances of modern American industrialization and its overwhelming effects upon those that lived and labored within its metropolitan crucible. In 1909, Paul Kellogg described it this way: "Pittsburgh is the capital of a district representative of untrammeled industrial development, but of a district which, for richer, for poorer, in sickness and in health, for vigor, waste and optimism, is rampantly American."[6] Perhaps nowhere else in the world did the commingled powers of industrialization, urbanization, and immigration play out upon and shape such an extreme, visible topography. Recognized in its contemporary moment as a capital-driven city distilled to its purest and most brutally efficient form, Pittsburgh was intensively studied and documented by a diverse group of urban planners, Progressive reformers, and social engineers who saw the city to be at once exemplary and representative of modern industrial society in all its problems and possibilities. Offering a detailed microcosm of the very sort of rough-and-tumble, working-class, urban environment often assumed to be the wellspring of American movie culture, Pittsburgh provides a fundamental site in which to assess cinema's historical narrative and to test that narrative's truths, mythologies, and invariably messy complications and contradictions.

ON AUGUST 26, 1786, an anonymous writer in the *Pittsburg Gazette* presciently predicted: "The town must in future time be a place of great manufacturing; indeed, the greatest on the continent, or perhaps the world." In fact, by 1914, Pittsburgh led the world in the manufacturing of iron, steel, glass, electrical machinery, cork, aluminum, tin plate, rail cars, turbines, air brakes, fire bricks, white lead, and pickles. Situated at a point of natural confluence where the Allegheny and Monongahela Rivers flow into the Ohio, Pittsburgh was an ideal location from which white settlers could trade their goods—at first with the area's Native Americans and, by the turn of the twentieth century, with much of the rest of the world. Perhaps America's true gateway city, Pittsburgh provided the country with a commercial entrepôt centrally located by train or barge within twelve hours of the Atlantic Ocean and the Mississippi River and within six hours of the Great Lakes.

The efficient shipping possibilities offered by the region's three rivers was matched by a cheap and seemingly limitless power source: extensive bituminous coalfields stretching outward from Pittsburgh for miles in all directions. Both high in quality and close to the earth's surface, these fields were easily strip-mined. By 1900, investments by local corporations in modernizing production processes and transportation systems resulted in a Pittsburgh region that supplied 64 percent of the nation's structural steel, 50 percent of its coking coal, and 26 percent of its steel rails.[7] The enormous size of these new, technologically advanced steel mills led manufacturers to absorb increasingly larger tracts of riverside real estate, and "population followed industry."[8] The efficiencies resulting from this intersection of rivers, men, and mills led to Pittsburgh's world primacy in the production of heavy industrial goods, transforming it into a place contemporary commentators described as "capitalism's key city."[9]

The workforce required to turn that key also changed considerably over the second half of the nineteenth century. Trained craftsmen, primarily of British, Welsh, Irish, and German heritage were slowly displaced as a result of a number of interrelated factors, including: an almost total shift from iron to steel production, the increased mechanization of all phases of millwork, and the collapse of the union movement, violently marked by the demise of the Amalgamated Association at Homestead in 1892. In their stead, a less highly skilled immigrant workforce was required to labor longer hours for considerably less pay—although wage rates constantly fluctuated both up and down during this era, common labor in the mills earned on average 16.5¢ an hour, or $1.98 for a twelve-hour day.[10] Most of the men receiving this pay were recent immigrants from less industrialized regions of the world, including the American South, southern and central Italy, and central and eastern Europe, especially Russia and Poland. The influx of these men, their families, and others caused the city's metropolitan area to nearly triple in population between 1880 and 1910 to over a million people, making Pittsburgh the eighth-largest city in the country.[11] Of that 1910 Pittsburgh population, over 271,000 were first-generation foreign immigrants, another 342,000 were the children of foreign-born parents, and 34,000 city residents were African American. Immigrants and their children accounted for between half and two-thirds of the city's residents between 1880 and 1930.[12]

The vast majority of these immigrant mill workers could neither afford the time nor the fare required for commuting from home to work, and overwhelmingly they lived within walking distance of their places of employment. This is particularly true for the steel industry, the largest single employer in the Pittsburgh region, where the seventy-two-hour workweek was often standard even after World War I.[13] By 1914, steel mills and their accompanying industries lined the riverbanks in the Pittsburgh region to a distance of twenty miles from the city's core. As these mills spread out, they gathered around them concentrations of workers and their families—and as many as 90 percent of the laborers in these steel mill communities walked to work on a daily basis.[14] This pattern of the city's development, along with the well-documented process of chain immigration, contributed to the creation of highly homogenous ethnic working-class communities, often crowded into housing built on the surrounding steep hills and other scraps of land considered unusable for mill operations. For example, by 1900, Polish immigrants in Pittsburgh had consolidated their employment in various steel mills, and a majority lived either within a mile or two of the mills on the Allegheny River in a neighborhood that became known as Polish Hill or up against the mills of Jones and Laughlin and the Oliver Iron and Steel Mills on the growing South Side. Other eastern and southern European ethnic communities including Lithuanians, Croatians, and southern Italians developed similarly homogenous communities around their places of employment.[15]

Conversely, the rapid expansion of a trolley system, while described by one local author in 1915 as "still far from ideal," was well enough established along certain routes to affect a nascent suburban lifestyle for Pittsburgh's growing "middling" class of corporate bureaucrats and small-business entrepreneurs.[16] Public transportation followed the path of least resistance, and so convenient transit access developed along the natural corridors formed by valleys and plains, primarily east and west from the city center. Separated by a distance of several miles from the mills and occasionally "even free from smoke," by 1914, the city's East End neighborhoods were composed primarily of upper- and middle-class single-family homes, and the business district on Penn Avenue in East Liberty correspondingly developed as a new and important hub of bourgeois commerce, drawing consumer enterprise away from the city's center.[17]

In direct relation to the consolidation of these industrial and housing patterns, the city's downtown commercial and business area, "peninsular Pittsburgh, some call it," was increasingly filled with the new "high-rises" of the region's corporate headquarters.[18] The insides of these brick, steel, and glass monuments to industrial modernity needed to be staffed accordingly, and by 1914, Pittsburgh's office staff accounted for over 12 percent of the working population, an amount more than twice the national average. This expanding core of mostly young men and women, a group social historian Ileen DeVault has aptly described as "the sons and daughters of labor," found themselves, in almost every way imaginable, somewhere in the complex middle.[19] Most boarded trolleys and left their millbound families and communities behind to take up a relatively new kind of work in the city's center. If their wages and working conditions reflected a marginally better standard of existence than their laboring brethren in the mills, the majority of these white-collar workers continued to reside and interact with the ethnically homogenous communities of their families: in 1915, only 6 percent of Pittsburgh's clerical and sales workers lived in the city's

FIG. 1.2.
"Penn Ave., looking East, East Liberty, Pittsburg, Pa.," postcard, circa 1914.
Courtesy of Q. David Bowers.

wealthier suburbs.[20] Film historian Robert Allen has rightly noted that "income overlap" between manual and nonmanual workers "blurred class boundaries" and helped produce "a kind of dual social identity." In Pittsburgh, these patterns of residency, based primarily on ethnic and familial relationships, continued to play a crucial and often central role in the formation of the city's social and cultural identity.[21] The complex transformations of social geography had significant implications for Pittsburgh's movie theaters and their moviegoers.

It was a city, regardless of where you lived or worked, dominated by a few companies and a single industry, and most of its residents soon found their own existence in some way subject to the steel mills' organization of life and labor. Driven by the growth of its master trade, Pittsburgh was in many ways less defined as a city than as a sprawling industrial region, less a civic entity than an economic one.[22] The industrial rationalization of the region prevailed in and took advantage of governmental and social fragmentation, and in the absence of any significant countervailing power, the mill owners were often largely free to structure the life of the city and its people at their will.[23] The result was that Pittsburgh's urban geography, social institutions, and labor relations were primarily shaped by the dominant needs of the metal industry and its owners. The subsequent mutilation and pollution of the area's striking topography was depressing in its totality, and living within the resulting tortured environment meant that basic requirements for food, shelter, and water were often impossible to meet. The workers who inhabited the resulting landscape "most frequently compared to hell," found that the massive wealth they helped bring forth from its fires was unequally distributed between labor and management.[24] According to the 1910 census, there were 2,369 industrial enterprises operating within the region, with 20,692 salaried employees earning average salaries of $1,204, while 139,285 wage earners received annual average paychecks of $646. In comparison, after total amounts paid for salaries, wages, materials, and other expenses were accounted for, profits that year for the metropolitan's industrial establishments both publicly and privately held equaled almost 59 million dollars.[25]

It is this atmosphere of stark inequality and the resulting widespread and highly visible problems that resulted from this imbalance of capital that led in the late 1900s and early 1910s to the publication of the landmark *Pittsburgh Survey*. Instigated by a small group of the city's business and welfare leaders in conjunction with the Charities Publication Committee of New York (later largely financed by the Russell Sage Foundation), the survey was a massive-scale exercise in Progressive reform and social research. Beginning in 1908, a field staff composed of authorities from the emerging disciplines of social work and labor relations descended on the region to investigate conditions of environment, workplace, and home; in the following six years they produced a thick set of documents, articles, and exhibits about the struggles of everyday life in contemporary Pittsburgh.[26] The survey was, and remains, distinctive in the breadth of its collaborative efforts to research, illustrate, analyze, and offer solutions to a staggering array of social, industrial, and civic issues.[27] Collectively, the resulting publications call for Pittsburgh to supply its citizens with safer working conditions, greener spaces, cleaner air and water, higher wages, shorter working hours, improved sanitation, and better housing. Despite its encyclopedic accounting of city life, however, there are significant and sometimes telling gaps in the survey's production of knowledge about the region and its residents. Of particular interest is the survey's surprising disinterest in the economic, cultural, and social dimensions of Pittsburgh's commercial amusements. In its thousands of pages, only once, in the survey's second volume, entitled *Homestead: The Households of a Mill Town,* is there an extended description of the role that the movies played in the life of the region's people. According to sociologist Margaret Byington, who authored the volume as a study of immigrant family life across the Monongahela River:

> Practically the only public amusements in Homestead . . . were the nickelodeons and skating rinks. Six of the former . . . sent out their penetrating music all the evening and most of the afternoon . . . Men on their way home from work stop for a few minutes to see something of life outside the alternation of mill and home; the shopper rests while she enjoys the music, poor though it may be, and the children are always begging for five cents to go to the nickelodeon. On a Saturday afternoon visit to a nickelodeon, which advertised that it admitted two children on one ticket, I was surprised to find a larger proportion of men in the audience. In many ways this form of amusement is desirable. What it ordinarily offers does not educate but does give pleasure . . . for five cents the nickelodeon offers fifteen minutes' relaxation, and a glimpse of other sides of life . . . As the nickelodeon seems to have met a real need in the mill towns, one must wish that it might offer them a better quality of entertainment.[28]

As hinted at in Byington's description, the nickelodeon was a central site of working-class entertainment in this period and reformers were often conflicted about the movies and their cultural primacy. In general, reformers understood the neighborhood movie theater as a site of largely unfulfilled Progressive potential, which, on one hand, offered a much-needed public space of respite from the traumas of the real world. On the other hand, however, the movie theaters too often, according to at least one other Pittsburgh researcher, presented images and stories that "play up the base qualities of life, showing reels upon reels of highly sensational love stories, infidelity of husband or wife."[29] This researcher, unlike Byington, was not part of the official survey force. The Reverend R. Earl Boyd of the city's Protestant Trinity Temple was a resident of Pittsburgh, and his self-published work focused on the Strip District, a rough but busy stretch of narrow ground running east of the city's core, bordered by the Allegheny River to its north and the passenger yards of the Pennsylvania Railroad on its south. Boyd's research included an accounting of the area's five movie theaters, summarized in a section devoted to neighborhood institutions labeled as "harmful social agencies." All was not lost for the movies, however, according to the minister, for once the Strip's exhibitors could be convinced to resist the medium's more "anti-social features" and offer pictures with a more "educational, wholesomely recreational message," the nickelodeons could then provide a "helpful" experience to the Strip's residents, 83 percent of whom were immigrants or their children.[30] Conversely, the minister perceived the two other primary local forms of "harmful" leisure, the saloon and the pool hall, to be well beyond the reach of any positive social transformation. In comparison to its five nickelodeons, the Strip offered its residents seventy-eight licensed saloons, ten "chartered clubs," and "eight drug stores notoriously selling liquor without a prescription," along with "ten or fifteen 'fly by night' speak-easies and about a dozen 'white line' and 'dope' joints where alcohol and drugs are obtained."[31] Although Boyd does not enumerate the Strip's pool halls, which he describes as chiefly patronized by young men having "long been recognized as ... thugs, petty criminals and loafers," another social survey from the following year gave a total metropolitan count of 332 pool rooms.[32]

While bars and pool halls were perceived by reformers as dangerously unrepentant sites of working-class immorality, other sites of commercial leisure and amusement in the city were marked (to varying degrees) as less socially problematic, many of which were included in a popular guidebook

FIG. 1.3.
View of the Strip District, circa 1925. Photograph by Mettee Holmes.
Courtesy of Carnegie Museum of Art.

of the same period, *Pittsburgh, How to See It*. Authored by local historian George Fleming, who wrote a regular weekly column devoted to the history of the city for the *Pittsburgh Post-Gazette*, the guide's list of entertainments for potential visitors included two amusement parks: Kennywood, downriver on the Monongahela opposite the mill town of Braddock; and West View Park, located on the northern side of the Allegheny River. Neither of these "fine natural park[s] with the usual amusement features and devices," charged an admission fee, but each required a ten-cent trolley ride to access their various pleasures. Or for twenty-five cents, you could sit in the top bleachers of Forbes Field, hallowed home of the Pittsburgh Pirates baseball team, described by Fleming as "the finest ball park, in matter of situation and construction, in the baseball world." If you preferred to be entertained indoors, you could instead turn to one of the approximately twelve legitimate theaters spread throughout the metropolitan area, including five in the downtown district: the Nixon, the Alvin, the Grand, the Davis and the Duquesne. Collectively, according to Fleming, they offered the region's citizens and visitors alike "a good variety of . . . elaborate productions of modern classic drama and comedy . . . and the highest class refined vaudeville" at admission prices ranging from twenty-five cents to two dollars and more.[33]

But if one could not afford such prices, or simply favored the movies to the stage, the choice of venue was virtually limitless. While the exact figure is unknown, and likely unknowable, the approximate number of movie-only theaters in the Pittsburgh region by the mid-1910s is somewhere in the range of two hundred.[34] In Pittsburgh the movies were everywhere, and "except in exclusive residential sections, visitors will not have to go far to find entertainment from moving films . . . for there are many five cent shows, or 'Nickelodeons.'"[35] It is these many shows, their owners, and their audiences that are the primary focus of this book's following chapters.

2

THE EPONYMOUS NICKELODEON

> A nickel is an insignificant coin; the whole great picture theater business is built upon the people's disregard for it as a piece of money. Almost anything is worth five cents.
>
> Editorial, *Nickelodeon*, 1909

Poor Sol Leight. All he really wanted was to collect "as many nickels as possible while the rush [was] on." On June 19, 1905, John P. Harris and Harry Davis had opened on Smithfield Street in downtown Pittsburgh a theater they called the Nickelodeon. Unlike those already successful showmen, however, in the fall of 1905 Leight could not afford to pay the rising rents in the city's downtown Golden Triangle. So instead he leased a small storefront from Hy Gerwig on Penn Avenue in the Strip, just around the corner from the Chautauqua Lake Ice House, in a busy area that mixed light industry with small businesses, sweatshops, saloons, and tenement housing. With his projector on the floor at the front of the store, near the drapery-darkened entrance, the resulting "theater" was only some eighteen feet wide and could accommodate just about sixty nickel-paying customers. Son of a Lithuanian-born Jewish tailor, Leight and his optimistically named

Grand Moving Picture Theater fits flawlessly within traditional historical assumptions about the nickelodeon as a potent site of immigrant entrepreneurship and proletarian commercial leisure. Nickelodeons like the Grand Moving Picture Theater, so history goes, was where American dreams were made for exhibitor and audience alike. And for a brief moment on Friday, November 17, 1905, such appeared to be the case. Upon opening the doors to his new, one-room enterprise, Leight immediately found himself, according to local newspaper reports, doing a "thriving business," primarily due to the district's many women and children.[1] Unfortunately, his potential gifts as a showman were not matched with an ability to manage "the mechanism of a moving picture machine," and when his young projectionist went to dinner that first busy Saturday night, things quickly took a turn for the worse. As the *Pittsburgh Post* described on its front page the next day, Leight, apparently unfamiliar with the flammable properties of cellulose nitrate, allowed the "machine to stop while the strong light was being thrown on the films," causing "an explosion and the building, machine and draperies [to catch] fire." The ensuing blaze and panicked rush to escape in the smoke-filled darkness resulted in injuries for "more or less" half of the audience. Included in the *Post*'s list of the burned and bruised was the show's youngest attendee, nine-month-old Mary Broski. Mary, who had been at the theater with her older brother and sister, was saved from a worse fate by Patrick Sullivan, a local passerby, who upon seeing the smoke and flames from the street, kicked the theater's front door down and rushed into the "struggling mob, carrying many of the children to a place of safety."[2] Less than a week after the fire, which appears to have prematurely ended Sol's dreams of cinematic fortune, the city's superintendent of building inspectors, Samuel Dies, began an "official inspection" tour of the city's remaining popular "five-cent shows."[3]

Dies made his well-publicized rounds in the evening, when the majority of these nickel enterprises were open for business, bringing along with him a number of local newspapermen. The superintendent and the press arrived unannounced at the dozen shows then located in various parts of the city, including at least one, a Lawrenceville storefront theater near the busy American Bridge Works, that Dies immediately ordered closed until "better equipment had been provided."[4] One of the accompanying journalists, a reporter for the *Pittsburgh Leader*, wrote the next day of his travels with the inspector and the palpable evidence he saw of a "craze" for the moving picture shows, "nickelodeons" as they were now being called for the first time. In the article, he detailed the "throngs" located at one particularly busy downtown location:

> The necessity for strict supervision over these little amusement places was demonstrated last evening by the scene at the establishment on Smithfield street . . . crowded to suffocation . . . over a hundred people were standing in the alcove entrance waiting for a chance to get in. There are seats for ninety people and back of the rail, a space about eight by fifteen feet in which over one hundred persons were packed tight . . . Three hundred people were standing around and this crowd tried to squeeze into a room intended to accommodate about one hundred. Although the exits and other arrangements are the best that can be provided there was a serious element of danger . . . about the place.[5]

Although never specifically named in the article, "the establishment on Smithfield [S]treet" would have been easily identified by the paper's readership. The theater with "arrangements . . . the best that can be provided" was not simply another anonymous nickel show, but rather the Nickelodeon, the moving picture house started by John P. Harris and Harry Davis, from which an era, and arguably the movies as we know them, first began. Admittedly, such an originary claim is a lot of weight for two men and a single, if crowded, storefront to bear. For many substantive reasons, many historians have come to face the very idea of any kind of beginning with significant trepidation or even outright dismissal. Transformations in the philosophy of history—what history is, who it is for, and what it has wrought—have taught us much about the intrinsic malleability of representation, the unstable nature of facts, and the slippery role of subjectivity in historical argument, and have driven home the role that power always plays in the construction of history's narrative.[6] Of all of history's difficulties, origins are among the most problematic.

The existing history of Pittsburgh's original nickelodeon in no way escapes this fate. Over the last one hundred years, many tales have been told by many men (it's almost always men), claiming some part of the nickelodeon's success, all a result of their personal roles in choosing its location, designing its front, playing its music, collecting its nickels, running its show, and, perhaps most important of all, arriving at its melodious name. Harry Cohn, for example, is erroneously sometimes credited as the nickelodeon's first manager. He was fourteen at the time, however, and living in New York City and, like others credited with the nickelodeon's birth, has no real part to play in this historical pageant.[7] Publicist Eugene Connelly, the unnamed plaster artist who transformed the empty downtown storefront into an attractive movie theater, and other local characters have minor—if affecting—roles in the collective performance of the nickelodeon's beginning. But in the end, Davis and Harris are the stars of this show.

Like Sol Leight, Harry Davis and John Harris were sons of immigrants. But they were otherwise very different men from very different places, whose intertwined lives and careers (if ultimately separate histories) offer an alternative framework for understanding the formative moment of the nickelodeon era. The traditional history of the nickelodeon boom and the rise of the American movie industry has emphasized men more like Sol Leight, working or merchant-class Jewish immigrants with nontheatrical backgrounds, who begin their showmen careers with a single storefront moving picture theater.[8] Such a "from the bottom up" narrative fits a not insignificant number of Hollywood's eventual moguls, men like Adolph Zukor, Marcus Loew, Lewis Selznick, and Harry Warner (the latter two of whom began their initial affairs with the movies in Pittsburgh). As a result, even many revisionist historians, like early cinema scholar Ben Singer, have continued to foreground the centrality of the "small-time" ethnic businessmen to the urban nickelodeon boom.[9] Men (and even a few women) who entered from the margins, men like Leight seeking swift success, would, as the Pittsburgh newspapers make visible, quickly follow Davis and Harris into the nickelodeon fray. It is crucial to this originary narrative, however, that Davis and Harris were distinctly different in their personal and professional backgrounds from men like Leight. One by choice and one by paternal folly, both grew up immersed in the commercial amusement world and were thoroughly versed (if not always successful) in its practices and possibilities. While both men became, in the later parts of their careers, best known for their various successes operating legitimate theaters and family vaudeville, their lives from an early age were saturated with the sights and sounds of the lower ends of the entertainment spectrum: carnivals, pool halls, freak shows, and dime museums. Arguably, these more youthful experiences and knowledges were central to the Nickelodeon and its success in 1905.

The histories of Davis and Harris, both separate and combined, are problematic. As both real lives and as cultural matrices through which the forces of their time and place were expressed, their narratives are overwhelmingly constructed from memories individual and collective, occasionally firsthand, but most much further removed. The resulting stories of self-made men who overcome considerable challenges create a troublesome situation for a historian charged with ethically reconstructing the past through a critical analysis of documented evidence. As film scholar Tom Gunning has pointed out, it is the job of the historian to "unmake stories as much as to create them."[10] Unfortunately, with few exceptions, when the stories of Harris and Davis and the Nickelodeon are unmade, what remains is often another layer of fabulous tales, told just a bit earlier than the last. The reason for this absence of empirical evidence is in itself somewhat revealing. In its inception, the Nickelodeon was never intended to be particularly meaningful, influential, or revolutionary, just profitable. No celebratory photographs were taken on opening day, no newspaper ads were placed, and no business records appear to have been saved. Simply put, the Nickelodeon was not started by these men with an explicit plan or a distinct vision to change the course of film history. Instead, the Nickelodeon was part of a larger set of overlapping businesses in which two hustling entrepreneurs relentlessly experimented with their pitch and product, shows and theaters. As a result, the historiography of the Nickelodeon was largely assembled retroactively by showmen, their pressmen, and their families, whose gains were derived from this nickel theater's surprising and rapid excessive success.

However, if the stories of the Nickelodeon, which began to appear in print as early as 1906, are often just stories, they nonetheless provide us with one of the medium's founding narratives: a tale of the transformation of the movies into mass culture and entertainment. Ultimately, therefore, the stories that are told are as important to the history of the movies as the movies themselves.

Faced with all the contradictory evidence, the multiple layers of hearsay, legends, and outright falsehoods, and the well-grounded theoretical resistance to "the metaphor of biological paternity," it is not surprising that many film historians have balked at the possibility of granting the Harris and Davis Nickelodeon a discernable originary role.[11] For instance, Douglas Gomery, in *Shared Pleasures*, one of the more comprehensive histories of American movie exhibition, adopts a safer universal narrative when he suggests: "There had been nickelodeons from the start . . . Edison's agents in the 1890s franchised a number of business leaders, who in turn rented storefronts and showed movies there. But . . . [a]cceptance—seemingly everywhere at once—would not come until 1905."[12] In this model, nickelodeons were old news, until 1905, when they were suddenly, for some reason, big news: "everywhere at once." Kenneth Macgowan, another traditional historian of American film, even more bluntly asserts, "the Nickelodeon was not the first store theater . . . nor the first successful one."[13] There is some evidentiary logic and appeal to Gomery's and Macgowan's versions of movie history, which studiously choose to refuse the Nickelodeon on Smithfield Street in downtown Pittsburgh as the initial epicenter of that 1905 acceptance.

There is even a measure of truth to Macgowan's claim, particularly if his definition of "success" includes something that is brief or transitory in its duration. Certainly there is a body of material evidence, consisting chiefly of advertising in various local newspapers, that confirms that in the mid- to late 1890s, entrepreneurs of early projection systems—in particular the Edison-branded Vitascope—operated short-lived storefront moving picture shows at a number of urban sites across the country. According to a study by Charlie Musser, the populace of many American cities developed a taste for movie-only exhibitions in these initial years, such as the "[r]esidents of Providence, Rhode Island—including the mayor and the city's leading citizens . . . [who] flocked a storefront show during the first part of June [of 1896] to see ten films for twenty-five cents."[14] Among the best documented and most influential of these prescient movie exhibitors was "Professor" William T. "Pop" Rock. In 1896 Rock, along with his partner at the time, Walter Wainright, bought the Louisiana state rights to Edison's patented machine for fifteen hundred dollars, and charged ten cents a show to New Orleans residents for a successful run during the summer and early fall of 1896. Rock and Wainright's storefront show is said to have been profitable for at least three months, but when sustained interest in the city began to taper off, Rock took his projector and films on the road, traveling throughout the Southwest. By the following year, various newspaper accounts showed the two partners exhibiting their "Pleasing Vitascope Pictures" in various towns and cities in Arizona, New Mexico, and Texas, including shows at the Music Hall at the annual Texas State Fair.[15]

Although almost half a dozen years later, 1902 advertisements placed in the *Los Angeles Times* by Thomas L. Tally for his version of a storefront picture show have also been frequently employed by historians to demystify Pittsburgh's nascent place in the development of the movie-only theater. Tally, a former circus performer, was much like Rock—a showman with a diverse entrepreneurial streak. He operated, bought, and sold commercial entertainment operations in Los Angeles around the turn of the century. In just one classified ad from 1902, Tally offered other Los Angeles residents the opportunity to become showmen, promoting his ability to "start you in business . . . if you have a little money . . . I have motion picture outfits, phonograph outfits and also have a fine soda fountain to sell at a bargain."[16] While accounts of the success and longevity of his storefront movie show vary widely, there is clear documentation that by late 1902, Tally was operating "The Electric Theatre. For Up-to-Date High Class Motion Picture Entertainment" in downtown Los Angeles.[17] Advertised as open for "continuous" performances in the evenings from 7:45 to 10:00 p.m., Tally offered, in return for ten cents admission, a program of short actualité and fiction films "lasting one hour and fifteen minutes."[18] In the most prevalent account of the Electric Theatre's demise, Tally shut its doors after a run of a couple months and turned (once again) to a more itinerant style of showmanship, exhibiting Edwin S. Porter's *The Great Train Robbery* (1903) as a traveling road show. Storefront theaters operated for relatively brief periods by Tally, Rock, Wainright, and other less well-known exhibitors were, without a doubt, a significant formative element in the creation of the modern moving picture experience, and the stories of these short-lived theaters are not simply a precocious proto-history for the Pittsburgh Nickelodeon. Despite Gomery or any other historian's assertions, however, these earlier storefront theaters should not be defined or understood, whether singularly or collectively, as nickelodeons. While labeling them as such may absolve film historians from the problematic task of assigning an originary moment, such claims of "everywhere at once" dehistoricize significant forces and determinants that were required for the widespread acceptance of this exhibition space and the experience first offered in Pittsburgh.

If storefront theaters had previously existed, what happened almost a decade later, in Pittsburgh in 1905, to explain how the commercial exhibition of motion pictures so suddenly became a profitable craze? What exactly had changed? Eugene Lemoyne Connelly's answer, given at a 1939 luncheon to the members of the Historical Society of Western Pennsylvania, was: "it took that long . . . for the germ of an idea to incubate in the minds of showmen steeped in the lore and traditions of the theater, alive in every opportunity for money-making and skilled beyond all others in the difficult art or science, whichever you chose to call it, of sensing the public's desire for entertainment."[19] Such an eloquent explanation might be expected from the onetime publicist for both Harris and Davis. According to Connelly, his own participation in the endeavor included "supply[ing] the name for . . . this parent picture theater."[20] Of all contemporary historians, Charles Musser offers the most productive set of other, less personified determinants that first allowed for the "opportunity" of a successful Pittsburgh movie-only site to develop in the second half of 1905. Musser's meticulous research shows that storefront theaters became nickelodeons that year because "changes in motion picture practice had created new conditions," which included, "a large and growing audience base, a minimal

FIG. 2.1.
Thomas L. Tally, circa 1900.
Author's collection.

level of 'feature' production, a rental system of exchanges, the conception of the film program as an interchangeable commodity, frequent program changes, a continuous-exhibition format, and cinema's relative independence from more traditional forms of entertainment."²¹ This is a good list, but there is at least one crucial element that Musser leaves out, and its absence is why, in the end, Gomery and others are wrong in their belief that there existed "nickelodeons from the start." For storefront theaters, plainly put, cannot become nickelodeons until they begin charging a nickel for their show.²²

Claiming the defining characteristic of a nickelodeon as its entry fee is, perhaps at first glance, a premise seemingly too tautological to be of much historiographic use. After all, it is widely (if often unthinkingly) acknowledged that the nickelodeon as an exhibition format succeeded precisely because its nickel admission enabled "working-class men and women to discover the wonders of the motion picture machine."[23] The nickel, however, should be understood as a powerfully signifying object in and of itself, a coin imbued with cultural as well as economic value, particularly in the later parts of the nineteenth century and the first quarter of the twentieth century. Arguably, in fact, the nickel's cultural capital was significantly larger than its monetary value, precisely because of its limited economic power. Harris and Davis's Nickelodeon succeeded in large part not just because it was cheap but because it was a bargain. This is an important, if subtle, distinction in that the nickelodeon was able to extend to its varied patrons the belief that regardless of their class position, they were being offered something more for something less.

As such, the nickelodeon, in its entrance fee and its name, can be understood as representing the acme of "popular price" amusements. This phrase of democratic accessibility, "popular price," is historically associated most closely with the New England entrepreneur Benjamin Franklin Keith, whose revolutionary development in the 1880s of low-priced "refined vaudeville" helped significantly expand the American audience for popular commercial entertainment. Keith, a contemporary of the Pittsburgh theatrical entrepreneurs, began his showman's life as a circus grifter selling quack novelties, but he made his fortune with the successful exploitation of the growing market for casual inexpensive entertainment performed in a respectable venue. Twenty years later, the Nickelodeon opened by Harris and Davis similarly offered the city's burgeoning urban market of come-and-go audiences an attractive space, a short show, and an even lower price. The nickelodeon followed a lengthy list of modern commercial amusements wrought by an evolution in discount pricing, including: the penny presses of William Hearst and Joseph Pulitzer, *Munsey*'s illustrated magazine (fifteen cents), "family" vaudeville, and the 10-20-30 melodrama (ten cents for a balcony seat).[24] The Pittsburgh Nickelodeon, like Keith's chain of theaters, offered an entertainment site that was readily accessible to both the laboring class and the city's rapidly developing white-collar "middling" class as well. As such, the nickel would play a significant role in the rapid generic development of "democracy's theater"—so much so that it eventually became extremely difficult to end the association between its appellation and its admission cost. As W. Stephen Bush lamented in 1908, "may Heaven forgive the man who invented this abomination of a name!"[25]

Of course, Bush, the influential editor of *Moving Picture World*, was not simply cursing a single Pittsburgh theater, but rather the word's long lasting persistence as a common reference and entrance fee for all American movie theaters. At least in regard to the name "nickelodeon" there is little cause to offer creative laudations for Harry Davis and John Harris or any of the others such as Eugene Connelly, Charles Bochert, or Howard Royer who all, at one time or another, have been endorsed with or taken credit for inventing the word.[26] This seductively denotative name, derived from the combining of *odeon*, the Greek word for theater, with the nickel, was, despite Connelly's and others' claims, not a term newly *coined* for the Harris and Davis theater on Smithfield Street (although it is likely that it was the first movie-only theater to bear this name), nor even one originally fashioned as a general descriptor for a cheap moving picture show. While the word's exact origins are unknown, it came to life in Boston in the fall of 1888 when entertainment impresario Colonel William Austin announced the opening of his "nickel-plated" nickelodeon.[27] Austin was a successful local entertainment entrepreneur, now known primarily as the initial theatrical business partner of Benjamin Franklin Keith.[28] Austin's nickelodeon was a "curio hall," a literally half-price version of the city's popular dime museums, offering its patrons such pleasures as a miniature diorama of a Japanese village, performances by male impersonator Kitty Randolph, Tom Morrissey and his "kid glove" sand dance, and "exciting bouts" between "the expert Lady Fencer [Anita Millenori] and swordsman Professor Castroni." Unlike the city's nearby Grand Dime Museum, whose ten-cent admission gave entrance to its "large exhibit halls" and shows that included "freak[s] never seen before" and displays of "large menageries," Austin's self-proclaimed "cozy" nickelodeon was a more intimate exhibit space that required of its patrons only "a five-cent piece . . . as [its] open sesame."[29] Although it is difficult to ascertain how much success Austin actually achieved with his bargain museum, it is clear from newspaper descriptions of the site and its offered entertainment that the Colonel believed that there was a large potential audience who desired the pleasures of the museum but who were unable or unwilling to part with a dime for the experience. Dime museums, which cultural historian Andrea Dennett has described as "distinctly American," can be seen in many regards as a direct entertainment antecedent of the moving picture version of the nickelodeon, offering a spectacularized blend of affordable amusement to a heterogeneous urban audience.[30] Keith in Boston and Davis and Harris in Pittsburgh owned or managed a number of dime museums. For a variety of reasons, including the success of the moving picture theater, by the turn of the century the dime museum was in decline as a popular entertainment form. The name "nickelodeon" would soon relocate from Austin's bargain museum to even more intimate venues.

As early as 1890, the word "nickelodeon" can be found in advertisements in a number of northeastern newspapers for various small theaters offering "family" vaudeville, an amusement form that was on the rise.[31] By 1897, the owner of one nickelodeon located in Trenton, New Jersey, had removed all of his museum displays and changed to a "continuous performance format" of vaudeville acts, although he continued to offer his nickel prices, gamely declaring, "I started as a Nickelodeon, and as a Nickelodeon I will continue!"[32] A brand-new vaudeville theater named Nickelodeon opened in Fitchburg, Massachusetts, in 1904, presenting its local patrons with five live acts including the museum-like spectacle of May Lamont, the "Moss haired Lady," and "Alfonso, the Human Ostrich."[33] Ironically, despite its name, the Fitchburg nickelodeon appears to have initially charged its patrons a dime admission. By 1906, however, as news of the success of Pittsburgh's movie-only Nickelodeon began to spread, its name caused a kind of titling ripple effect, which started in western Pennsylvania and rapidly spread across the country. From that year on, the word "nickelodeon," almost exclusively, came to signify either the generic or specific identity of a nickel-charging moving picture show.[34]

Regardless of its commercial evolution or precise site of origination, the word belongs to a broader trend of entrepreneurially heightened rhetoric, designed to blend words of American origin with real or ersatz Greek and Latin terms and prefixes, resulting in what one New York newspaper of the era derided as "high sounding appellations."[35] As film scholar Lee Grieveson has illustrated in regard to the later creation of the term "photoplay" as a respectable signifier for the movies, "nickelodeon" reflects cultural meanings and social practices that extend far beyond its basic etymological implications.[36] Exactly whoever, and whenever, the name was first used, the nickelodeon's rhetorical melding of the "high" of the theater and the "low" of the nickel successfully sought to bind a bargain and its pleasures to the more refined discourses of cultural acceptance and moral authority. It was this ability to offer a gratifying entertainment experience at a lower entrance price, in both economic and ideological terms, that proved to be the key to the success of the Pittsburgh nickelodeon and all that followed.

The commercial exhibition of movies, of course, showed up in Pittsburgh long before 1905—on September 4, 1896, to be exact, four and half months after their initial New York commercial introduction at Koster and Bial's Music Hall. Despite many later claims otherwise, however, it was neither Davis nor Harris who first gave Pittsburgh the movies, but rather R. M. Gulick, manager of the Bijou Theatre and one of Davis's regular local competitors.[37] According to an article titled "The Marvelous Vitascope," which appeared on the front page of the *Pittsburgh Dispatch* on September 5, 1896, after a preview offered to the local press:

> Manager Gulick . . . last evening gave a private performance to newspaper men and friends in [sic] the Edison Vitascope entertainment. . . . Those who have seen the Kinetoscope will be somewhat prepared for the marvelous invention and those who have not can have no conception of the wonderful accuracy with which life is reproduced. It seems like witchery to look at the life-sized figures of stage, dancers, whirling, kicking, and bowing, while the drapery floats about their nimble forms. It is the acme of instantaneous photography and mechanical accessory to imitate life.[38]

Davis, however, was not far behind, quickly booking the Cinématographe from the French Lumière Company for his own theater, the Avenue:

> The marvelous *Lumière Cinématographe* will be seen for the first time in Pittsburg. It is, in brief, the perfection of instantaneous photography. It is the

original of all the life photography inventions, and was first shown in Paris in 1895. The Cinématographe's great success in Paris . . . prevented its being brought to this country sooner. . . . Among the many views which will be exhibited at the Avenue tomorrow is "Babies Quarrel" which is said to be wonderfully natural. It is a picture of two babies at a table where all is happy and tranquil for the moment, when suddenly selfishness is shown. The babies quarrel and unhappiness is the result.[39]

The tenor of the article in the *Pittsburgh Dispatch* makes evident that Davis was less than thrilled with second place in the constant showman's race to offer new and exciting attractions. At least Davis was able to promote his offering as the "original." Regardless of order of arrival or conception, the new movies and their competing projector systems were apparently popular at both theaters, and for the rest of the year, Gulick and Davis each regularly programmed the new machines and their films into their shows, which were otherwise dominated by live vaudeville or stock theatrical performances.

While Davis continued to show movies in some form in most of his theaters through the rest of the decade and into the 1900s, it was almost nine years later, on June 19, 1905, that John P. Harris, in a vacant storefront owned by Davis, opened a nickelodeon on the west side of Smithfield Street in Pittsburgh's bustling downtown business district. As Charles Musser has rightly stated, "[t]he significance of this theater is not that it was some official 'first' but that it was to some degree responsible for the rapid proliferation of theaters across the United States."[40] If Davis and Harris weren't first, what exactly was it about this specific theater, and these two particular men that were responsible for its creation, that facilitated such quick and sustained growth?

Born in England, Harry Davis arrived in the United States in 1870 at the age of nine and settled with his family in Pittsburgh's Twelfth Ward. His father, John Davis, a highly skilled millwright, succeeded in a series of jobs designing and managing iron and tin-plate mills in the region. From childhood on, however, Harry showed little interest in his father's trade, and, when the time came, he refused to train as an apprentice. School did not hold much appeal, and Harry Davis quit at age eleven for a job as a florist's delivery boy. In his mid-teens, Davis began spending his summers

FIG. 2.2.
Bijou Theatre (Interior), Greater Pittsburg's Most Popular Theatre, R. M. Gulick, Manager," postcard, circa 1900. *Courtesy of Q. David Bowers.*

touring the Midwest as a carnival "fakir" (hustler), running a cane-rack toss, a game of chance that customers had little chance of winning.[41] According to Davis in an interview many years later, he was drawn to and excelled at, from an early age, the "high pitch," the ability to talk "unwilling nickels from the pockets of yokels at country fairs and carnivals."[42] Arguably, this itinerant education was a seminal experience in his life as a showman as Davis continually revisited lessons he learned hustling on the midway and the kind of profits that could be gained just a nickel at a time. Every fall, as the carnival season came to a close, he returned to Pittsburgh to play and work in the city's bowling alleys, amusement parlors, and pool halls. Davis purchased his first bowling alley in 1884. It was located in Diamond Alley, a downtown street largely devoted to low-end commercial leisure. A year later, Davis, who considered himself something of a pool shark, bought a nearby billiards parlor where throughout the 1890s he regularly promoted high-stakes tournaments involving many of the country's best pool players.[43] Like Thomas Tally, Davis was broadly inclusive in his interests in all things commercially amusing and sought out opportunities to own a variety of leisure operations in Pittsburgh. His next chance to expand his holdings came in 1888, when he secured the lease of the nearby Old Tivoli Garden, an amusement hall in the basement of the city's largest legitimate theater, the Grand Opera House. The previous management had built an indoor track and was holding a series of poorly attended "walking matches." Popular in the United States since before the Civil War, walking matches were competitive "races" in which the participants attempted to out-distance each other over a lengthy period of time, typically three or six days. On taking possession of the Tivoli, Davis transformed the previous owner's losses into his own profits by lowering admission costs to a dime—the old management had charged as much as a quarter—and by utilizing his carnival pitchman's know-how to promote the event. Davis provided larger prizes for the contestants and giveaways for the spectators, generated national press attention by enticing international stars of the sport to compete in the Pittsburgh events, and offered racers and audiences an ever-changing set of variations on the walking theme for each of the matches, including one "Go-as-You-Please" race in which women participated alongside the male competitors.[44] Eventually, Davis managed the entire Opera House and installed and operated an ice-skating rink in its basement where the walking matches had been held. Charging less, offering more, and heavily promoting both price and spectacle subsequently became the standard Davis model for commercial entertainment throughout his career, although the costly contradictions of this formula resulted in failure as often as success.

At the Tivoli Gardens, his invest-for-success economics worked well, and Davis was able to take the profits from this venture and, in 1891, lease from "the elderly and amiable" John W. O'Brien the nearby Casino, a then-

FIG. 2.3.
"New Grand Opera House—Fifth Avenue, Pittsburg," circa 1900.

failing dime museum. Unlike Davis's first bowling alley, the Casino, on Fifth Avenue near Wood Street, offered Davis a location in the heart of the city's primary entertainment district. In order to renovate the space on the "magnificent scale" that he felt necessary to transform it into the self-appointed Harry Davis Eden Musee, Davis turned to Frank McCann, a man Davis described to a local reporter as his "big butter and egg man."[45] Taciturn and unassuming in public, McCann was anything but a showman, and while his name rarely surfaced in the pages of the local press, county government archives and records of property transactions from the period show that this local investor was an extremely powerful force in Pittsburgh's rapidly expanding real estate market.[46] McCann influenced in a number of critical ways how Davis developed and managed his growing portfolio of Pittsburgh real estate and entertainment operations.

One of the many unknown aspects of Davis's career is to what degree his business actually belonged to him. Perhaps the most illuminating glimpse into this particular puzzle is an event that occurred in the summer of 1899. One day in early August, Davis chose to barricade himself inside the Grand Opera House, the city's largest legitimate theater at the time, alongside six Pinkerton detectives he had hired as part of a failed attempt to maintain control of this and another nearby stock-company theater, the Avenue. Such antics make for good news, and the national press, reporting on the underlying cause of the unfolding spectacle, revealed that Frank McCann had, in fact, recently fired Harry Davis from his services as manager of these two theaters. Up until that moment, McCann's name had never been publicly attached to the theaters—both had been presented and promoted as wholly owned and operated by the "Harry Davis Syndicate."[47] Later reports, however, exposed that Davis had from the beginning been only a minority partner to McCann, and that he had been further reduced to the position of paid employee when forced to sell his share to McCann in exchange for "an indebtedness of $175,000 to secure [Davis's other] creditors."[48] McCann had Davis and his Pinkertons arrested by city detectives, and the courts found that Davis's firing was warranted under the terms of his contract with McCann. Surprisingly, however, the two men's relationship did not end there.[49]

The Harry Davis Eden Musee, managed (if not owned outright) by Davis, was profitable for its first half-dozen years. In 1897, the heating system of the cage that held the museum's signature attraction, Old Rube, a twenty-six-foot python, caught fire and gutted most of the building.[50] Until that time, Davis promoted his museum by presenting not only Old Rube, "a magnificent specimen of the mastodonic reptile," but also Jo-Jo the dog-faced boy, Laloo the two-headed woman, and other attractions. Using the business model that had worked for him at the Tivoli, Davis succeeded in this amusement enterprise where previous attempts had failed by spending more on the museum's appearance, including a series of lavish new murals installed at the building's entrance, and promoting new entertainment, including a contract with the Keith vaudeville circuit for a regular schedule of performers. On the ground floor of the three-story museum, Davis opened the Café Royal and installed the city's best-known restaurateur at the time, Albert Menjou (father of future Hollywood star, then-infant Adolph), the "first to introduce to Pittsburg the European style of dining."[51] If Menjou's popular café, seating two to three hundred customers at lunch, helped situate the museum as a site of refined luxury, the White House, a saloon located at the other end of the building offering horse racing and baseball pool gambling, gave its operator access to a more "sporting" type of patron. The Eden's success led Davis to run and/or own at least five other dime museums in the western half of the state throughout the 1890s: the New World in nearby Allegheny and other smaller versions of the Eden in Harrisburg, Altoona, McKeesport, and Johnstown.

Unlike Davis, John Harris was a native, born in Pittsburgh's Fifth Ward in 1871 to Bridget (Gaughan) and John Harris Sr., a British immigrant. Harris's father literally thrust his young son into the life of a showman, pushing him into the boxing ring at the age of seven. By the early 1880s, the senior Harris, whose previous employment had included attempts at schoolteaching and cigar-making, was a partner in the "Comedy & Specialty Company of Harris and Willoughby," a minor barnstorming burlesque show whose specialty was the performance of "travesty" matches, "prize" bouts staged between two boxing midgets. If John Jr.'s recollections are to be believed, his first job in show business was as a last-minute replacement for one of the company's diminutive pugilists, who unfortunately turned up to work too inebriated to fight. Dressed by his father to look like "an impish dwarf" and set into the ring to triumph over the remaining boxer, General Andy Sweitzer, whether "little Johnny" truly "walloped the stuffings" out of the General is impossible to verify, but in the story's telling Harris grounds the beginning of his own entrepreneurial life in the display of less-than-refined amusements.[52] Harris's father later claimed to be "the foundation" for his son's success. In fact, Harris Jr. was able to secure a steady job for his itinerant father by purchasing a franchise to run the concessions for the city's baseball team, selling Pirates scorecards and souvenirs at Forbes Field. Harry Davis, only seven years older than "Little Johnny," was, in truth, a much more lasting influence on Harris's career, at least in the entertainment business.[53]

Considering the significance of their eventual relationship and the number of stories around and about their individual lives, it is somewhat surprising that there are no existing accounts of Harris and Davis's original meeting. Harris eventually became director and vice president of Harry Davis Enterprises, but he began working for Davis at the very bottom, standing on Fifth Avenue and selling tickets at the entrance to the Eden Musee. At some point in his late teens, Harris met and fell in love with Davis's younger sister, Eleanor.[54] Eleanor and John wed in the summer of 1894, and relocated to Johnstown, a mill town east on the Pennsylvania Railroad route, to manage that city's branch of the Harry Davis Eden Musee. Eventually, Harris began to take ownership of his own amusement houses. He purchased the McKeesport Musee from Davis in 1898 and renamed it, of course, Harris' Musee Theatre. Harris did not, however, leave his position in the Davis operation then or later, and continued to run its theaters both in and out of Pittsburgh.

The development of Davis's career to this point can be seen as a reflection of a showman's confidence in the power of the pitch as well as a businessman's pragmatic belief in the financial security of a diversified portfolio. Davis had, in the intervening years, bounced back from his losses of the Grand Opera House and the Avenue; by the summer of 1903 he had amicably purchased both of them back from McCann, proudly announcing "Harry Davis, sole owner and manager" near the top of all his newspaper advertisements and playbills for the two houses he now owned outright.[55] By the following theatrical season, Davis had amassed, in addition to several still-operating dime museums in the region, a collection of six Pittsburgh theaters: the Grand Opera House, which provided "continuous family vaudeville"; the Avenue, which featured the Harry Davis Stock Company in a different legitimate play each week; the Alvin, in which Davis experimented with a musical company; the Empire and Bijou, which both featured a mix of "family" burlesque and popular melodrama; and the Duquesne Garden, which, as an outdoor theater offering light opera, was one of the few venues to remain open during the summer months. In virtually all of Davis's theaters and museums, motion pictures had, since 1896, played a fairly regular supporting role in their various programs. By 1904, for example, Davis consistently used the year-old Edison/Porter sensation *The Great Train Robbery* to conclude the show at the Opera House. According to an account in one of the local papers: "The bill is closed by the realistic bank robbery portrayed by the kinetograph [sic], and very few people left their seats until it was concluded."[56]

The quick success of Harris and Davis's Nickelodeon, which opened only six months later, was a sum total of all that came before it: a substantial body of showmen's wisdom that began with both partners' youthful membership in the low-end amusement world; almost twenty years of theater and museum management; prior experiences using motion pictures within a theatrical setting; and both men's working knowledge of Pittsburgh's growing market for commercial leisure. But there are at least two other significant aspects of their shared business model that bore a direct relationship to the success of their first storefront theater. As theater historian Laurie Stepanian first documented, between 1902 and 1905, Davis had become a major participant in the city's rampant real estate speculation and development.[57] County deed records reveal that beginning in 1902, Davis steadily purchased Pittsburgh properties and land, typically located in and around the city's central downtown district.[58] Initially, these were limited purchases of narrow or odd-shaped lots that were nearby Davis's already established businesses, but, by the summer of 1903, Davis began to enter the heart of the city, paying $150,000 for a small piece of Fifth Avenue property, only fifteen wide, but well situated only one door away from his Avenue Theater.[59] From that moment on, real estate investment became a central and profitable element of Davis Enterprises, and in the beginning of June 1905, only two weeks before the nickelodeon opened, the *Pittsburgh Press* reported that Davis had bought the entire *Chronicle-Telegraph* office building at 347–349 Fifth Avenue for $490,000. In the previous three years, Davis's real estate purchases had come to "aggregate something like $6,000,000," in addition to leases on "a great deal of property which is earning him a great deal of money in addition to the theater properties." The article concluded: "Taken all in all, although one of the youngest investors of the city, he has driven good bargains and is in possession of some of the best property in the city."[60]

At the turn of the century, most prime available real estate was located in and around the city center. It was here, in Pittsburgh's Golden Triangle, that one could find a cadre of modern department stores, including The Joseph Horne Company, "devoted to fashion and merchandise of the high class," and Kaufmann's "Big Store," twelve stories tall, a block wide, and employing three thousand workers.[61] The new giants of steel-based capital and the industry-yoked city politic filled the downtown with increasingly larger (and more ornate) corporate headquarters and civic offices. Location, location, location—this relatively small and finite piece of land at the rivers' juncture forced interested parties to compete fiercely for property, causing prices to soar, driven in part by speculators like McCann and Davis. Davis, in fact, during this period was so active that he was individually credited by one local newspaper as having "caused the [city] boom through his deals."[62] Davis's model of speculation was not based on passively waiting for the wider real estate market to drive up the value of his own properties. Instead, he worked actively to improve and then lease or sublease his downtown properties, sometimes even to his own various busi-

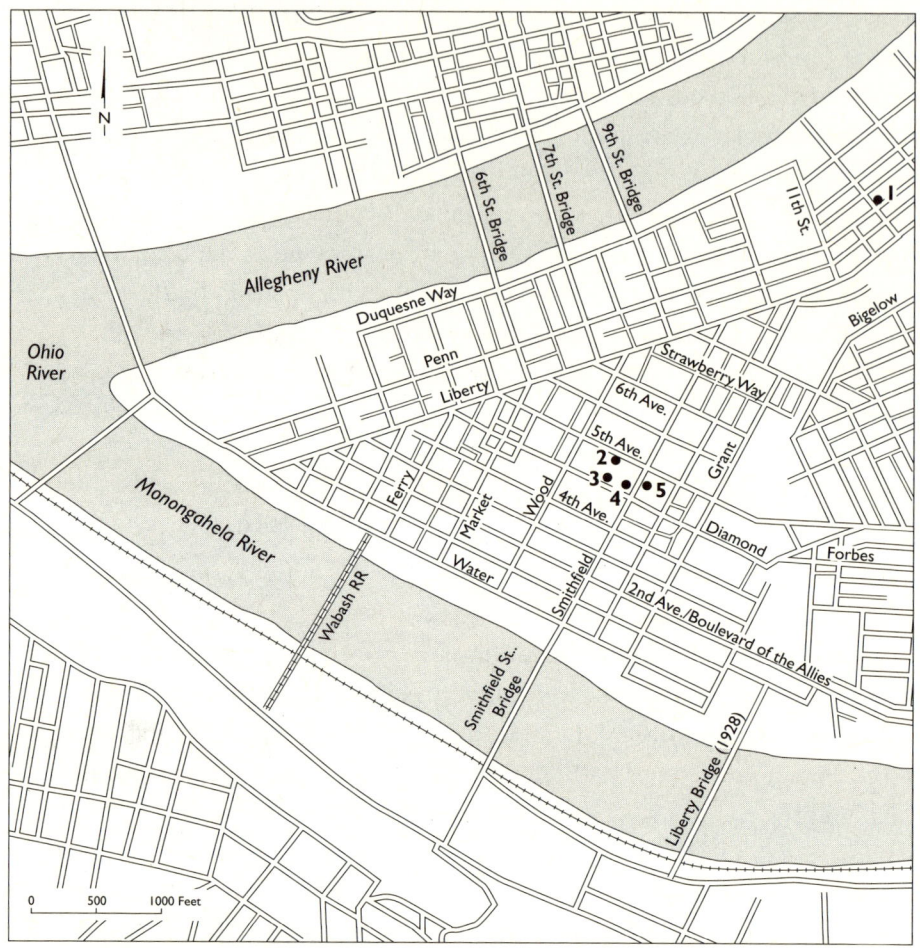

Map of downtown Pittsburgh, circa 1905.
1. Sol Leight's Grand Moving Picture Theater, 1302 Penn Avenue, Strip District
2. Avenue Theater, 330 Fifth Avenue, Downtown
3. Grand Opera House, Diamond Street, Downtown
4. Kaufmann's "Big Store," Smithfield Street, Fifth Avenue and Diamond Street blocks
5. Harris and Davis's Nickelodeon, 433–435 Smithfield Street, Downtown

nesses, at higher rents than had been required by the previous owner/ leaseholder. Once those increases had taken hold, he often sold the property to another landlord for a substantial profit. Not every property that Davis desired was available for direct sale, and in the late spring of 1905 he "acquired a 99-year lease on the entire block on Smithfield Street from Fifth Avenue to Diamond." It was in this particular stretch of buildings, across from the Kaufmann's store and its three thousand employees, that Harris opened the nickelodeon in a space he subleased from the Davis Company for an inflated rate of ten thousand dollars per year.[63]

While Davis apparently had found a key to successful realty profits in the Pittsburgh boom market, it was not something every investor was able to so easily accomplish. A lengthy article in the *Pittsburgh Post* that summer entitled "To Improve Property Is Problem" acknowledged that many "downtown [real estate] holders are perplexed with ideas in reference to betterments for their property." Frank McCann was not at a loss, however, and the article's author credited him with the "original idea" of developing a popular arcade-style building on his Fifth Avenue property. Although the author suggested that other investors in downtown property might succeed as well by creating office and light-industry spaces, it was "innovation that counts," and the article presciently suggests that it would be "the man who can offer the public something which no one else has [who] will be the one to rake in the profits for a long time to come."[64]

In the beginning of June, only two weeks before the nickelodeon opened, Davis decided to formally split his entertainment business in two, incorporating "his bowling alleys, shooting galleries, slot machine parlours, billiard rooms and kindred amusements into a new company to be known as 'Harry Davis Enterprises'"[65] These "kindred amusements," which had been Davis's initial entry into the business of commercial leisure, represent the least-regarded factor in the success of the Pittsburgh nickelodeon—his long-tested belief in the power of the lowly nickel. Even during periods when his legitimate theaters were profitable, Davis imagined new ways of hustling small change, at one point supposedly devising a chewing-gum machine for streetcars that he marketed to the various local traction companies operating in the busy city.⁶⁶ That particular project was short-lived —too much used gum stuck to the seats of the cars—but it underscores Davis's primary business model, structured around a popular philosophy: "if dollars are hard to get, go after profitable nickels.... You'll find they soon amount to *dollars* of profit.... It's little nickels, largely profit, that count toward dividend dollars."⁶⁷

In 1905, five cents carried considerably more purchasing power than it does today—it could buy you a one pound loaf of bread in most places in the country, a single-fare trolley token on Pittsburgh's interurban lines, or a large glass of draft beer in almost any of hundreds of mill-town saloons— but its power for the amusement businessman was due to "the inconsequence, the utter insignificance of the five-cent coin."⁶⁸ While for many of Pittsburgh's working poor, a nickel remained a coin of not insignificant value for quite some time, industrialization and the slow rise of real wages had led to a moment where increasingly larger portions of the city's population, even women and children, had occasional access to small amounts of money not intended for food, shelter, or savings. Pittsburgh in 1905 was in the midst of a massive growth spurt that had increased the city's population by more than 150,000 people in less than five years. That year, in particular, was by many accounts extremely productive for the region's steel industry, and weekly mill reports in the area's newspapers regularly pronounced "all mills working, none idle, prospects, good."⁶⁹ The resulting overall industrial prosperity helped precipitate the Pittsburgh region as a preeminent environment for the combining of business and pleasure, the massing and commercialization of amusement on a level not previously seen before. The nickel was the perfect symbol for the entrepreneur of these cheap amusements, because "for the very reason that we value a nickel lightly, we are apt to value lightly whatever we buy with that nickel."⁷⁰

Early in both their careers, Davis and Harris had used their various museums to enthusiastically chase dimes, but both were happy to pursue these coins of even smaller consequence by selling a form of leisure even more casual and low-cost than the museum or vaudeville theater. At this lower economic threshold, profits were dependent on the popularity of a form of entertainment that required no advanced planning on the part of the patron, requiring minimal investment in time, money, and cultural capital. The penny arcade was obviously home to the cheapest of cheap amusements, providing those whose work took them through the city's busy streets "a momentary break from routine that was so unobtrusive it could be seamlessly interwoven into the fabric of daily life."[71] Prior to the nickelodeon, Harry Davis found the penny arcade to be one of the most consistently lucrative of his leisure businesses; in 1904 he opened three such amusement parlors in the city's central downtown district.[72] Owners of parlors, including Davis, often promoted their arcades as offering the experience of an "Automatic Vaudeville," which allowed visitors the opportunity to build their own entertainment program by picking and choosing from a selection of mechanized amusements. Although the arcades did provide some diversions at a penny a piece, the majority of these coin-in-the-slot machines—the phonographs, shooting galleries, punching bags, strength and lung-testers, weighing scales, gambling machines, metal embossers, stationary bicycles, orchestrions, player pianos, self-playing banjos, and, of course, the Kinetoscope and Biograph peep shows—mostly required a nickel each for their pleasures.

While there are several conflicting reports about the exact timing, it seems certain that Davis, like other arcade owners across the country, used a section of a parlor he owned on Diamond Street, next door to his first bowling alley, to carve out the smallest of moving picture theaters. As early as 1902, and no later than the fall of 1904, one of his various managers—either Howard Royer, J. G. Foley, another Davis employee, or maybe even John P. Harris himself—operated a standing-room-only space for thirty-two customers who paid their nickel to enter a small space at the back of the penny arcade and watch a show which consisted of "a reel of film 300 to 400 feet in length . . . lasting four or five minutes."[73] Howard Royer, who, like Eugene Connelly, later asserted personal "credit for evolving the idea [of the nickelodeon] and carrying it to successful fruition," claimed that the backroom theater was "an instant hit" and that he "at once looked around for a larger location . . . decid[ing] on a storeroom on Smithfield street."[74] Royer may or may not have chosen the new space which extant records show was leased to Davis. Regardless, what more likely set Davis and/or Harris looking for a new location for their little movie show was the massive fire that burned down Davis's Alvin Theatre on June 2, 1905, destroying it along with much of the facade of the Grand Opera and the Diamond Street amusement arcade, which was located just around the corner in the adjacent building.[75]

Although it was Davis who owned the long-term lease on the storefront that would become the nickelodeon, whose initial idea it was to open a movie-only show in that space remains unknown. Davis was the more established showman who had an enduring belief in cheap amusements and deep pockets with which to take bigger risks. Harris was still on the road to success, still an employee of Davis's, and still much better known in McKeesport than Pittsburgh, but his time spent managing commercial amusements in the region's various mill towns had trained him in the successful operation of small-space, cheap-admission amusements. The two men were not competitors, they were family and friends. Harris and Davis's sister had just named their second son Harry Harris after Harry Davis. Just over a week before the nickelodeon's opening, the two men were seen together in McKeesport, eagerly discussing potential "shared real estate opportunities."[76] For more than a hundred years, both men have, at various times, been credited either individually or collectively with the resulting nickelodeon, and there is little documentation to support one particular narrative over the other.

The Pittsburgh Nickelodeon was one of a multitude of commercial experiments conducted in this period by the men, who both held a strong belief that "small sums lead to more than seldom large ones."[77] The nickelodeon was also, at least at first glance, more an amusement evolution than revolution. The first verifiable mention of the Nickelodeon on Smithfield Street does not materialize in a local newspaper until May 1906, almost a full year after its successful opening, by which time the citywide boom had clearly begun in earnest. By that spring of 1906, forty-five nickel theaters were paying for annual city operating licenses. The brief article,

"The Festive Nickelodeon" appears on the editorial page of the *Pittsburgh Sun*, an afternoon paper that had just begun publication a few months before. It reports an account that is seemingly intimate with the moment of the theater's origination: "A year ago John P. Harris a native Pittsburgher . . . conceived the idea of opening a room in the downtown section of the city, installing a moving picture machine, renting the films from an Eastern syndicate, changing the picture once or twice a week, and charging 5 cents admission. He went to Mr. Davis with his idea. Mr. Davis said he had the money to back the idea. So the theory became a fact."[78]

The story's unusual lack of hyperbole and support by existing documentation makes it a particularly appealing account, well within the realm of possibility and with just enough specific details and unanswered questions to persuade. It also offers up a lovely circular narrative in which Harry Davis, who not so long ago had required financing by a real estate–investing silent partner, offered up his own money or property (or both) at the request of another showman in need, his brother-in-law. How the resulting theater's costs or profits may have been divided, or even whose company actually controlled the Nickelodeon, remains unknown. But everything points to the Nickelodeon as a profitable partnership between John Harris and Harry Davis.

Whether it was Davis or Harris who eventually picked its location, the Nickelodeon at 433–435 Smithfield Street was specifically chosen to maximize the profits and pedestrian traffic associated with one of Davis's penny arcades; although rarely mentioned, the movie theater was opened right next-door to one of his "Automatic Vaudeville" parlors.[79] Capitalizing on the same transient market present in the business district, the nickelodeon presented a new kind of amusement bargain, the quickest of modern show experiences. And in classic Davis style, the Nickelodeon's "popular pricing" did not preclude a sense of luxury.

Almost from the beginning, a get-rich-quick mythology of the nickelodeon business was propagated by how-to books such as David Hulfish's *Motion Picture Work*, industry trade journals like the *Moving Picture World*, and national magazines and newspapers including the *Saturday Evening Post*. All described the generic nickelodeon as a seat-of-the-pants operation that could profitably be run by entrepreneurs of little means and experience, with total costs ranging from $83 to $200 a week, including rent for the storefront, estimated at only $10 to $40 a week, and in which patrons were to be uncomfortably seated, according to one trade magazine, in "ordinary kitchen chairs, not fastened."[80] Davis, however, like other local landlords, was raising rents on all his downtown property, and at $10,000 a year, the lease alone on the nickelodeon amounted to $210 a week, more than the total operating expenses being suggested by these various national journals. "More for less" was a Davis mantra, reflected by even the Nickelodeon's upholstered "opera chairs."[81] Such increased expenditures were economically feasible for the operation because, unlike Sol Leight and the many other potential exhibitors that started from nothing, Davis and Harris had easy access to the accoutrements and labor necessary to efficiently convert an empty storefront into a moving picture theater. This transformation included work by the aforementioned plaster artist who Davis kept on regular retainer for all his commercial properties. The earliest surviving images of the theater's interior and exterior show the exterior lobby and the exhibition space decorated with ornamental flourishes—crown moldings, ceiling ornamentation, fanciful rosettes around entrances, pilasters decoratively framing the screen—all more closely associated with the later development of the movie palaces than an early nickel-charging storefront show.[82] One trade paper article written in 1907, recounting the success of the Pittsburgh nickelodeon, set the cost of the five-cent theater at a considerable forty thousand dollars, although there are no records as to how exactly the money was spent.[83]

By all accounts, the expenditures were a worthwhile investment. Open seven days a week from eight in the morning until around midnight, the theater could accommodate approximately two hundred paying customers at a time, half up front in the seats, the rest standing along a rail in a raised section in the back. At the height of its popularity, if reports are to be believed, as many as seven or eight thousand nickels a day may have rolled in, a total that would have required a new set of patrons every twenty-four

FIG. 2.5. The exterior of Harris and Davis's Nickelodeon. *Moving Picture World*, November 30, 1907, 629.

FIG. 2.6. The interior of Harris and Davis's Nickelodeon. *Moving Picture World*, November 30, 1907, 629.

minutes.[84] Exactly what movies these earliest audiences saw for that nickel remains a mystery, although film scholar Richard Abel has convincingly shown that the majority of films exhibited in the United States during this period were overwhelmingly of French origin, usually from the Pathé Company.[85] Later accounts associate any number of different films with the very first show, including the now two-year-old sensation, *The Great Train Robbery*, which Davis had regularly shown at the Grand Opera House.[86] What *is* well documented is that by the fall of that same year, around the time of Leight's disastrous attempt at exhibition, Davis had already opened at least two other nickel theaters in the downtown district—but neither these, nor any of his other subsequent movie theaters, were named "Nickelodeon." Why would he so quickly abandon the term that would bring him fortune and fame? It is possible that the name was not his to keep, because Harris or someone else had come up with the powerful moniker. Equally likely is that Davis did not want his reputation as Pittsburgh's premier showman becoming too closely associated with the rising tide of cheap entrepreneurs of the type personified by Sol Leight and his Strip storefront theater. Davis instead named most of his new moving picture theaters either Dreamland or the Bijou Dream, both in and beyond Pittsburgh. A *Variety* article later that year reported: "Harry Davis, it is rumored, will invest about $500,000 in establishing moving picture theaters in every city of importance in the country. Every detail of the business, even to the manufacturing of his own machines and the making of films will be handled by Mr. Davis in his Pittsburgh headquarters. Locations have already been secured in Rochester, Toledo, Cleveland, Detroit, Buffalo, Boston, New York, Grand Rapids, Dayton and other cities and work on some of the theaters has already commenced."[87]

Over the next two years, Davis opened other nickelodeons in many, if not all, of these cities mentioned by the article, as well as Washington DC, Philadelphia, and throughout a number of Pennsylvania's smaller towns and cities. The majority of these were described, like the Pittsburgh theater, as offering patrons the "most elaborate" show, and the "finest in the land."[88] Davis did not go to the trouble of building his own cameras or projectors, but he did attempt to produce a number of his own movies and also opened

FIG. 2.7.
Pittsburgh's Bijou Dream, owned by Harry Davis, postcard, circa 1906.
Courtesy of Q. David Bowers.

FIG. 2.8.
Last known image of the Nickelodeon, from across Smithfield Street, circa 1909. *Courtesy of the Western Pennsylvania Historical Society.*

a film rental service, the "Harry Davis Exchange," which by 1907 was regularly advertised in a number of national trade journals.[89] Harris, meanwhile, in addition to remaining vice president of Harry Davis Enterprises, began to open his own moving picture theaters in Pittsburgh as well as in Johnstown, Altoona, and a number of other the region's many mill towns.

Harris and Davis were not alone for long, and as Sol Leight and others started to emulate the two successful showmen, the battle for Pittsburgh's nickels began in earnest. As early as the fall of 1906, some of the competing exhibitors were forced to provide additional inducements to attract a regular audience to their shows. According to one Pittsburgh reporter: "Others . . . who are not so favorably situated . . . give good long shows and in one establishment four different sets of views were given for a nickel, including illustrated songs with phonograph accompaniment. The competition is already becoming keen and the boom of the 5-cent theater has nearly reached its zenith."[90]

This was not nearly true. The nickelodeon and its business, in Pittsburgh and across the country, continued to grow exponentially during the following years; complete with its own new trade journal, the *Nickelodeon*, which described the boom as "a tremendous, whirling, dizzy multiplication of picture theatres; an industrial growth so rapid and startling that nothing else had a chance to happen."[91]

3

THE WRONG KIND OF NICKEL MADNESS

IN 1914, THE *Pittsburgh Moving Picture Bulletin* began with two goals: to sustain development of a local community of men (and a few women) who shared the movies as business and passion; and to promote the long-needed increase in theater admission prices in Pittsburgh beyond the profit-thin nickel. Almost a decade after Harris and Davis helped spark nationwide nickel madness, virtually every movie house in Pittsburgh continued to charge its patrons the same five cents, regardless of size of theater, type of neighborhood, or length of show. From the grandest new theater in the city's wealthiest enclave to the smallest storefront in a mill-side neighborhood, exhibitors were unable (or, in some cases, unwilling) to depart from nickelodeon pricing. Nickel pricing was so ubiquitous in Pittsburgh that it earned its own poem, written by "Miss A." of the Independent Film Exchange and published in the *Bulletin* on August 3, 1914:

THE NICKEL SHOW

Now old "Si Perkins" came to town,
With nickels and dimes to spend,
He stood at the corner of Fifth and Wood—
Had a date, no doubt, with a friend.

He looked at the buildings so awful tall;
They almost made him sick—
When all of a sudden, he said, "By Gosh!
If there ain't one of the nicks."

The name "Olympic" looked pretty good,
The cost he thought was a "dime"
But on the window it read "five cents";
"I'm lucky," he said, "this time."

The show let out in an hour or so,
And from there he crossed the street;
"The Minerva" charged likewise "five cents"
Si chuckled, "This can't be beat."

From there he went to "The Wonderland"
He saw "five cents" admission,
He asked the boss of "The Cameraphone,"
"Do you guys work on Commission?"

He had one more he wanted to see
"Columbia," I think is the name
Where funny Keystones reign supreme,
"The price," of course, was the same.

Well the very next day when "Si" got home,
He was tired, he was almost a wreck;
He couldn't get over such shows for "five cents"
"Pretty soft boys"—"By Heck!"[1]

In her joshing familiarity with the Pittsburgh film world, Miss A. makes visible a community otherwise unseen—the region's exhibitors, exchangemen, moviemakers, suppliers, postermen, salesmen, exploiters, lecturers, and all the many others. This merely partial list underscores a simple yet significant point; the local experience of the movies was then (and still is) affected by a diverse institutional array of people, parties, and practices. While in the last two decades it has become a historiographic truism within film studies that exhibition is a key site for making meaning, and that exhibitors and their theaters have shaped the medium as much as its stars and their directors, the broader spectrum of local film history has largely remained outside the boundaries of this otherwise productive belief. If the formative role of exhibition and its diversity of local practices is now firmly located within the arc of film's institutional history, we still have yet to really come to grips with what "exhibition" actually means and who exactly was involved in its definition.

In stopping to study this small poem, we can see what structural changes created these local specificities, and what place bookkeepers, their bosses, and the other "invisible" characters in the local film business had in the formation and evolution of movie exhibition and its resulting culture. Thus, we can begin to understand why a place like Pittsburgh (or anywhere else for that matter) might develop its own particular movie culture, through the social process through which lives, relations, and institutions of a particular kind are created.

In Pittsburgh, a clerical job at the Independent Film Exchange, keeping track of films coming in and films going out, was one likely attended to by thousands of equally anonymous women and men—like "Miss A."—in an unknown number of exchanges across the country.[2] It was no secret that the Independent's manager, "Ab" Davis (no relation to Harry), along with many of the city's other exchangemen, thought that the exhibitors were "spoiling" the local movie business with their excesses and that they must be somehow taught to "use rational business methods" in order to more profitably run their picture shows.[3] Neither was it a mystery within the local trade that the *Bulletin* by and large agreed with the exchangemen in locating the blame for nickel-pricing with the exhibitors. As such, the journal's editors were more than happy to publish the poem. Just like Davis and Harris's Smithfield Street nickelodeon, Miss A.'s verse is the real result of a lived-effort to negotiate and express the particular opportunities and difficulties of Pittsburgh's movie business at a critical moment in time.

The *Bulletin* Begins: An Intimate Journal of Local Film Facts

In April 1914, only six months before publishing Miss A.'s poem, brothers William and Charles Mayer announced that they were about to "launch a new craft on the journalistic sea—the *Pittsburgh Moving Picture Bulletin*."[4] Although both were neophytes to the movie business, the brothers brought with them more than twenty-five years of experience in the local printing business. William and Charles, sons of a German immigrant carriage-maker, started their family company in Pittsburgh's East End in 1887. Initially, Mayer Publishing and Printing was a small, single-press outfit, but by the 1910s it had grown into a "medium-sized, if well equipped" plant that prospered by printing everything from "monthly religious journals" to wholesale jewelry catalogs and drugstore price lists.[5] The company's primary income depended on these general print jobs, but, from the very beginning, the brothers were also active publishers and distributors of their own materials. William, who never finished grammar school, having left home at an early age to escape their abusive alcoholic father, acted as editor-in-chief for four different self-published local periodicals over the span of forty-two years.[6] Beginning in 1887, the brothers published: the *East End Journal* (1887–1897), a weekly review of local affairs; *Remarques* (1897–1904), a "coat pocket sized home news-magazine" offering local, social, religious, and fraternal news at three cents an issue; and the *Pittsburgh Herald* (1904–1914), a more ambitious, citywide, daily paper best known for its extensive coverage of the Pirates baseball team.[7] Although the *Herald* never achieved financial success, in general, these publications offered reasonable economic benefit to the Mayers. Besides profit, publishing and editing their own journal provided the brothers with the kinds of "fun, excitement and headaches" that their just-for-hire work rarely offered, something that William, in particular, seemed to have craved for much of his professional life. Startup and overhead costs for each of these local ventures were relatively low since all the printing was done using the Mayers' own equipment. The publication of each of these local papers relied primarily on advertising sales, which resulted in a continuous stream of additional revenue for their company. Perhaps most importantly, the regular circulation of these papers acted as an efficient form of marketing for the brothers' primary business, offering "a most effective means of contact for printing orders" for the numerous concerns of their readership.[8]

Upon closing down the *Herald*, sometime early in 1914, the two brothers were, for the first time in a long time, without a local periodical to call their own. The *Herald* had required a fairly large percentage of the city's daily readership for its success, resulting, the brothers agreed, in more work than fun. A new publishing project was in order, and what could be more fun than the movies?

According to William Mayer's introductory editorial in the *Pittsburgh Moving Picture Bulletin*, the journal's mission was to "disseminate information" regarding films and equipment, "foster friendliness" between exhibitors and exchangemen, and help "combat adverse legislation" that might affect the health and growth of the local moving picture industry.[9] Prior to the arrival of the *Bulletin*, Pittsburgh exchanges, if they wanted to advertise their services to regional exhibitors, were forced to take out ads in the mainstream Pittsburgh city newspapers, an inefficient and likely expensive undertaking. Unlike all the Mayers' previous publications, a subscription to the *Bulletin* was free, provided weekly to 1,500 of the region's movie-related businesses and individuals, and so its costs and profits were derived solely from advertising purchased by the city's exchanges and supply houses.[10] With few exceptions, the advertisers came from the local end of the movie business, and from the very beginning Mayer made clear that his new enterprise was not designed to compete with established national trades like *Moving Picture World*, *Motion Picture News*, or *Variety*: "The Bulletin has no lofty aspirations to fulfill; it does not desire a national field of operation—we have other

FIG. 3.1.
The cover of the inaugural *Pittsburgh Moving Picture Bulletin*,
picturing James B. Clark, April 15, 1914.

publications which fill the bill—its ambition is to fill a want—for a local publication."[11] The local, magazine-styled journal ran consistently (with only a few weeks of inactivity caused by the flu pandemic of 1918) for fifteen years.

Later, looking back at his career, William Mayer boasted that theirs had been the first regional trade journal devoted to its local film business. In fact, the *Bulletin* belongs within a group of a yet unknown number of periodicals contemporarily described as "zone" papers, regional trade journals that began their publication in the 1910s and early 1920s.[12] William and his brother, within a year of introducing the *Bulletin*, were simultaneously publishing similar weekly trade papers for the Cincinnati, Cleveland, and Detroit areas, which was an indication of the success of their regional model. While there are no known surviving examples of these other Mayer publications, there are, in addition to the *Bulletin*, extant copies of at least three other regional trade journals produced elsewhere in this era; the Minneapolis-based *Amusements* (1916–1944), the *Exhibitor* of Philadelphia (1918–1954), and Atlanta's *Weekly Film Review* (1920–1930).[13] The seven cities that sustained known regional journals had in common a thriving local exhibition scene that included plenty of theaters and lots of regular customers. The key determinant, however, that made the *Bulletin* and these other regional publications possible (and profitable) was not movie exhibition per se, but rather exhibition's local relationship to the film exchange.

All of these cities, from Detroit to Atlanta, were regional urban hubs with developed infrastructure and transportation systems, and each had, at various moments, developed into a primary site for trade between what the *Bulletin* describes as "filmmen," the owners of the exchanges, and "picture men," the theater owners and exhibitors.[14] In each of these seven major municipalities, a "Film Row" subsequently developed, an area, street, or downtown block dominated by the exchange offices and the supply houses required for the daily business of running a moving picture show. In Pittsburgh, it was initially the downtown stretch of Forbes Avenue between Ninth and Twelfth Streets that became the institutional heart of the city's movie business, although, because of changes to the city's fire-safety codes, most had moved by 1915 to Fourth Avenue. Harry Davis was the earliest entertainment entrepreneur active in downtown real estate, but he was not the only one, and in more than a few cases, substantial properties, like the seven-story Seltzer Building, were developed specifically for the local moving picture business. The Seltzer family located their primary business—selling player pianos and pipe organs to the region's theaters (and churches)—on the first two floors, and leased the rest of the offices to a variety of movie-related occupants, including: a supply house; Hollis-Smith (seventh floor), which specialized in the sale of used projectors; and as a number of exchanges both major (Selznick Productions) and minor (Square Deal Film Company). The presence of these and the dozens of other companies that supplied the region's theaters with everything from feature films and movie posters to ticket rolls and toilet paper meant that Pittsburgh was a productive site at which to start a regional trade journal. As Stanley Mayer, William's son, suggested in 1937: "The film exchanges of Pittsburgh needed a method of communication with their customers, the motion picture theater owners of Western Pennsylvania and the *Moving Picture Bulletin* . . . fit the bill."[15]

The kinds of "communication" required, were specific to the exchanges, which operated in this period in a significant number of different ways and offered a surprising variety of services and products. Film historians, with very few exceptions, have largely disregarded the role of the regional exchange in the development of the American film industry.[16] At best, if mentioned at all in the history books, the exchange is described at its rhetorical face value—a place where exhibitors swapped old films for newer ones.[17] While without a doubt, this material transaction was an ongoing part of the exchange environment, the actual physical processes of transfer was only one aspect of its work and influence. Today, we describe this basic transfer function as product "distribution," but this is a term that almost never appears in exchange discourse from the period. A distributor, as typically defined, does not really alter or affect the possible meanings and uses of the product he or she handles, whether it is a Chaplin short or canned meat. Distribution is a middleman's job, often profitable, but not exactly rich with authorial intention or creative control. Arguably, this apparent

DIRECTORY
OF THE
SELTZER BUILDING
Liberty Ave. and Twelfth St.
Pittsburgh, Pa.

T. P. HOLLIS — H. J. SMITH

HOLLIS-SMITH CO.

Machines, Booths, Chairs, Carbons—Everything needed to equip and conduct motion picture theatres. SEVENTH FLOOR

LEWIS J. SELZNICK PRODUCTIONS

C. F. SCHWERIN, Mgr. — SELZNICK PICTURES — PHONE 3479 GRANT, FIFTH FLOOR

"The Common Law," "The Foolish Virgin," "The Price She Paid," "Panthea," "The Law of Compensation," "The Argyle Case," all taken from known writers' books, enacted by the screen's greatest artists.

LEON D. NETTER, Gen Mgr. — GEO. P. JACOBS, Mgr.

MASTERPIECE FILM ATTRACTIONS

Presenting

In Ohio—"Garden of Allah," "Beware of Strangers," "The Ne'er Do Well," "The Libertine." In Northern Ohio—"Purity." In Western Pennsylvania and West Virginia—"The Ne'er Do Well," "Neptune's Daughter," "The Spoilers," "Purity."

FOURTH FLOOR — PHONE 6117 GRANT

L. NEWMAN, Mgr. — PHONE 6117 GRANT

A. G. FONTANA PRODUCTIONS, INC.

NOW BOOKING

"20,000 Leagues Under the Sea" and "The Witching Hour" for Western Pennsylvania and West Virginia. FOURTH FLOOR

GENERAL FILM COMPANY, INC.

THIRD FLOOR

O. HENRY STORIES — "THE BARRIER"

PHONE 2380 GRANT

SELTZER MUSIC COMPANY

Sole Distributors for the Celebrated
SEEBURG PIPE ORGAN ORCHESTRA

Phone—Private Exchange 4870 Grant. · First & 2nd Floors & Basement

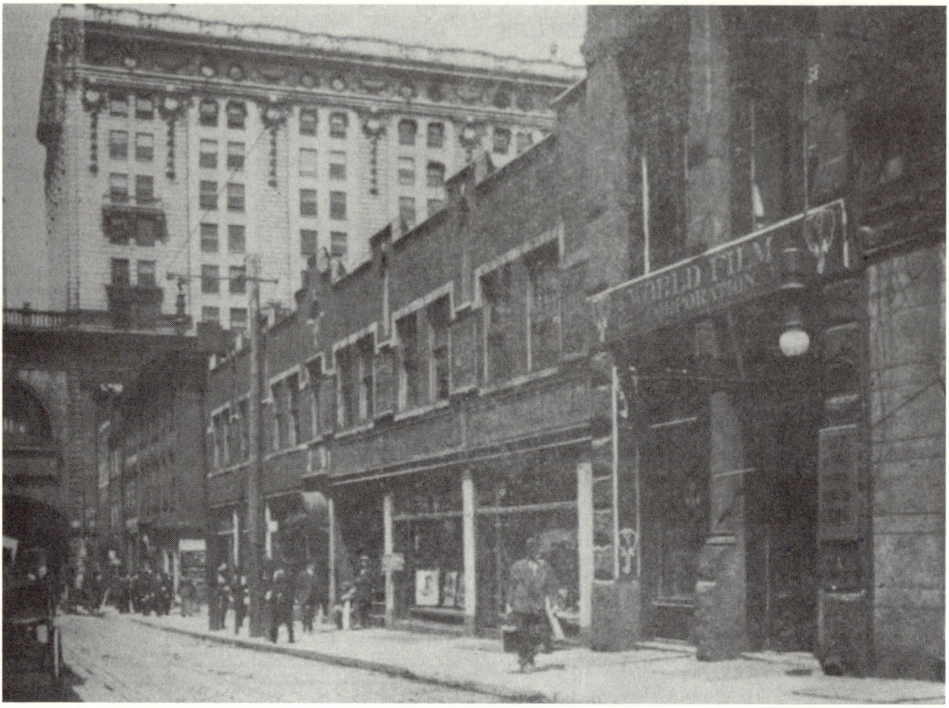

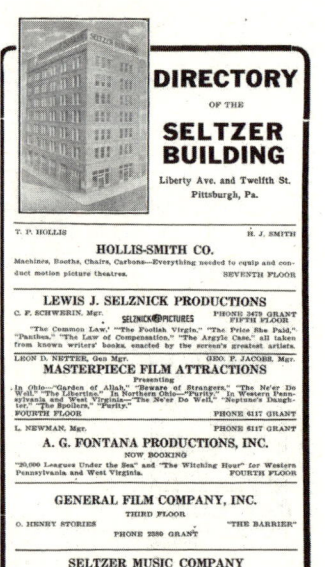

FIG. 3.2.
"The Fourth Avenue Section of Film Row," *Pittsburgh Moving Picture Bulletin*, May 13, 1914, 8.

FIG. 3.3.
"Directory of the Seltzer Building," *Pittsburgh Moving Picture Bulletin*, April 25, 1917.

lack of dynamic power is why historians of cinema have tended to intensively focus their research on production and exhibition, two places where movies and their meanings are more clearly made. However, for the first two decades of the 1900s, the exchange was both literally and affectively a central institutional site, and as such had a significant stake in the formation of local movie culture.

At least until the early 1910s, the exchange generally compiled the program offered to local exhibitors, creating the all-important mix of short films that a theater showed to its patrons. So while exhibitors were considered showmen in the early years of the nickelodeon boom, they rarely actually chose exactly what they showed. Instead, they typically had to rely on a particular exchange to provide a weekly supply of predetermined titles. By 1913 or so, theater owners had many more options and (briefly) a bit more control, but the exchange remained, throughout this period, a key participant in determining what kind of films exhibitors might choose and profit from. Never ancillary, the exchange was a principal and constant entity in the shaping of local movie culture. Who actually owned that exchange, and what he could/would offer in terms of the range and variations of form, content, and manufacturer, would shift quite dramatically over the early years of the twentieth century.

Charlie Musser's research has shown that theater owners in this country began the practice of renting films to project themselves, rather than purchasing films outright or hiring the services of an itinerant exhibitor, beginning around 1903.[18] In the years leading up to the nickelodeon, many of the films shown in Pittsburgh were shipped directly to its variety and vaudeville theaters from elsewhere, most likely either from George Kleine's substantial operation in Chicago or the Kinetograph Company in New York City.[19] But with its efficient railroad system and an extensive web of industrialized satellite towns spread across western Pennsylvania, northern West Virginia, and eastern Ohio, Pittsburgh was a "natural" site for regional film exchanges to develop. Although the exact date remains uncertain, the Stieren Optical Company, begun in the late nineteenth century by William E. Stieren to supply Pittsburgh-area engineers, architects, and surveyors with "optical, mathematical, meteorological, and electrical instruments," first began to

FIG. 3.4.
Richard A. Rowland.
Portrait by W. S. Wasburn,
in *Sketches Serious and Otherwise*
(1914), Pittsburgh [s.n.], 221.
*Courtesy of ULS Digital Research
Library, University of Pittsburgh.*

operate a film exchange sometime in early 1903.[20] Stieren, whose film rentals joined an already successful service supplying local theaters with magic lantern slides, was followed later that year by both a Pittsburgh branch of the New York Kinetograph Company and the local Pittsburgh Calcium Light Company,[21] run by a young Richard Rowland. In 1900, at the age of twenty, Rowland had inherited his father's profitable business selling rolls of tickets, boxes of limelight, and other supplies to the city's legitimate theaters, and of the early entrepreneurs who entered the movie exchange business, it was Rowland who took best advantage of the local potential and develop a sustainable film rental and supply service.

FIG. 3.5.
Calcium Light and Film advertisement. *Connellsville Daily Courier*, December 12, 1906, 7.

By the summer of 1905, the rapid spread of the region's nickelodeons and intense competition between many of their owners increased demand for an exchange service located in Pittsburgh that could consistently provide "new" films as often as three times a week. Rowland's business quickly grew. At the end of that first boom year, thirty-four-year old James B. Clark became Rowland's partner. Clark, a second-generation "native son" of Pittsburgh, had for the previous eighteen years been employed as a bookkeeper for one of the city's wholesale grocers, and had recently married Rowland's cousin, Gertrude. Together, he and Rowland changed their business name to Calcium Light and Film Company, reflecting the importance of the exchange to their growing concern. A 1906 invoice from the newly titled company showed one local nickelodeon owing eighteen dollars a week for a service that consisted of "one reel of film with one change weekly."[22]

In fairly rapid succession, the partners expanded their reach, opening five Calcium Light branch offices in Rochester, Des Moines, Omaha, Cincinnati, and Wilkes-Barre. With such a large operation, Clark and Rowland required a steady supply of films, and overall consistency was more important than the story or subject of any particular title. According to Clark in a later interview with one of the national trade journals: "We bought our films outright from firms like Pathé and Méliès, and we paid so much a foot for them. We did not have to look over the picture to see what it was all about before taking it. The producers got out a catalogue with the lengths and descriptions of the pictures, and we ordered from that, and we ordered the book through several times."[23] Between 1906 and 1907, competition to supply the region's nickelodeons swiftly grew as a number of other entrepreneurs, many former local theater owners, opened rival exchanges, including: the American Film Exchange, the Fort Pitt Film Company, Regal Amusement Company, the Pittsburgh Cut-Rate Exchange, Davis's self-titled Harry Davis Enterprises, as well as the pre-studio Warner brothers, whose downtown Duquesne Amusement Supply Company was managed by the eldest brother, Harry. Harry's younger brother Albert was also involved in this new aspect of the family business, operating a branch of the Duquesne exchange in Norfolk, Virginia.[24]

That Pittsburgh could support all of these exchanges was, in large part, due to a culture of exhibition that had developed among its nickelodeons, at least those within the city, where theater owners changed their program multiple times a week. As early as 1907, competition was fierce enough that some theaters switched their program every day, Monday through Saturday. This, in turn, required Pittsburgh exchanges to stock enough different titles to supply their exhibitors with "new" films every day but Sunday, when theaters were closed due to the city's strict "blue" laws.[25] "New" did not necessarily mean newly produced or even new to Pittsburgh, but unseen within the exhibitor's neighborhood or theater. Although the exact number of titles being produced and distributed worldwide is unknown, Richard Abel has convincingly shown that companies like Pathé-Frères, at the time the largest international manufacturer of motion pictures, were dramatically increasing production to meet demand, releasing as many as five to ten new films every week.[26] Newly produced films were the most costly type for an exhibitor to rent, and a local theater owner who ran a completely different program—averaging two to four reels each—six days a week typically could not afford this expense. Older films typically recirculated, sometimes for years, and exchanges, which most typically purchased the films outright from the manufacturers, often kept them in circulation until their emulsion was worn out. Exchanges generally offered exhibitors a choice of programs that provided a "blend" of old and new stock (the more new stock the higher the rental fee). A surviving business card circa 1907 from J. G. Foley, a salesman for Harry Davis's new film exchange business, provides a sense of the rental costs a potential local exhibitor was faced with: "Film Rental: $15.00, $18.00, $21.00, $25.00 . . . Take Your Choice . . . Three Changes Weekly. You get what you pay for."[27]

The original source of the films was as varied and inconsistent in this early period as the films themselves. Harry Davis, always open to new business opportunities, attempted to enter the production field in 1906, establishing a small rooftop studio on a building he owned in the city's downtown district. Sparsely staffed, the studio was rather ineffectually run by two of Edison's former personnel, one of whom was Gilbert M. Anderson who had held a minor role as one of the horse-riding bandits in *The Great Train Robbery*. Although no studio records remain, Davis's publicist later claimed that Anderson produced only three or four shorts in the year he spent with Davis, including a nonfiction view of a local pageant for the consecration of Pittsburgh's Saint Paul Cathedral and a one-reel chase film, shot in Hazelwood, a nearby mill town.[28] According to a recent biography of Anderson, he was unhappy with Davis's demand for primarily nonfiction films of the Pittsburgh region, and so soon left for Chicago.[29] If the recollection of one of Davis's employees is to be believed, however, Anderson was actually more interested in "chasing Pittsburgh's beautiful daughters" than making movies.[30] Regardless, Anderson's career dramatically changed after heading westward to Chicago—he reinvented himself as Western hero Broncho Billy Anderson, and became one of the medium's earliest "stars" as well as half-owner of the soon-to-be prolific Essanay Studios.

For Pittsburgh theater owners, local production was clearly never going to be a complete solution to the need for continuously new product, although the practice remained an active aspect of the region's movie culture well into the studio era. Instead, Pittsburgh's exchanges were required to seek out literally dozens of individual manufacturers working in a number of other cities across the country and around the world. Those manufacturers that were even fairly dependable in their output earned high regard, and their films were eagerly sought. In Pittsburgh, one of the smaller but ultimately influential exchanges in this period was Duquesne Amusement, operated by the Warner Brothers. The brothers, who hailed from Ohio, entered the local exchange business sometime in late 1906 or early 1907, after a number of other exchanges were already well established within the city. While Harry and Albert Warner's business letterhead claimed their rental operation as "The Largest Film House in the West," the letters often told a different story. In April 1907, for example, Harry Warner wrote to William Selig, who ran a successful Chicago production company. This letter illustrates that Duquesne Amusements was struggling to find its way:

> Dear Sir:
> We are as yet waiting for a reply to our communication regarding films, and now we understand you just issued a new subject, "The Banded King"[sic] which we expected you would send to us as soon as you did to any one else in our city. It is true we are just beginning and unable to use one dozen prints of a subject, but we expect in a short space of time to be able to compete in quantity with any of them. . . . We have received courteous treatment from all Eastern manufacturers namely: Pathe, Vitagraph, and the Mutoscope, and we trust you will treat us in the same way. . .
> Yours very truly,
> THE DUQUESNE AMUSEMENT SUPPLY CO.
> H. M. Warner, MGR.[31]

It is evident from other correspondence that Selig continued to ignore Harry Warner's requests for titles, in large part because the Warners apparently made a regular habit of not paying their bills on time. In comparison, all of the other exchanges operating in the city in 1907, including Davis's, consistently purchased and received every one of Selig's titles, including *The Bandit King*.[32]

Calcium Light and Film, Selig's best Pittsburgh customer, consistently rented out a dozen prints of each of his new titles, and in the winter of 1909, Clark and Rowland were the first to be licensed by the Motion Picture Patents Company (MPPC), also known as the Edison Trust, to distribute its members' films. The broad institutional effects of the Trust are well documented, as well as the concurrent rise of the independent manufacturers, but the fate of the local exchange in these litigious years of deal making and law breaking is less well known. Under the twin auspices of profit and Progressivism, the Edison Trust is credited with facilitating the rationalization of the industry, particularly in its ability to organize film manufacturers, stimulate dependable production, and regularize print circulation. The MPPC sought to turn film into a standardized commodity by controlling and regulating the economies of production, distribution, and exhibition. The result required each of the Trust's manufactures to regularly provide new films, consisting of a fixed number of reels, on a specific weekly release day. Calcium Light, or any other licensed exchange, could then offer a regular and consistent service to their local customers, the exhibitors, who also were required to be licensed by the Trust. Under this system, it soon became feasible for a Pittsburgh theater that contracted with licensed exchangemen to create a program consisting of all new, truly unseen titles every week. Most, however, continued to pay for and utilize a "blended" program that mixed both the relative age and the genre of titles. Initially, Calcium Light profited from its exclusive deal with the Trust in large part due to decreased exchange competition for local exhibitors. But what happened to other exchanges in Pittsburgh, particularly those that either did not choose or were not chosen to distribute MPPC product? How could a local, non-licensed exchange survive with little or no access to new films when the Trust effectively, if only temporarily, disrupted most American non-licensed production? Some, like the Allegheny Film Exchange, joined start-up trade organizations, particularly the Independent Film Protective Organization and the Film Renters Protective Association, both of which attempted to link independent exchanges with unlicensed film producers and equipment manufacturers. Others, like the Pittsburgh Cut-Rate, whose name does not inspire much fiscal confidence to begin with, simply did not survive; no record of the company appears after 1909. A few non-licensed exchanges endured, and even thrived, by converting themselves into something else, such as the local Fort Pitt Company, which became a successful regional production company specializing in the growing province of educational and industrial filmmaking.

If the owners of struggling Pittsburgh exchanges were jealous of Calcium Light during the initial years of the Trust, the reason for their envy would be short-lived. In spring 1910, the MPPC threatened Calcium Light with its fourteen-day, no-fault cancellation clause, in effect ending Clark and Rowland's access to the Trust's licensed films. This move had the intended result of forcing Clark and Rowland to sell their exchange and its branches to the General Film Corporation, the MPPC's newly created distribution arm, which was intended to operate as an efficient national exchange network for its producers' combined release schedule.[33] Resignedly, the two Pittsburgh men accepted the forced buyout and, for a time, left the local rental business. Unlike Warner Brothers, however, whose exchanges were also bought by the General Film Corporation, Rowland and Clark chose to remain a part of the continuing transformation of the movies' regional landscape.

Exchange Madness

As a number of other historians have shown, the policies of control and regulation that allowed the MPCC and General Film to stabilize the chaotic world of film production and distribution also contributed to their demise, as they were significantly limited in their ability (or desire) to react quickly to shifts in market conditions. Although the rationalization of business and filmmaking practices led to dramatically increased output by the production partners of the Trust and General Film, the resulting yield still was inadequate to meet the nickelodeons' unceasing demand for rapid changes and fresh titles. Thus, independent companies grew stronger as demand for pictures increased. This market, coupled with resentment on the part of "licensed" exhibitors who were required to pay Trust patent royalties (for their projectors), and those exchange owners disenfranchised by the strong-arm tactics of General Film, led to multiple opportunities for increasing numbers of independent-minded entrepreneurs to develop and exploit. Non-licensed production burgeoned in this period, particularly as new companies gained access to necessary quantities of raw film stock. Initially, most of these companies imported film from the French manufacturer Lumière, but in spring 1911, Eastman Kodak broke off its exclusive arrangement with the Trust and became available to supply anyone. Lawsuits and countersuits centering on infringements of Trust-controlled camera patents initially held independent producers somewhat in check, but in the summer of 1912, a U.S. Court of Appeals judge rejected the Trust's legal claims to the underlying technology and threw out its rights to one of the crucial patents.[34]

With material support in place, the number of independent producers increased, the weekly number of titles offered expanded, and as nickelodeons spread throughout the nation, the shows that exhibitors offered grew longer and longer. One result was that its audiences, in Pittsburgh and elsewhere, became comfortably habituated to sitting down and watching the movies for an hour or so, whether it was a series of shorts or a "feature" film, all for the same nickel price.

It was in this atmosphere of a rapidly changing industry that the *Pittsburgh Moving Picture Bulletin* was born. At the time of the *Bulletin*'s arrival in the spring of 1914, General Film was still in Pittsburgh, operating out of the third floor of the Seltzer Building, but it was forced to compete in an increasingly open market with thirty-one other companies. Only a few weeks into his tenure as the *Bulletin*'s editor, William Mayer expressed how dramatic this shift was, and its effect on local practices: "What a change has been wrought in one short year in the way of arranging programs! A year ago a 'licensed' exhibitor was not allowed to show 'independent' films in his house under penalty of losing his franchise.... Now all is changed. You pay your money and take anything you want—or can get. The exchanges have ceased to worry themselves about it and the exhibitor has a free hand."[35]

The offerings of the Pittsburgh exchanges at that time can be divided into four general categories: the schedule, the bargain exchange, the feature service, and the "states' rights" contract. The Trust was the first to develop a business model that provided exhibitors with a dependable balance of shorts composed primarily of single-reel titles, but by 1912 it had been joined by two successful independents, Universal and Mutual. Each of the three offered exchanges and their exhibitors a service so reliable that they became known in the trade journals simply as the "film schedule."[36] Each of these umbrella corporations aligned a group of production companies under a single distribution system whose combined output provided exhibitors with a dependable mix of comedy shorts, newsreels, and dramas. In Pittsburgh, where exhibitors were required to sign an exclusive contract for an exchange service, those who signed with General, Mutual, or Universal could find considerable comfort in knowing exactly when his films were coming, who made them, and their typical quality, but, at least initially, he could not choose the actual titles. However, as more and more manufacturers produced films outside of the confines of the "Big Three," the collective leverage of the "schedule" companies over exhibitors rapidly declined.[37]

Pittsburgh exhibitors who wanted to pay less than what General, Universal, or Mutual might charge sought out one of a number of local "bargain" exchanges, which offered their own library of titles for rent by the day or week. Although a few of the bigger bargain exchanges in Pittsburgh had a large enough collection of films to provide an entire program (or at least that is what they advertised), more generally this type of rental house offered exhibitors an economical way of choosing one or two films to balance, enhance, or partially substitute for films from one of the established service programs. Balancing a program was seen as a requisite for a successful show, and the ability to do so was a skill in which many exhibitors took great pride. "Balance" usually referred to the program's ratio of actualities (news or views) versus comedies and dramas, as well as their overall order in the show. Although General, Mutual, and Universal all promoted their weekly assortment of titles as "pleasingly perfect in subject," there were any number of reasons that an exhibitor might wish to alter that mix. One large motive was cost, and a local exhibitor could save considerable money by lowering his weekly rental of new films from one of the film services and then supplement his total with an older, cheaper title from a bargain exchange. Charlie Chaplin was almost as iconic a figure then as he is now, and the local availability in the 1910s of his one- and two-reel comedies provides perhaps the best example of this cost imperative and its resulting exchange practices. Chaplin was everywhere in Pittsburgh theaters, and his short comedies were practically considered a requisite by local exhibitors for a successfully balanced program. In 1915 and 1916, his new films were released by Mutual as part of their regular service, but in Pittsburgh, exhibitors could easily choose Chaplin without choosing Mutual by renting his older films, particularly those produced while he was at Keystone (1914) and Essanay (1915). The August 1915 edition of the *Bulletin* illustrates just how pervasive this practice of renting older films had become; in this issue, six local exchanges were all simultaneously advertising their ability to offer Chaplin films. William Mayer, in an editorial that same summer, wrote that this "abundance of old Chaplin pictures" was actually depressing the market for Chaplin's newest work for Mutual, which was "not pull[ing] quite as strongly as anticipated."[38]

The Western Film Company, the largest "bargain" exchange in Pittsburgh, made the attention-getting claim in its first *Bulletin* advertisement that "Dealing with us is like making love to a widow. You can't do enough of it. And then it makes you feel good," it explained, "for it reduces your film service and increases your box office receipts."[39] Western, the filmic equivalent of a used-car dealership, belongs to an aspect of the industry that escapes our typical historiographic attentions, because its success was based on stasis rather than change—selling the old rather than the new. For these very reasons, Western was a necessary element of the established institutional system of this period. If William Mayer is to be believed, this type of "Bargain service with a big 'B'" was of critical use to the region's "exhibitor in the country town" whose smaller houses with smaller audiences could not afford to compete for the newest, most expensive, feature films.[40] In fact, Western never actually bothered to advertise specific film titles, preferring to advance its cause based on price or occasionally genre categories—"26 two-reel Western films at Western now available."[41]

Many of the small bargain exchange houses, like the J. Frank Hatch Film Company, explicitly promoted their focus on even shorter films. Mayer presented Mr. Hatch's service to his readers as "having an elegant line of single reels on hand, which come in mighty handy when arranging your program. Comedy, western, society, military, Indian and many other subjects are covered. The make includes independent and licensed productions and posters are on hand for most of them."[42] The *Bulletin*'s brief editorial pitch—likely quid pro quo for the one-eighth-page ad placed by Hatch in the same issue—provides a telling description of this bargain library. Hatch's small operation was clearly not part of the General Film exchange family, and yet he and the editor of the *Bulletin* were happily promoting his ability to provide exhibitors anywhere in the city with the Trust's supposedly exclusive films. Some historians have claimed that General Film was generally effective in its ability to limit the circulation of old prints and eliminate the duping (illegal copying) of popular ones.[43] But Hatch received his "licensed films" from somewhere, most likely in the form of both old prints and new copies, directly or indirectly from a General Film exchange, or one of its local employees.

Hatch owned all the films that he rented to Pittsburgh exhibitors, as he had originally purchased them for his string of seasonal airdomes, open-air moving picture shows, mostly located in mid-sized southern cities such as Macon, Georgia. He operated this semi-itinerant operation only during the hot, humid summer months when the idea of sitting in a brick-and-mortar, non-air-conditioned theater became unbearable to all but the most

> **DEALING WITH US IS LIKE MAKING LOVE TO A WIDOW**
>
> You can't do enough of it. And then it makes you feel good, for it reduces your film service, and increases your box office receipts.
>
> ONE OR MORE A DAY. ONE OR MORE A WEEK.
>
> Our Motto: What we say we do, we do do.
>
> Correspondence Solicited.
>
> **Western Film Co.**
>
> Bell Phone Court 1951   127 FOURTH AVE., PITTSBURGH, PA.
> Second Floor

FIG. 3.6.
Western Film Company advertisement. *Pittsburgh Moving Picture Bulletin,* June 17, 1914, 11.

crazed movie fans. Although airdomes and other alternative exhibition practices remain largely absent from traditional histories of American moviegoing, Hatch—who went on in 1919 to write and produce at least one feature film[44]—is not atypical of this period. Like many others in the business, Hatch sought, often all at once, to engage in multiple aspects of an industry in which occupational and institutional boundaries remained permeable and the costs to participate remained relatively low. Exchanges like Pittsburgh's Western and entrepreneurs like Frank Hatch survived and thrived in this era in part because films, old and new, long and short, were both in plentiful supply and high demand.

While Pittsburgh bargain houses sometimes claimed "feature" status for their better-known films, typically, the bulk of their titles were generic one- and two-reelers. An increasing number of companies in the city, however, focused their efforts primarily on distributing feature films. These feature companies can further be divided into two categories, those that offered and contracted with the region's exhibitors for a regularized weekly schedule of feature films, and those that rented their features on a more singular basis, and which operated under a slightly older but still popular system defined by the "states' rights" contract.

Of the thirty-two "exchanges" listed in the *Bulletin*'s index in 1914, a half-dozen or more did not seek to provide exhibitors with a regular exchange of films, but instead worked within the states' rights system to circulate and rent films. Under this distribution strategy, a person or company purchased the right to exhibit, or sublicense others to exhibit, a single film in a particular territory. Although its name suggests state borders as territorial boundaries, the system was usually structured as a pyramid of rights that cascaded downward in a geographic range of licensees, from territories that could be as large as everything east of the Mississippi, to as small as an individual city. Pittsburgh and Philadelphia, for instance, were almost always separate territories. Although many of the topmost rights holders, who typically profited more from subleasing than actual exhibiting, resided in the cities where the films were produced—Chicago, New York, and increasingly in Los Angeles—foreign films could be imported and brokered by almost anyone operating anywhere.

As Michael Quinn and Richard Abel have shown, the states' rights system became an important distribution strategy in the United States as early as 1911, but in Pittsburgh, the practice first became widely visible with the arrival of the *Bulletin* in 1914.[45] Michaels and Freeman, a short-lived, small, local company, was one of the first to advertise in the *Bulletin* as the owner of "exclusive United States and Canadian rights" to a set of films; three "great money-makers," all foreign imports, that were now available from them for "offers from all States' Rights buyers."[46] The states' rights system was an important developmental step that offered producers and exhibitors several significant advantages: it had the ability to provide a filmmaker a return on investment prior to exhibition, it allowed more expensive films to become profitable through an extended period of circulation and exhibition, and it offered the possibility for extensive marketing and featuring of individual titles both to potential exhibitors and their audiences.

Two Pittsburgh exchanges with offices on the fourth floor of the aforementioned Seltzer Building illustrate how the states' rights contracts worked. In winter 1917, Leon Netter's Masterpiece Film Attractions, the larger of the two tenants, promoted a total of seven feature films in three distinct territories, including: for the state of Ohio, the William Selig nine-reel *Garden of Allah* (1916); for just northern Ohio, *Purity* (1916), a six-reel drama of self-sacrifice and nude modeling produced by the American Film Co.; and in the cross-border region that consisted of western Pennsylvania and all of West Virginia, *Neptune's Daughter*, a two-year old, seven-reel Universal film that is best known for being the first movie to capture the attentions of psychologist and film-theorist-to-be Hugo Munsterberg.[47] Netter's seven feature films (the shortest was five reels, the longest eleven) constituted a substantial number of properties for a local states' rights enterprise to advertise and distribute at the same time. More typically, because the licensee's success was dependent on booking the individual titles into local theaters, a states' rights company would heavily promote only a few titles at any one time. In part, it was the states' rights system, along with the road show, that helped regularize the now-standard practice of advance promotion and advertising for each individual movie released.

On the other hand, A.G. Fontana Productions, Inc., whose offices were just down the hall from Netter's, was, during that time period, promoting just two recent productions: *20,000 Leagues Under the Sea* (1916) and *The Witching Hour* (1916). In both these cases, Fontana was the licensee only for the Western Pennsylvania/West Virginia territory. The bulk of his potential customers, owners of local theaters, came directly from his city's own exhibitors.

While it would be wrong to collapse all states' rights films into a single thematic or generic category, there are certain shared characteristics that are present in many of the titles that both Fontana and Netter booked into the region's theaters. As opposed to a "regular" shorts-based program, in which individual film content was less important to an exhibitor than genre or star and overall quality and consistency, states' rights films had to be marketed to a theater owner as having something special that could draw a larger crowd, often for a longer run at a higher price. That something was typically spectacle, or sex, or both. Whether it was undersea monsters prowling the deep in *20,000 Leagues*, violent gangsters blackmailing the virtuous in *Beware of Strangers* (1917), or the profligate fantasies of a suicidal virgin in *The Libertine* (1916), the states' rights films and their often lurid posters were designed to capture exhibitors' and audiences' attentions.

In late 1914, Joseph Katz, a Pittsburgh exhibitor who employed a Universal schedule for his regular programming, was in the market for just such an attention-getter, which was known in the business as an "opener." In this case, Katz needed a "re-opener" for his Pearl Theater, a three-hundred-seat downtown nickelodeon that he had been forced to close for seven weeks due to a fire on the upper floors of his Fifth Avenue building. New paint, new chairs, and even a new automatic piano were, he feared, not enough to draw back his old customers in the competitive downtown environment. So to kick things off, he rented from Mayer Silverman, another exchange owner, *The Lure of New York* (1913). Shot on the streets of New York, the four-reel states' rights film offered complete with "big paper" was an action-packed melodrama that offered the promise of both spectacle and sex—giving Katz's audience voyeuristic access to the Bowery and its nefarious underworld, and the graphic, if ultimately failed, attempted rape of the film's naïve and beautiful heroine by a vicious criminal, her new American "father."[48]

The film that the exchangeman rented Katz resulted in a "big success," but unlike Masterpiece or Fontana Productions, Silverman's Liberty Film Renting Company did not actually specialize in states' rights features. While Silverman occasionally purchased a regional license for a title like *The Lure of New York*, in general he operated self-sufficiently, going to the source to directly buy copies of films outright from their actual manufacturers. Silverman, by all accounts an energetic and voluble entrepreneur, appears and reappears throughout the *Bulletin*'s publication history as a primary figure in the life of the local film community. The *Bulletin*'s editors credit

> **BIJOU Tonight**
>
> The Sensational 4 Part Feature
>
> ## "The Lure of New York"
>
> See the Bowery, Chinatown, Coney Island and many other great scenes.
>
> **ADMISSION 5c ANY SEAT**
>
> **Special Thursday**
>
> **MEXICAN WAR SCENES AT VERA CRUZ**
>
> Also the 4 Part Feature
>
> **"THE DREAM WOMAN"**
>
> Admission (This Night Only) 5c and 10c

FIG. 3.7.
The Lure of New York advertisement. *Piqua (Ohio) Daily Call*, May 6, 1914, 8.

Mayer Silverman with being the first in Pittsburgh, as early as 1908, to market and rent multiple-reel pictures, "which have since become known as the 'feature.'" According to Silverman, that first feature was *The Price of Beauty*, a three-reeler imported by Great Northern, the American representative of the Danish Nordisk Company.[49] Nordisk was one of the first independent companies to take on the Edison Trust; it filed a legal suit against Biograph, one of MPPC's primary members. Silverman also operated his exchange autonomous of the Trust, Mutual, or any other major concern, and by 1914 Liberty was the largest non-affiliated independent exchange in Pittsburgh, able to offer regional exhibitors 150 "features" for rent on an individual or service basis.[50] Where all of those films came from, exactly who made them, and when remains unknown, but traces of Silverman's purchasing habits are visible in the pages of the *Bulletin*, which illustrate how the Pittsburgh exchange business was simultaneously wide-open and competitive during this time.

In 1914, Mayer boasted that as many as three new features a week were coming into his Pittsburgh office, all according to him, the product of "high-class companies."[51] In some cases, Silverman had a standing deal with such producers for their entire feature output—as soon as the film was finished, the company sent it to Silverman. This was the case with Apex Film Company, a New York–based manufacturer. Apex was one of dozens of short-lived production and distribution companies that from 1913–1915 made upward of a dozen features of their own while simultaneously importing films from Bioskop, a German manufacturer.[52] Silverman could not rely on this single small producer/importer, so he also regularly went on buying trips to New York and Chicago to call on independent production companies and view their newest wares. Returning from one such trip in the spring of 1914, Silverman declared in the pages of the *Bulletin* that he had "corralled some good ones," including *Winning His First* Case (1914, four reels) and *The Folks from Way Down East* (1914, five reels), both from another historically ephemeral producer, the Photodrama Picture Company. A consummate salesman, once back from this particular sojourn Silverman announced a series of "demonstration banquets." These well-attended occasions became regular events for Silverman, for which he rented out local auditoriums and invited the region's exhibitors, as well as other local exchangemen, to partake in serious repasts of "gastronomic treats" while screening, and then, hopefully booking, his newest films.[53]

Silverman was, by nature, a social man. But he also had to work hard to stay competitive with the other local feature exchange houses. Among his competition was Miss A.'s Independent Film Exchange, which was the official exchange of the rapidly expanding Universal pictures, and the Weiland Film Company, which promoted its ability to provide Pittsburgh exhibitors with "a big feature every day," the type that would "make your house the envy of your competitors."[54] Moreover, Silverman had to con-

FIG. 3.8.
A "demonstration banquet" held by Mayer Silverman. *Pittsburgh Moving Picture Bulletin*, October 28, 1914, 3.

tend with the recent arrival in the city of two national weekly feature film services: Famous Players in 1913, and in the fall of 1914, the prodigal-like return of Harry Warner, this time under the banner of his family's recently created United Program Service.[55] Unlike the former Duquesne Amusements, the *Bulletin*'s report announcing the newest Warner enterprise made clear to its readers that there was "nothing local about this new proposition."[56] Instead, the Warner brothers now promoted their ability to provide exhibitors across the country with at least three different three-reel features every week, a program composed of European imports and American independent producers, including the now long-forgotten Ambrosia, Superba, Premier, Luna, and Mittenthal Studios.[57] While Richard Abel has found that the Warners promoted their service for its ability to distribute "American features, made in America," the first set of films they made available to the Pittsburgh market were Italian in origin, a series of four three-reel films—

Zingo and the White Elephants, Zingo in Africa, Zingo of the Sea, and *Zingo's War in the Clouds*—telling the adventures of a Tarzan-like hirsute caveman who visits Western civilization. According to Abel, the Warners' company was an important element in regularizing feature distribution and exhibition, but there is little indication that it became very popular in the Pittsburgh region, although it continued to sporadically advertise in the *Bulletin* for another two years.[58] Although Famous Players Film Service started in Pittsburgh slightly later, it became a more regular advertiser in the pages of the *Bulletin* than Warner Brothers, and grew to be the most powerful feature distributor in the city.

Famous Players topped the Seltzer Building, formerly the biggest edifice on Pittsburgh's Film Row, in 1914 with the construction of its own seven story, twelve-thousand-square-foot purpose-built office. William Mayer alliteratively described it as "convenient, commodious, complete in every detail." In fact, what later became known as the Paramount Pictures Building was, according the *Bulletin*, the largest film exchange in the United States.[59] Famous Players, founded by Adolph Zukor, himself a former nickelodeon and exchange owner, was in part responsible for regularizing some of the most significant production and distribution strategies of the 1910s, including the star system, the regular feature service, and, eventually, vertical integration of the industry. Zukor founded the company to produce motion pictures that were both profitable and "uplifting," resulting primarily in expensive, feature-length adaptations of legitimate stage plays performed by the likes of Dustin Farnum, John Barrymore, and Mary Pickford. Rebuffed in his approaches to General Film, Zukor joined forces, in the spring of 1914, with a number of other companies, including Bosworth Film and Jesse Lasky's Feature Play, to form the newly organized Paramount Pictures Corporation, created to distribute their combined output in a regular and profitable manner. Like General Film before it, Paramount, in what would later become known as run, zone, and clearance, limited access to its new films to certain theaters in each region and city. Paramount also originated a percentage fee, whereby both the producer and the distributor received back a percentage of the exhibitors' gross box office for their films.

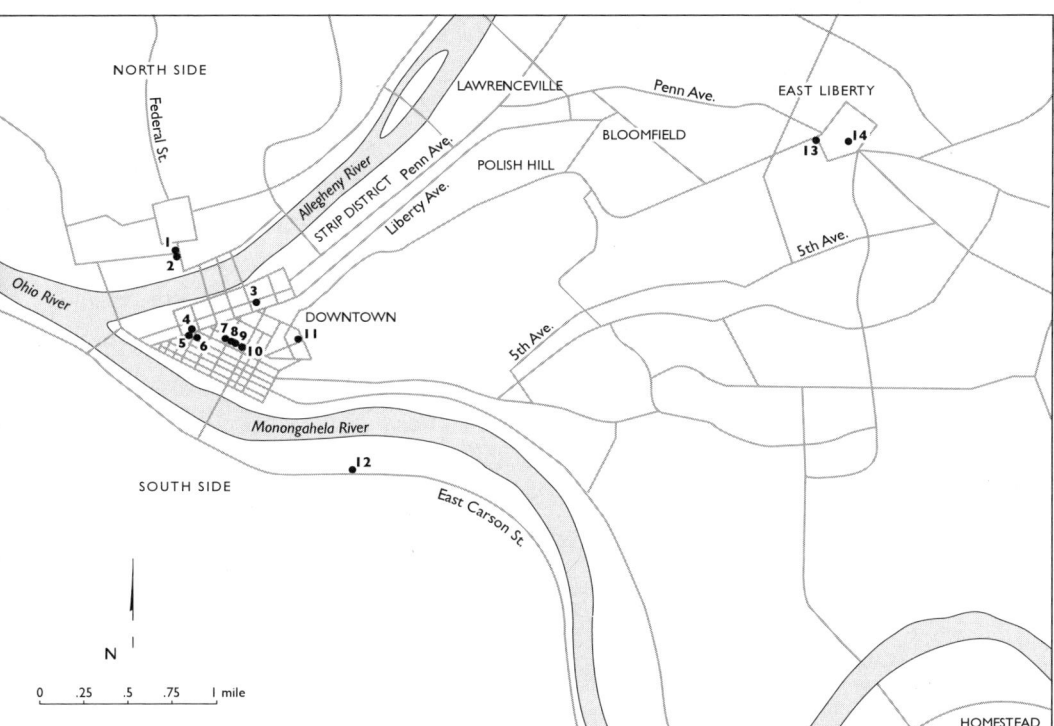

FIG. 3.9.

Map of Pittsburgh, circa 1914.

1. Casino Theater, 304 Federal Street, North Side
2. Elite Theatre, 309 Federal Street, North Side
3. Pitt Theater, Penn Avenue above Seventh Avenue, Downtown
4. Pittsburgh Calcium Light Company, 715 Empire Building, corner of Liberty and Stanwix Streets, Downtown
5. Liberty Film Renting Company, 105 Fourth Avenue, Downtown
6. Famous Players Film Service, 404 Ferry Street, Downtown
7. The Wonderland, 219 Fifth Avenue, Downtown
8. Olympic Theater, 318 Fifth Avenue, Downtown
9. Minerva Theater, 319 Fifth Avenue, Downtown
10. Cameraphone #1, 347 Fifth Avenue, Downtown
11. Court Theatre, Wylie Avenue at Sixth Avenue, adjacent to Downtown
12. Royal Theater, 1715 East Carson Street, South Side
13. Offices of the *Pittsburgh Moving Picture Bulletin,* 231 Collins Avenue, East Liberty
14. The Regent, 5941 Penn Avenue, East Liberty

Zukor employed Joseph Steele, previously the manager of General Film's Pittsburgh exchange, to run his new Pittsburgh operation. It was Steele who gave William Mayer his inaugural tour of the local Paramount facilities. Along their winding route of the bookkeeping, stenographers, sales and shipping offices, telephone exchanges, poster rooms, "where millions of sheets of paper [i.e., posters] are stored," film storage, projection and rewind stations, the *Bulletin*'s editor ran across many other former employees of General Film, including Mary Jones (wholesale department), Hilda Lissman (bookings), Russell Smith (manager of Family Players releases), and Fanny Acktenheil (slide and photo loans). If General Film was the past, Paramount was the future. Shows made up of anonymous, if dependable, short genre films were on their way out; features with stars were on their way in. Things were changing on the exchange side, but, as Miss A.'s poem reminds us, for the Pittsburgh exhibitor and his moving picture theater, some things remained very much the same.

There's Something about a Nickelodeon

In October 1914, the *Bulletin* reported that James Clark and Richard Rowland were putting the finishes touches on Pittsburgh's newest moving picture theater, the East Liberty Regent. Four years previously, when the two partners were forced out of the exchange business by the General buyout, they had almost immediately turned to local exhibition. Under the auspices of their new company, now simply called Clark and Rowland, they began to acquire moving picture theaters around the city and its region. The Regent brought their total theater holdings in the area to an even dozen, but this was the first theater that they, along with prominent local architect Harry S. Bair, designed and built from the ground up. At around nine hundred seats, the Regent was not nearly the city's largest theater, but it was perhaps the most luxurious to open in the region, offering Pittsburghers "a note of refinement and an atmosphere of elegance such as seldom attained."[60] Its facade was covered with cream-colored, ornamental terra cotta, its ticket booth made of art nouveau–styled brass, and its exterior lobby decorated

FIG. 3.10.
Regent Theater, exterior, postcard, circa 1915. *Author's collection.*

FIG. 3.11.
Regent Theater, interior lobby, postcard, circa 1915. *Author's collection.*

in murals of Faience tile imported from Italy. Rising more than three stories above the building itself, the theater's sign displayed "the massive figure of a maiden" holding in her upwardly stretched arm an antediluvian vessel from which, every evening, an eye-catching wellspring of electric light erupted. Once inside the front doors, continuing the theme of aquatic plenty, patrons were greeted with an elaborate, goldfish-filled marble fountain topped with the bronze figure of a naked cherub, this one spouting real water. Two large and lavishly decorated "retiring rooms for ladies and gentlemen" flanked each side of the foyer and allowed entrance directly into the actual theater. Upon entering the auditorium, decorated in Italian Renaissance style, one had the choice of two seating options; the 606-seat main section, which gradually rose toward the back in a traditional manner, or the 309 remaining seats, which were located in an unusually steep bleacher-

FIG. 3.12.
Regent Theater, interior, postcard, circa 1915. *Author's collection.*

style section in the rear. Once settled, patrons found, under their upholstered opera chairs, fresh-air inlet tubes designed to provide them with the "newest in sanitary ventilation . . . producing an optimum flow of air cooled with a special refrigerating device" in the summer and "soothing heat" in the winter. Music was furnished by both a live orchestra and a Moller pipe organ, played by the city's best-known organist, Professor C. A. Graninger. Exclusive of the professor's wages, this new theater cost Clark and Rowland the then-considerable sum of seventy-five thousand dollars. What was most striking about the Regent, and deemed most worthy of the *Bulletin*'s headlines, was not its price tag, nor its architectural design, nor the quality of its musical accompaniment, but rather what the editor described as the theater's "radical" and "revolutionary" plan to charge ten and twenty cents a show.[61]

FIG. 3.13.
C. A. Graninger. Caricature by George S. Applegarth, in *Men of This Big Town of Ours as Seen by 'Appy'* (Pittsburgh: Iron City Trades Journal, n.d.), 697. *Courtesy of ULS Digital Research Library, University of Pittsburgh.*

C. A. GRANINGER.

BENEATH his touch the ivories seem
  To wake as from a fairy dream,
    Spring into vibrant life and fill
Each bosom with responsive thrill.
His magic baton draws a sound
From all the echoing voices 'round
  Until the chorus swells and rolls,
  Stirring emotions in our souls,
Till all our being seems to be
Swept by a flood of melody
  That sways us with the same deft ease
  With which he plies the ivory keys.

Why, in 1914—nearly a decade after nickel madness had first begun—was it so radical for an expensive new theater in "the most important section" of town, run by two well-established members of the local movie business, to begin charging a dime a show, a "lousy two jitney's [sic] instead of one"?[62] If a dime constitutes a radical change then what was the status quo? Miss A. knew the answer. She poked poetic fun at the five large downtown theaters still charging nickelodeon prices, but they were clearly not alone. This is troubling, in part, because with few exceptions, the dominant historiography of early cinema depends on a more or less similar chronology that claims the end of the nickelodeon era no later than at this very moment, and often much, much sooner.[63] By this time, or so the traditional narrative goes, there should be nothing radical about a theater such as the Regent charging ten cents a show. As Robert Allen has noted in his critique of Ben Singer's work on Manhattan exhibition:

> As early as April 1908, W. Stephen Bush was already proclaiming The Coming of the Ten and Twenty Cent Moving Picture Theater: "Scattered all over the Union are numerous places to-day that have broken away from the sacred nickel, have offered more than the average nickelodeon ... and are making more money by charging more and are in addition blessed with a better and cleaner patronage."[64]

While most historians, including Singer, would, quite rightly, be skeptical of the institutional agenda behind Bush's hopeful claims, even some of the most compelling contemporary scholarship posits a core teleological narrative that remains essentially unchanged. It goes something like this: The nickelodeon was a popular but chaotic and relatively short-lived phenomenon with a diverse audience primarily comprised of urban, working-class immigrants. The Trust, although temporally restricted in its own success, led in rationalizing this mass marvel into a structured business, a model taken up and perfected by efficient corporations like Paramount. The resulting accelerated rate of production and exhibition of feature-length films, presented in Regent-like palatial surroundings, helped to produce a leisure form that attracted the immigrant wage-earner but also the salaried worker and his respectable wife and family. The East Liberty Regent with its upstanding location, advancing admission prices, plush opera seats, and Paramount's feature film service would appear to fit nicely, if perhaps a few years late, within this established model. The Regent, in may ways, can be understood as a substantive sign of the end of the nickelodeon era.

But the Regent's new admission policy of ten and twenty cents was a loser. Only a brief month after the theater opened to great acclaim it quietly joined the city's other movie-only houses in charging its patrons that same profit-thin nickel. Clark and Rowland, according to available evidence, failed to regularly raise their prices at their theater until almost two years later in the spring of 1916. The Regent was certainly not the last local theater to double its admission price; Pittsburgh's large downtown theaters took almost another year to arrive at a consistent dime price plateau, and it appears likely that many of the city's smallest neighborhood theaters continued their nickelodeon pricing in some cases until almost the end of the decade.[65] Although the city's "legitimate" theaters and the largest of Pittsburgh's movie-only theaters were occasionally, prior to 1916, able to charge much higher admissions prices—from twenty-five cents up to two dollars for road show "spectaculars" like D. W. Griffith's *Intolerance*[66]—the citywide *normalization* of pricing above and beyond the nickel did not occur nearly as early as most histories have stated.

If reports in the national trades are any indication, Pittsburgh and its theaters were not alone in their inability to move quickly beyond the nickel, although this city's nickelodeon culture seems to have lasted as long as, or longer, than almost anywhere else. While movie theaters in other parts of the state and country were able to charge a dime or more, Pittsburgh's nickel problem was part of a general reaction to an industry-wide struggle occurring in the mid-1910s over who would, and how best to, define the moving picture show and its theater. In the summer of 1916, when the editors of *Motion Picture News* asked "What Is a Picture Theatre?" they were not simply raising a rhetorical question—developments in production, exchange, and exhibition practices were causing the industry's always slightly schizophrenic personality to cultivate a major identity crisis.[67]

Ironically, it was an identity crisis precipitated by success: movies had become the most popular and profitable commercial leisure form in America, and larger, fancier theaters now projected longer feature films to higher-paying audiences. But the institutional model assumed necessary for this type of success, one built upon "great photodramas and spectacles" presented to middle-class audiences in "big show places," was in many ways in apparent contradiction with the needs and profits of the nickelodeon, the already well "established community theater" and its "changing program of composite interests."[68] Many of the debates taking place in the industry—features vs. programs, longer runs vs. daily changes, 1,200 seats vs. 200 seats, downtown vs. neighborhood, fixed show times vs. come-and-go-as-you-please, a quarter vs. a nickel—were bifurcated elements of a much larger struggle over what and who the movies were for, as the *Motion Picture News* declared: "It behooves us to dip under the surface and know more definitely about today's picture theater—what it signifies, what its functions are, what the future has in store for it."[69] While history reveals which choices were made and which battles were won, in the 1910s the answers were uncertain and the results unknown. Although much of the debate and its strategies are historically unrecoverable, the traces of its trajectory in Pittsburgh can best be seen in the *Bulletin* and its struggle to get the city's exchangemen and exhibitors beyond its nickel show.

From its very first issue and editorial, one of the *Pittsburgh Moving Picture Bulletin*'s raisons d'être was to persuade local theater owners and managers to produce exhibition environments and programs that would appeal to the deeper pockets of the city's expanding moviegoing populace, or, in William Mayer's words, to "Rise Up and Get the Gold."[70] Of course, the *Bulletin*'s editors were, by the very nature of their printing business, highly invested in the kind of moving picture show that could charge, if not gold, at least a dime. Programs, posters, flyers, and "cuts" were part of the Mayer Publishing and Printing Company's stock-in-trade—but it was nearly impossible for an exhibitor to afford such ephemera when his profit margin was based on nickel prices. According to an ad placed in their own *Bulletin*, Mayer's company charged twelve dollars for printing one thousand copies of an eight-page program, a cost that would have eaten up more than 20 percent of a nickel-charging exhibitor's gross.[71]

The resulting rhetoric of fiscal persuasion printed in the *Bulletin* involved a variety of articles, images, and editorials designed to gently, and occasionally not so gently, "educate" its readership. Although subscribers included both the region's exchanges and exhibitors, the local exhibitors, at least in this initial period, most often found themselves under editorial review as admission prices, theater promotions, and actual programs were all ripe subjects for critiques.

In his first editorial, William Mayer lamented over local exhibitors' inabilities to promote an up-to-date show—defined here as a show where the movies alone could take center stage: "Some of our Pittsburgh nickelodeons are running the old-style museum stuff and one of the largest in lower Fifth Avenue is not without blemish in this respect. A midget lady one week and an armless violinist the next brings us back to scenes of our childhood days. Cut it out, boys! The pictures are strong enough."[72] Just weeks later, Mayer wrote that this type of old-fashioned dime-museum–like ballyhoo should be replaced by more "modern" techniques: "Advertising will help your business more than all the schemes in the world."[73] In this case, the particular "nickelodeon" utilizing such ill-conceived antics was, as we learn in a later edition of the *Bulletin*, the downtown Olympic, which, at almost 2,500 seats, was actually at that moment the city's largest movie theater. Nickelodeons, at least as we historically imagine them, do not seat thousands at a time. Thus, Mayer's reports of the Olympic's activities stands in contradiction to scholar Robert Allen's understanding that by 1910, "it is *only* the remaining and rapidly diminishing storefront shows that are referred to as nickelodeons."[74]

In fact, the rhetoric of the *Bulletin* consistently groups together, often uncritically, all the city's movie theaters as nickelodeons: "While the larger houses, those which run the 'legitimate' during the winter season, have everything in their favor in the way of ventilation, capacity and prestige, still there seems to be something about a nickelodeon that attracts. It may be a Bohemian spirit which permeates the small house and then it may be the superior knowledge, gained by experience of the public's desires in the picture line, that renders the exclusive picture house more satisfactory to the public."[75] This language undeniably positions the "small house" as a vigorous and still significant element within the city's commercial leisure landscape, contra to Allen's "rapidly diminishing storefronts."

The industry's national trade journals, in particular, in the *Motion Picture News*, paint a somewhat different picture regarding the state of nickelodeons at this time. At practically the same moment that Mayer was celebrating Pittsburgh's "small house[s]" the *News* printed a series of articles and editorials optimistically declaring that "the day of the five-cent show is passing [to] be succeeded by commodious, well ventilated houses, at which the admission price will be from ten to twenty five cents." Even the *News*, however, used the future tense in its 1914 article, "predicting that the 'nickel show' is *soon* to disappear" and that "the big houses showing pictures *will* play to a scale of 10 and 20 cents" (my emphasis). Such language makes clear that the nickelodeon remained a significant feature of the national landscape as well. Perhaps even more significant, it was not just the "small houses" that continued to charge their patrons nickel prices.[76]

More striking in its consistent lack of discursive disparagement, the *Bulletin*'s editor regularly refers to his Pittsburgh exhibitors as "nickelodeon men," regardless of house size, and with no apparent social stigma attached.[77] And in a sense they all were, for despite what must have been significant qualitative and quantitative differences in their houses and shows, they were all apparently obliged to still charge a nickel.

The concept of the nickelodeon remains a slippery one. The descriptive language of the trades, both in the *Bulletin* and the national journals, and the economics and culture of exhibition in Pittsburgh and elsewhere, proves "nickelodeon" to be a word (and site) loaded with material, discursive, and historical contradictions. By 1910, according to Allen, the term as used in New York referred to a storefront theater of apparent professional derision and diminishing cultural and industrial importance. Yet in 1914, in Pittsburgh, a person who owned such a place belonged to a large and professionally well-respected group of exhibitors whose theaters ranged from 150-seat storefronts to elaborate picture palaces that accommodated thousands. That an exhibitor in Pittsburgh might take pride in the descriptive label, while one in another city might shrink from the moniker, makes clear that the nickelodeon was a site of contestation, and as such, its definition shifted as the polemic of discourses ebbed and flowed. If we are to accept the material evidence that someone considered all of these spaces at some time, and at someplace, to be nickelodeons, then as scholars we need to be careful about retroactively attempting to force one definition or one period to fit them all.

The vast majority of previous work around the nickelodeon has often focused itself on questions surrounding the ethnicity, gender, and class of its audience. These are crucial questions to ask if we are to understand how the social processes of American moviegoing fit into the larger practice of our shared cultural lives, and these are questions that obviously must be answered, or at least addressed, for Pittsburgh as well as Manhattan. However, the resulting historiography has, in chasing these questions of reception, largely replicated a discursive formula visible in the national trade papers of the era, which presented a direct and causal relationship between size of theater, quality of show, price of admission, and type of patron. As claimed by one New York editor, "there are three things upon which every film man agrees: Larger theaters; superior productions; higher admissions."[78] For many in the film business at the time, and for many later historians, such a formulation appeared seductively rational in its theory. *Moving Picture World*, for example, remarked on the striking difference in character and audience between the "picture houses" and the nickelodeon: "The vast investments, the gorgeous arrangements and the painstaking management of the modern picture houses have attracted to the pictures the attention of thousands of people who have never entered a nickelodeon."[79]

At the exhibition sites in Pittsburgh, however, particularly in the case of the East Liberty Regent, the numbers unfortunately do not quite add up. That is, if the Regent and other like theaters of the era were designed to attract the deeper pockets of those supposed "thousands of people who have never entered a nickelodeon," then the Regent's failure to raise prices—in 1914, six years after the trade papers say this process began—problematizes the existing definition and periodization of something that has become known as the "nickelodeon era."

In and About the City

In the expanding Pittsburgh metropolitan area, most of the city's moviegoers could choose between walking to a local neighborhood theater or traveling farther afield to one of a number of entertainment "strips," made up of multiple theaters, most often residing alongside or within the city's larger business districts. These districts each represent distinct, if sometimes overlapping, components of the city's social and cultural milieu. Downtown had become the burgeoning center of the region's corporate interests, as well as home to department stores and many of the city's larger "legitimate" and vaudeville theaters. Just a short walk or trolley ride over the Allegheny's Sixth Street Bridge, the North Side, a mixed-class residential neighborhood, was the location of the city's most compact movie district with at least nine theaters "within a stone's throw of each other" on Federal Street.[80] Across the Monongahela River, East Carson Street on the South Side was a focal point for many of the communities that spread up and down the mill-polluted waterway, east to Homestead and west to McKees Rocks. Trolley lines connected many of these otherwise surprisingly isolated towns with the South Side, providing the immigrant wage earner and his family with a busy centralized district of merchants and commercial amusements. Meanwhile, East Liberty had become, in the years leading up to the war, an area of merchants and businesses geared toward the city's expanding (sub)urban periphery—the place to procure those fashions declared stylish in New York and Philadelphia not too long ago.

Pittsburgh's extreme river-and-hill-bound geography and the resulting development of its urban-industrial topography allows for some insight into the demographic composition of the city's movie theaters, especially those neighborhood theaters located in and around the mill communities.

A theater such as the small, 250-seat Eagle, located in the heart of Polish Hill, would have attracted largely an ethnically Polish and "working-class" clientele, especially considering that the theater's namesake was the national "white" eagle of Poland rather than its bald American cousin.[81] While Bill Uricchio and Roberta Pearson have noted in their work on New York City nickelodeons that neighborhood theaters such as the Eagle probably attracted "several different audiences depending on the time of day or day of the week," it is crucial to recognize that at least in Pittsburgh, with its sharply defined geographic and cultural landscape, each theater's patrons would have been overwhelmingly from the surrounding community, and that the theater would have been understood as an object collectively belonging to that community.[82]

Additionally, the *Bulletin*'s editorial coverage, or rather, the absence of it around certain neighborhoods and theaters, implicitly works to mark out the potential patronage available to the city's various theaters. In the case of East Carson Street, the overall lack of mention of South Side exhibitors and their venues on the pages of the *Bulletin* is a telling sign of the class composition of these theaters' audiences. In a trade journal that exhorted its readers to "get the gold," theaters whose primary audience could likely not afford an admission increase received little, or no, attention. In fact, the occasional mention of South Side theaters on the pages of the *Bulletin* occurred only when a change of ownership transpired, or in one case when W. J. Bernardi, the manager of the Royal Theater, chose to "join the ranks of the program issuing houses."[83] Since the Mayers printed the theater's programs, such a story was to their advantage—and they described Bernardi's move as a smart one. While landscape and transit development in flat, grid-like cities such as Manhattan may have allowed for a more fluid movement of its amusement-seeking populace, Pittsburgh's geographic features accentuated and hardened the socioeconomic boundaries that played an undeniable role in the populace's commercial leisure practices.

These borders, however, were not absolute, and the citywide pricing structure suggests that at least a portion of Pittsburgh's populace regularly traveled for their entertainment. That is, while the neighborhood theaters in Polish Hill and the South Side had potentially fewer dime-wielding patrons to draw upon, theaters in other parts of the city should have had access to the type of patrons who could afford to pay "two jitneys" instead of one. Yet the nickel persisted across the city, in all neighborhoods.

The downtown was where the nickelodeon first began and apparently stayed. With its commercial districts and rapidly expanding corporate presence, undoubtedly it contained the area's highest volume of pedestrian traffic, and it was the one section of the metropolis that continued to serve as an environment open to a broad spectrum of the city's populace. The Penn Avenue stretch of East Liberty was another area of the city where both commerce and commercial entertainment had developed and were thriving side by side. This was not an unusual feature of only Pittsburgh, nor even a particularly new one. As Allen has said of Manhattan's development: "As early as the 1890s Keith and Proctor cemented the relationship between shopping and theater-going by locating their palatial new vaudeville theaters at urban nodes where shoppers, especially women, were drawn from around the city, many of them via public transportation . . . *Moving Picture World* speaks on several occasions of a 'floating clientele' for the movies as well [as] patrons drawn from outside the immediate neighborhood of the theater."[84]

East Liberty had, by this time, developed into just such an "urban node," and no doubt Rowland and Clark were assuming a certain portion of this city's "floating clientele" to help fill the Regent's dime-worthy seats.[85] Who were these potential floating patrons? Who might have been willing and able to consistently dress themselves in acceptable finery, to pay a nickel and board the trolley (or often two or three, East Liberty not being directly connected to most of the more industrialized neighborhoods), and to travel to a landscape dramatically different from the one they were daily accustomed to? The most likely answer is the group social historian Ileen DeVault has described as the "sons and daughters of labor," the unusually large number of this city's clerical workers and other nonmanual laborers who were in the active process of literally learning how to travel—learning what social and economic boundaries could and could not be crossed.[86]

Even this group, however, seems to have been unwilling to pay that extra nickel for the experience of cool air rushing beneath their seats. Facing intense competition from other nearby theaters still charging a nickel, it seems the Regent was unable to convince these city travelers what extra pleasures a dime could buy them.

It was not, however, only competition or the low wages of the city's clerical workers that kept admission prices low, as other significant determinants were also in evidence in the pages of both the *Bulletin* and the national trades. One such crucial factor, as the critique in Miss A.'s verse attests to, was that Pittsburgh's moving picture shows were not just too cheap, but also too long. Theater owners who were no longer locked into exclusive exchange contracts could now pick and choose from a growing selection of relatively inexpensive films. Although the local exhibitors' proximity to so many exchanges in this city offering both new and old pictures may have exacerbated the problem, Pittsburgh was not alone in its struggle over "long programs." Both *Moving Picture World* and *Motion Picture News* present a series of editorials and articles that declare "it is not quantity but quality that counts" and bemoan the exhibitor who, by presenting his audience with an eight- to twelve-reel show, was "trying to replace a lack of ability with inert film."[87] And it was not just film that was offered, as other inducements were increasingly added in hopes of attracting a crowd. In May 1915, according to William Mayer, the Royal Theater provided the following, "all for a nickel": "Seven reels of pictures, a chance on a 'Big Live, Red Rooster,' and United Profit-Sharing Coupons. Can you beat it? Last Saturday's bill for instance, consisted of *A Prince of India*, four reels; *The Lost Heir*, two reels; a Keystone comedy with Charles Chaplin, 1 reel—seven big reels—count 'em yourself."[88] The editorial goes on to state that an exhibitor of "this caliber" will go bankrupt as will all other houses in his area forced to compete with his prodigious output. The Royal's weekend program as described by Mayer provides a sense of how richly eclectic movie exhibition had become by the 1910s—features alongside shorts, action and melodrama next to comedies—as well as how much theater owners relied on older titles to fill their programs. Not one of the three films represented here was less than a year old, including the four-reel feature debut of "Smiling" Billy Mason in *A Prince of India*, a fast-paced romantic adventure that was first released in October 1914 by the Eclectic Film Company, an American exchange owned by the French Pathé Company. In its totality, this abundant program, which also incorporated the live performative aspects of poultry and prize giveaways, is important to consider for two reasons: its low price and the competition-based anxiety that it represents.

The cost of admission to the nickelodeon, five cents, has overwhelmingly been (mis)understood as simply an economic amount that allowed working-class patrons affordable access to commercialized leisure. Yet what was ultimately most sacred about the five-cent admission was its psychological, not its economic, value. Once the nickel became popularly bound to the moving picture show—both the beauty and curse of the nickelodeon appellation—in essence the sign turned into the signifier. The resulting associative meaning became and remained tightly wrought, regardless of social or class considerations, for much longer than has been traditionally assumed.[89] The existing historiography attributes a number of determinants to the formation of a middle-class audience for the movies: the rise of the picture palace and its accompanying higher admission prices, the increased production of feature-length films, and the effect regulation and reform had on the moral acceptability of both the site and object of cinema. Rarely, however, is the power of the bargain addressed.[90] The supposition that those who could afford to pay more for the movies would want to bears closer examination because little work has been done to explore whether the psychological value bound to that five cents was a significant determinant for new audiences.[91]

Because in the mid-1910s, this psychological value was large and its economic value was small (theater owners could ill afford to lower prices any further), product size became a primary way for exhibitors to differentiate their theater and attract an audience. Their show was their product, so offering more and more films (and the occasional rooster) became the norm.[92] Pittsburgh exhibitors and others across the country found themselves in a vicious cycle, as this ersatz monologue that begins a March 1914 article in *Motion Picture News* attests to: "I can't afford to give my patrons any more for their money than I am giving them now. . . . I can't afford to let my competitors give more for the money than I am giving. . . . My competitor can't afford to give as much for the money as he IS giving. . . . But can he, or can I, afford to raise our prices?"[93]

The national trade papers consistently pushed for cooperation between local exhibitors so that the answer might be a resounding "yes." They editorialized that the continuation of exhibition practices that simply emphasized the length of a show would hurt the cause of an industry that was, in the face of potential federal and growing state-sponsored censorship, desperately seeking to be associated with progressive uplift. "The public is not demanding the quantity program. On the other hand, the public is clamoring positively so, for a quality program," claimed one editorial in *Motion Picture News*. While the *News* suggested that selectively choosing and showing "better pictures" would enhance the movies' cultural standing, the authors also attempted to sell to theater owners on the economic advantages of "uplift," stating that such films have "a commercial meaning, as well as a moral and educational one."[94]

Compared to the national trade journals, these issues of uplift and morality are less directly visible in the pages of the *Bulletin*. William Mayer was, at least in print, worried more about the direct economic effect the local exhibitors' cinematic excesses had on the city's movie industry: "Pittsburgh exhibitors, as a rule, are showing too much film for the price of admission charged. We know of houses where six and often seven reels of good pictures are shown for a nickel. The object in most cases, is, of course, to keep the patron out of the other fellow's house, but if the first exhibitor would only stop to consider the fact that the other fellow is doing identically the same thing, he might take a tumble to himself."[95] Showing "too much film" was easy for the city's exhibitors to do at this moment because the mid-1910s were probably the most prolific period of American film production, in terms of footage produced and number of movies released and remaining in circulation. With the feature "photoplay" and its related exchanges quickly ascending in both production and popularity, and the shorter single- and double-reel pictures not yet in productive, distributive, or receptive descent, it is not surprising that, according to a report from the Pennsylvania State Board of Censorship, the European and American industries combined were producing an average of four hundred reels of film a week in 1915–1916.[96]

The relative newness and novelty of the feature film additionally complicated the structure of programming that most exhibitors in Pittsburgh had previously followed. In effect, the audience *and the exhibitors* had to be taught the economic and psychological value of a feature film in relation to the shorts and single-reels that they had grown accustomed to in the preceding decade. William Fox, a man with an obvious investment in the outcome of the final definition, noted in a interview with the *Bulletin* that both economic and social distinctions must be made between "high-class multiple reel production[s] adapted from a big play featuring a famous star" and those falsely popular "sensational clap-trap feature[s] with the 'yellow poster' display."[97] Yet average exhibitors remained confused about such economic distinctions. Even the *Bulletin* could not easily clarify: "You might ask how are you to know what features are worth a boost in price. It is a hard query to answer. It depends on yourself, and you must use your wits and best efforts to find out by watching the trade papers and inquiring of those managers who have used the films you figure on."[98] One of the primary reasons for this bewilderment is that, as Michael Quinn has asserted in his research into early film distribution, the development of the feature film market was "not merely a mode of production, but . . . an endeavor to differ individual motion pictures from the standard single-reel program."[99] Such an undertaking was the result of structural and economic developments within the industry, and the evolving production and distribution practices of Paramount and others, but it was also an issue heavily inflected by concerns about audience class. That the single-reel program was still very much a viable form of exhibition, while feature production was becoming more regularized, fueled an industry debate over which format patrons most desired—a debate that that took place on the pages of the trades and in the seats of the theaters. What side of the debate you fell on had less to do with which branch of the industry you belonged to than on the kind of audience with which you hoped to fill the theater: "the big picture has without exception made its converts to the cause of cinematography who refused to take seriously the ordinary pictures.... It is not uncommon to hear a prominent man or woman, who has heretofore tabooed the film theater ... declare their amazement at the possibilities of what they had considered a cheap and more or less harmful amusement of the masses." Those in the industry, like this *Motion Picture News* author who posited such a correlation, assumed that people of prominence embraced the feature, particularly those made by the "large producing companies," because that type of film tended to "enlist stars of the legitimate stage" and re-create stories based on adaptations of plays and novels.[100]

Others in the business complained that the increase in feature production was moving the industry away from the very format that attracted "the millions who go *each day* to picture theaters."[101] The theater that ran short programs was typically situated as a community center and "not a show place, not at least in the sense that people go to it at infrequent intervals and with considerable forethought—as they go to see a stage play or to some other show place."[102] Its charm, according to its advocates, and its ability to attract a working-class audience, was based on a continuous format of short subjects that allowed for an informal and varied program. As one columnist, under the bizarre pseudonym "Goat Man," wrote for *Motography* in 1914: "I will always believe that good, single reels should constitute the bulk of regular program. It comes more nearly filling all requirements. You go to a picture show for a short entertainment. When you breeze into the middle of a multiple reel, you don't get the drift of the story—you sit it out to the finish ... and have a look at the beginning."[103] Exhibitors of short-based programs often took great pride in their ability to arrange the reels and their corresponding subjects to create a show that met the specific needs and desires of their neighborhoods. As early as 1910, the editors of *Nickelodeon* optimistically claimed that longer shows "[gave] a greater promise of pleasing everybody, and allows the exhibitor to exercise some ingenuity in arranging it, thus giving the cleverest man the most attractive show."[104] The authors admitted, however, that the real problem was that once the show was lengthened, an audience would not seek out a shorter one, and that increasing admission prices to ten cents was the only available alternative for a theater to operate on a profit.

This option was precluded in much of Pittsburgh during much of the 1910s for the simple reason that exhibitors rarely had the luxury of operating in areas free from competition. From Mayer's many disparaging editorials and business reports in the *Bulletin*, it is obvious that there was little consensus among the city's exhibitors on the issue of admission price, at least prior to the Regent's opening in the spring of 1914. Even in the often less sharply self-critical news that was reported about Pittsburgh on the pages of the *Moving Picture World*, there is strong evidence that local competition was fierce and cooperation was minimal:

> The inability to operate a motion picture theater in Pittsburgh with an admission of ten cents while all the other houses are charging but five, was plainly shown recently by the lowering of the admission to the new Harry Davis Theater.... With six other downtown theaters within a few squares showing similar exhibits at an admission of only five cents, the ten cent admission was doomed.... There have been several propositions taken at various times by the local exhibitors for a general advance of admission charges, but each time the attempt has fallen through.[105]

This competitive atmosphere was in apparent contradiction with the spirit and mood of the regional and national economy. After all, this was the golden age of monopoly and oligopoly capitalism, with Pittsburgh arguably its key city, and vertical integration of the movie industry was beginning to affect exhibition practices in many other areas of the country. The national trades often happily reported that exhibitors in other cities and towns successfully set community-wide levels for movie theater admission. From El Paso, Texas, "always ... a ten-cent picture town," where the city's nine theater owners were "in complete accord," to Louisville, Kentucky, where the local "photoplay association" collectively advocated to raise evening admissions to a dime, to Philadelphia, where the city's Motion Picture Exhibitors' League "voted to adopt a uniform scale ...

charging five cents for a four-reel program and ten cents for program[s] from five to eight reels," exhibitors in these and many other places were, unlike Pittsburgh's film men, able to work together to raise their individual profit lines.[106]

The sheer number of theaters, both in the city core and in surrounding business districts and nearby mill towns, obviously accounted for part of Pittsburgh's pricing difficulties. P. J. Demas, owner of the Minerva Theater located downtown, noted with frustration that even when a group of exhibitors did get together, cooperation was often short-lived: "I was the first to suggest a 10-cent admission price on Fifth Avenue, and we all tried it for awhile, but one or two broke the agreement and we all had to come down."[107]

One potentially underlying reason for this lack of cooperation was the broad-based ownership of Pittsburgh's movie theaters. In 1914, no conglomerate controlled more than Clark and Rowland's dozen regional venues, with the majority of the local theaters being owned individually by a relatively socially diverse and ethnically varied group of businessmen. Unlike Ben Singer's evaluation of New York City's exhibitors, in which he found Manhattan's picture businessmen to be predominately Jewish, Pittsburgh's owners appear as a much more heterogeneous group.[108] The four biggest players in the local exhibition scene—Harris, Davis, Rowland, and Clark—were all of English descent and, except for Davis, American-born, and each had been previously involved in the city's amusement business in its earlier commercial forms. Many of the city's other exhibitors were immigrants or the children of immigrants, and the rest of Pittsburgh's owners included: Gerard Tess, a French native who changed his name to John in 1914, Harry Mintz, owner of the Evaline, a second-generation Russian Jew whose father David owned two other local theaters both in East Liberty; Pete Antonopolis, a Greek immigrant whose "museum" antics at his aptly named Olympic Theater caused the *Bulletin* so much consternation; and W. J. Bernardi, whose Italian immigrant father had worked in the nearby mills until he went to work in his son's Southside theater.[109] In a city of ethnically homogenous and geographically disparate neighborhoods, theater owners, whose ethnicity in many cases matched that of their regular

FIG. 3.14. P. J. Demas. Caricature by George S. Applegarth, in *Men of This Big Town of Ours as Seen by 'Appy'* (Pittsburgh: Iron City Trades Journal, n.d.), 657. *Courtesy of ULS Digital Research Library, University of Pittsburgh.*

P. J. DEMAS.

HE RAISES the roses because, you know,
    He loves to see them bloom and grow
    So everywhere that he may go
His path is strewn with flowers.
He also runs a "movy" show,
The place we all delight to go,
For he's the man to whom we owe
    So many happy hours.

patrons, may have been unwilling or unable to place the exhibition community's desire for a collective price hike over the ability or desire of the neighborhood community to pay more for a show.

From the "Nimble Nickel" to the "Diligent Dime"

By September 1916, these loyalties finally began to shift, as a headline in the *Motion Picture News* elatedly declared: "Pittsburgh Theaters Raise Admission Prices." The article stated that many of the city's downtown and East Liberty exhibitors had joined together and begun to regularly charge a dime admission, although Pittsburgh remained "one of the cheapest theater towns in motion pictures . . . and many of the owners of the theaters are afraid to boost their prices for fear that all of the theaters in their section will not do the same."[110] A month later, Mayer and his *Bulletin* gave their editorial approval of the city's price advance: "Apparently Pittsburgh's exhibitors are beginning to realize the fact that the 'nimble nickel' is not sufficient to meet the expenses of present day picture house and that the 'diligent dime' or more is essential to the success of a photoplay house, especially where the house is located in a high-rent district and where film rentals are soaring."[111]

Change was on the way, if unevenly. The construction in "high-rent district[s]," of theaters like the Regent, specifically designed as a "photoplay house"—built without a stage or dressing rooms—paved the way at the national level for the economics of exhibition to begin shifting in the years around World War I. Locally, issues such as battles with the Pennsylvania State Board of Censors and the state passage of legislation for increasingly tough zoning and safety laws produced a desire in exhibitors for the kind of influence and power that is best available in group form. The Pittsburgh Screen Club provided just such an assemblage when it formed in November 1914, with over 150 exhibitors and exchangemen paying their membership at the club's inaugural banquet. The Screen Club advocated both social fraternalism and industry camaraderie, but it did not attempt to hide its desire for economic cooperation, with its official charter requiring its new members to: "Lay aside all petty jealousies and unite for the good of all. We are not saying organization will eliminate competition, neither will it eradicate a certain amount of jealousy, but it will minimize those conditions and eventually eradicate the cutthroat competition now prevalent in some sections. At least it is worth trying!"[112] And try they did, although their successes were limited in the 1910s when Pittsburgh's moviegoing audiences regularly got what Mayer disapprovingly described as "maximum film for minimum price."[113] Eventual success meant better cooperation among local movie businessmen, but it did not necessarily mean the end of the nickelodeon. The rhetoric of the *Bulletin*, a full two years later, is still emphatic in its advocacy for the nickel show: "many picture men predict the extinction, in a few years, of the small house entirely. They contend that the large house will be the picture show of the future. Right here we should like to be placed on record as predicting that there will always be room for the small nickelodeon around the corner."[114]

Ultimately, the combination of the structural growth of the feature film and its studio system of production, the consolidation of theater ownership by regional and national chains, and the increasingly cooperative spirit of the local exhibitors would alter the economics of Pittsburgh's moving picture show. But for longer than has currently been imagined, that nickelodeon, and its price, remained just "around the corner."

4

SWATTING FLIES AND WINNING CHICKENS

In the first week of June 1916, the *Bulletin*'s editor had an inch left over at the bottom of page twelve. Into that otherwise easily missed space went a brief and somewhat bewildering accolade for exhibitor Harry Mintz. Mintz was the owner of the Evaline, a two-hundred-seat theater in the largely Italian immigrant neighborhood of Bloomfield. According to the *Bulletin*, Mintz was "running a Swat-The-Fly stunt that is doing him tremendous business."[1] No photograph was included with this odd if positive notice, and no further explanation of Swat-the-Fly was forthcoming in a later edition of the *Bulletin*. However puzzling this appears, most, if not all, of Mintz's fellow exhibitors would have needed no extra information to know exactly what this theater owner was doing. Effective stunts that had succeeded for another showman often took on lives of their own, and instructive details circulated widely, although rarely at the level of popular discourse.

Like magicians jealously guarding their trickery, the perpetrators of successful publicity shrouded their audience-seeking activities in secrecy. Within show business, however, the best stunts, schemes, contests, humbugs, hoaxes, and other forms of ballyhoo often became the stuff of legends (along with their creators), and good ideas were passed along from city to city by word of mouth or, on occasion, as published accounts in the trade press.[2] A *Motion Picture News* ad in 1924 urged exhibitors to share their promotional ideas, reminding the exhibitor that "the stunt which has been used in your town is no longer new, but it may be the very thing the other fellow needs."[3]

In Mintz's case, the fly stunt he was running was not new; its details were described in *Picture Theatre Advertising* (1915), an exhibitors' how-to manual written by Epes Winthrop Sargent.[4] Sargent, who helped found *Variety*, was a former vaudeville critic, a prolific screenwriter, and a familiar columnist for *Moving Picture World* on a range of cinematic subjects. His book, the first of two he wrote on the subject of promotion, offered a compendium of selling advice from the perspective of "the theater as an institution of entertainment." In his chapter on the practical working of various "Prize and Coupon Schemes," Sargent set out meticulous instructions for his own version of "Swat the Fly." Perhaps more accurately, Sargent lists "Swat the Fly" as a "scheme" rather than a "stunt," a showman's term typically associated with the production of a single spectacular crowd-drawing event rather than the ongoing contest that Mintz apparently held. The exhibitor's goal in this contest was to attract children to the movie theater during the hotter months of summer, an otherwise poor attendance period for non-air-conditioned theaters. In elaborate and rather loving detail, Sargent describes the scheme's pesky particulars:

> Swat the Fly crusades can be worked as a prize scheme in the early summer.... Get hold of one of the old Selig fly pictures if you can and run this and some comedies at a Saturday morning performance for the children. Charge no admission. Let someone lecture on the danger of the fly and then make your own talk. Tell the children that you want them to help rid the town of flies. Explain that a fly killed in May means the destruction of many flies in June. Tell them prizes will be given in proportion to the number killed ...

Have prepared a neat membership card. Make it as important looking as the heart of a small boy can desire. Have someone who writes a neat hand to take the entries and write the name of the child on the card. Do not get a card that does not require names to be written in. It has a value all of its own if the child sees his or her own name written in. The signature of the President (generally the manager) should be printed in facsimile. The President may be some minister or other well known person, perhaps the Health Officer.

Have weekly, monthly and season prizes. . . . Keep a ledger account of each name, working it on a card catalogue, and keep the standing of the leaders posted in the lobby. Require the flies to be brought to the theatre in bags. Weigh the flies carefully . . . Have a glass case and put all the flies in the case. . . Keep the case in the lobby and keep it locked. Take his membership from any small boy who tries to work in sticks and gravel.

And all the time keep talking of the fly crusade on your screen, in your advertisements, and in the lobby. Give cheap fly swatters for matinee souvenirs. Have weekly talks about the fly pest, and keep the interest up. Some night, after the collection of flies has become important looking, take them out, fasten a cigar box to the bottom, covering it with flies. As the collection proceeds you can add a cigar box from time to time.[5]

Reading Sargent's description today, it is tempting to simply dismiss the practical application of this promotional "crusade" with its anachronistic weirdness and strange amalgamation of pests and pleasures. Can we really imagine children at home, around the yard, on the stoop, or in the alley, swatters in hand, eagerly scooping up their flattened prey and dropping one after another into a paper sack? It is easy for us to doubt the contest's very possibility to engage, allure, and sell its young participants the experience awaiting them at the moving picture show. Sure, children like (killing) bugs, but could a rational adult businessman ever really think to profit from a display of dead flies? Empirical evidence tells us it is true, however, and Mintz's successful collection of flies, or rather his exhibition of those his young patrons collected, represents important issues and practices that have largely gone unnoticed and unconsidered in the existing history of moviegoing and its promotion.

"Swat the Fly" was, in fact, not a competition imagined up by Sargent, Mintz, or some other Barnum-like fakir seeking profits from throngs of amused children, but instead a Progressive catchphrase for a civic discourse linking "modern" science, public health policy, and social welfare to private behavior and hygiene. Beginning in the early 1910s, swat-the-fly campaigns were organized and promoted by both public institutions and government bureaucracies: ladies' auxiliaries, Boy Scout troops, county and municipal health departments, the federal Department of Agriculture, and even the occasional movie theater owner. Swat-the-fly was designed to educate the populace about how to "best combat the deadly pest . . . the undertaker's traveling salesman," the common housefly, a prevalent host to a variety of life-threatening diseases, including typhoid, cholera, and tuberculosis.[6] The underlying purpose of Mintz's fly crusade, then, was ultimately not just about bringing in larger audiences, but also about presenting the neighborhood nickelodeon as a site devoted to its community's well-being and the exhibitor as both a showman and a Progressive caretaker. In an era that often correlated social stability with personal well being, it was crucial for exhibitors to inscribe their theaters within "healthy" communal boundaries. Almost from cinema's beginnings, a widespread discourse on fears about the damaging potential of the moving pictures and their site of exhibition that led to metaphors of disease and infection; imaginary maladies such as *Spectatoritis* and *Serialitis* were routinely labeled as film-caused social illnesses.[7] Other contagions were more frighteningly real in their physical effects, and in a era where flu pandemics could and did quickly kill hundreds of thousands of people—more than half a million Americans died of Spanish flu in 1918–1919—the dark and often crowded space of the movie theater not surprisingly became marked as a site both socially and physiologically dangerous to the community's collective health. To combat such anxieties, tradesmen like Sargent and exhibitors like Mintz regularly developed and promoted routines and procedures that emphasized the movie theater as a healthy site of communal edification and benefit. "Swat the Fly," bizarre as it seems now, was a result of this underlying set of needs, and offered a productive form of advertising for a theater and its owner that was at once promotion and public service.

If the communal aspects of the dead fly campaign are linked to a Progressive discourse on good hygiene, the more promotional possibilities of Mintz's fly stunt/scheme—the glass case full of flies for instance—can be

FIG. 4.1.
"Swat the Fly" booklet illustration by Ernest Hamlin Baker, circa 1910.
Author's collection.

traced to the less socially-positive lineage of nineteenth-century popular leisure forms like the dime museum, the carnival, and the circus. Mintz's promotion was theater-based and exhibitor-driven and designed to attract customers, in this case children, primarily from within his own neighborhood. The scheme depended on his knowledge of this neighborhood and his potential patrons, and it involved no real financial cooperation or creative input from either national producers or regional distributors. Although Mintz may have, as Sargent suggests, given away some "cheap fly swatters," the stunt did not otherwise require elaborate tie-ins or tie-ups of merchants or their merchandise. And, significantly, Sargent's scheme did not rely upon nor promote a particular movie, genre, serial, or star for its success to draw an audience. As such, "Swat the Fly," and its productive use by Mintz (and apparently many other exhibitors in this period) seems to resist the institution of a more nationalized mass model of promotion in which the center of power was increasingly located within the developing studio system. Swatting flies, simply put, does not fit very well into the standard history of this period, what historian Jane Gaines has described as the process of "transformation [from] the crude showman's gimmick into the slick Madison Avenue campaign."[8] After all, what could be cruder than a bag of dead flies?

Gaines's underlying assumptions about this dichotomy—that the "gimmicks" of the local showman were crude and the national campaigns of the producers and distributors were slick—tends to rely upon and reproduce an institutional discourse put forth by those very segments of the moving picture business, the large manufacturers, that most greatly desired the end result of "slick" national promotion. This is the narrative put forth by the studios, and more often than not replicated in the national trades from this time period. It is true that significant capital and cultural investment by the developing studio system was increasingly directed toward efficient "picture exploitation," the centralized mass advertising of individual films and their stars. Eventually, these sustained efforts in intensive advertising led to the studios' collective ability to powerfully participate in the shaping of their shared public. However, particularly in the mid-1910s, this kind of persuasive influence was sought more often than achieved. It was exhibitors like Mintz that remained the most visible and active showmen for their local audiences and their moving pictures. Gaines, it should be noted, is not alone in accepting the producers' hopeful ambitions as on-the-ground reality. Within the limited existing history of early movie advertising, the 1910s have typically been marked as the moment of movie advertising's modern "transformation." According to studio historian Janet Staiger: "By 1915 . . . the film business had made several significant choices. Distribution would be predictable, benefiting advertising; feature films would be differentiated and stressed; brand names would be submerged to product features (genre, stars, plots, spectacle, or realism)."[9]

The institutional framework for these changes was no doubt emerging and affecting the range and scope of promotional practices in this period, both for the movies themselves and the theaters and their exhibitors that presented them. The structural determinants required for such streamlined efficiency, however, had not yet truly coalesced into a cohesive industry-wide system—vertical integration was still around the corner and many new films continued to come from many different places. So in 1915, and for some time after that, the multi-branch industry was unable, or more often unwilling, to make unified decisions about what it was selling and how to sell it. The film business remained too competitive and too fractured for much collective agreement. The manufacturers' increasing investments in various forms of production and advertising, particularly those possibilities offered by large-circulation newspapers, highlighted their desire to create a single national public rather than an endless multitude of local audiences, an institutional aspiration that ultimately led studios to seek greater control of exhibition through promotion.[10] Most exhibitors, on the other hand, continued to believe that "going to the movies" was best described as a casual but habitual act on their patrons' part, one that had more to do with the theater and the overall program than what specifically might appear on the screen. The exhibitor-based promotions, therefore, tended most often to focus on the site and its show even when the ballyhoo was ostensibly about a movie, serial, or star. Ultimately, what was at stake was the audience and its allegiance. Pittsburgh exhibitors, as well as many others across the country, were in no hurry to give up the control that came with their role as showmen. The result was an extended period of competing, if not necessarily uncomplimentary, promotional practices that ranged in size and shape from the smallest dead fly at the bottom of a case in a Bloomfield movie theater to national campaigns with big prizes and even bigger posters designed to attract the eyes and ears of twenty-five-million newspaper readers.

The Exchange, the Movie, and the Program

In the early years of the nickelodeon boom, filmmaking remained more a craft than an industry. Eileen Bowser describes the result for exhibitors: "a nickelodeon manager got films wherever and however he could . . . [and] film quality was not always so much a matter of content or style as of condition."[11] Unfortunately, it was not unusual for the condition of the film to be poor, as many exchanges rented out films until the emulsion was virtually worn away. Although trade reports of the period show that exhibitors routinely complained and producers worried about what was being presented to the public as their collective product, the exchange owners continued to make the most from such a "short" market. Because the rental companies could abuse the film and make considerable profits, sometimes higher than the film's actual manufacturer, producers began looking for a way to gain greater influence over the "regulation and improvement of existing business conditions." In November 1907, this goal led a group of some of the largest manufacturers (including most of the future members of the MPPC) to offer a "cordial invitation [to] the leading Film Rental Bureaus" asking them to come to Pittsburgh to "discuss matters of vital importance."[12] Pittsburgh as a growing center for these proto-exchanges was chosen for "its central location," but it was also likely picked for its relatively neutral topography, as it was geographically (and perhaps politically) situated between the powerful rental and import men of Chicago, including Carl Laemmle, and the major film manufacturers of the East Coast.

The result of the convention, which took place downtown in the city's Fort Pitt Hotel, was the formation of the short-lived United Film Services Protective Association. The manufacturers created this organization primarily to impose restrictions on a number of commonplace and profitable exchange practices including the duping, sub-renting (to other exchanges), and secondhand selling of prints. Exchanges doing business with United would agree to buy films only from association members and return worn prints to their original manufacturer.[13] The producers' explicit rhetoric surrounding these new rules spoke of protecting the reputation of the industry by taking films in poor condition out of public circulation. Implicit in these directives, however, was the manufacturers' attempt to regulate and retain primary control of the films and their profits. Surprisingly, most of the exchangemen seem to have been willing to accept a measure of producer control, likely in the hopes that it would discourage new competitors from entering their lucrative distribution business and undercutting their established rental charges. According to O. T. Crawford, who owned a film exchange in St. Louis, "If something can be done to stop price cutting, throat cutting, duping, it will be to the advantage of everybody."[14] These organizational goals for the exchanges remained in place throughout the 1910s, but this particular combine never really got off the ground. Biograph refused to join the association, which helped lead to Edison's year-long drive to form the Motion Picture Patent Company (which Biograph did eventually join) at the end of 1908.[15]

The MPPC and the creation in 1910 of its distribution arm, the General Film Corporation (GFC), is no doubt the most heavily researched institutional aspect of the first two decades of American motion picture history. The MPPC and GFC are generally credited with industrializing the cinema in the early 1910s by establishing a rigid set of corporate structures that regularized production and exhibition around the assembly line—like daily release of one- (and later multi-) reel films. According to the film history presented in most textbooks, the success of this regularization actually led to the Trust's demise, because the MPPC continued to stubbornly rely on short films and was unable or unwilling to respond to the independents' innovation of the developing feature film market. This historiography—

which typically ascribes the Trust's influence within the industry as prematurely ending a number of years before its final legal dissolution in 1915—overstates both the speedy transformation to a feature-based cinema and the industrial and cultural consensus that was required for such a radical reordering of the status quo. The definition of the feature remained largely ill-defined for a good portion of the 1910s—in that decade, "feature" did not necessarily signify a multi-reel film.[16]

Additionally, as the feature film market evolved, the short-film program and its theater did not immediately lose its economic or cultural efficacy. The Trust model of industrialized cinema was a rational reaction to the nickelodeon boom and its popular short-film format. The Trust, in molding itself to this existing leisure paradigm, was working from an exhibitor-based definition of the cinema that assumed that any individual film was less important than the regular provision of an overall pleasurable experience. As a collective whole, the Trust envisioned each of its manufacturers' films as an indistinguishable commodity to be produced, packaged, and sold as part of a standard, but ever-changing, package.[17] By agreement, the MPPC manufacturers sold their individual films for a set price per foot, regardless of genre or production cost, to the GFC, which then rented the films to exhibitors as a "complete service" at a per-reel price. The complete service offered licensed exhibitors an omnibus of enough films to provide for a "daily change of reels."[18] Obviously, such a continuous rotation of films had considerable consequences for exhibitor-based advertising and promotion. Although theater owners and managers could look in the national trades to find out which films were coming next, promoting a single film, or even a group of films, that would have only a one-day showing made little economic sense.

By 1910, a significant percentage of American exhibitors, regardless of size, location, or whether they were contractually aligned to the Trust or the independents, provided their audiences with a new set of films each day. The fact that individual films could not be promoted, or even really differentiated within such a rapidly changing framework, was not considered a serious liability because theater owners were driven by a desire for a regular moviegoing audience, and believed that the patron paid an admission for a show—or even just part of a show—rather than a specific film. According to one trade editorial of the period, "down-town theatres" typically attracted "the after-lunch and few-minutes-to-spare" crowd, of which a considerable portion of the "patronage never remains for the whole show, but departs after a reel or two." With no specific start times and a program that ran almost continuously from early in the morning to late at night, a viewer could enter his theater at any point, confident that, if the film on the screen was not to his liking, it would only be a few minutes before a new one took its place: "The boundaries between one show and the next, though definite, are not important, and the visitor may drop in at any time, whenever he and his family get ready or get the notion, and remain until the return of the scene which was showing when he entered. The diversity of subjects presented in the one program is largely responsible for his interest; for he is reasonably sure of finding at least one theme of interest."[19]

In a period of intense competition among moving picture theaters, whether located "down-town" or in the neighborhoods, the daily change of program helped sustain theater loyalty and consistent patronage by allowing the audience to pay admission to the same exhibitor every day without ever having to worry about seeing the same film twice. Although the rental costs required for such rapid turnover of new films were not inconsiderable, exhibitors in cities like Pittsburgh, with its dense concentrations of movie theaters, continued to state their approval for this "daily change" structure into at least the mid-1910s.[20]

The average nickelodeon exhibitor in the early boom years required three or four reels per day, although this total jumped to as many as ten by 1915, and, as already noted, the more first-run films the exhibitor used the greater his rental fees.[21] As Eileen Bowser notes, as a result of this pricing system, "[m]ost nickelodeons settled for a smorgasbord, getting one film absolutely fresh, one a day old, one a week old, one over thirty days, and so forth."[22] When the system was first put in place, this cinematic buffet could only be chosen from a single distributor's supply. By 1911, the success of the independents made it increasingly difficult for General Film to enforce its regulations. Numerous exhibitors began to sign multiple contracts with different exchanges, many of which offered unlicensed films. According to one *Bulletin* editorial in 1914: "The day is gone forever when an exhibitor can complacently accept and show a single schedule and expect the nickels and dimes to come rolling in."[23]

Although the MPPC and General Film did not invent the nickelodeon, initiate its market for short films, or create its neighborhood and transient audiences, the rationalization of program exhibition and daily changes that it developed and standardized had a profound effect on how movies were sold and promoted in the following years. Even as the Paramount Corporation began promoting a feature program service in 1914, formalizing the initial ascent of a new industry paradigm, at least four national and many smaller regional distribution companies continued to supply the short-based film program.[24] Trade reports from Chicago that same year describe the situation as a "division of picture exhibiting into . . . big and little shows." According to the writer, the theater in which the "little show" played continued to provide the dominant exhibition format: "There are a hundred of them to every one of the newly appointed feature houses. They continue to demand their daily change of program. . . . Thus the market for the common, ordinary, garden variety of film, the single reel drama or comedy, is still, and will continue to be, a thousand times greater than the market for the feature."[25]

Between the growth of the feature market and the maturation of the "regular" program, advertising the movies in the 1910s would evolve into a set of related but distinct spheres involving both the selling of a movie and the selling of the show. It was in this stratified exhibition environment that William Mayer first began publication of the *Pittsburgh Moving Picture Bulletin*.

The *Bulletin*, the Exchange, and the Exhibitor

In May 1914, a single paragraph on the back page of the Chicago-based trade paper, *Motography*, congratulated the Mayers for publishing the *Pittsburgh Moving Picture Bulletin*, "launching a new craft on the journalistic sea."[26] The *Bulletin*'s weekly format largely emulated the national trade papers upon which its film-related editorials, summary reviews, and industry news articles were based. Although information regarding industry issues at a national level was included in the *Bulletin*, the journal's copy focused primarily on the personalities and activities of those locally involved in the movies. While the majority of this local news revolved around business dealings—who was buying what films, what company had sold which theater, where to find the newest poster frames, when to attend the anti-censorship rally—a substantial percentage of the paper was devoted to the personal and public lives of Pittsburgh's movie community. The *Bulletin* included celebrations of marriages, sympathetic relations of illnesses, and even exaggerated accounts of fishing trips, complete with photographs of the fish and fisherman involved.[27] The Mayers' paper also regularly printed group and individual photographs of those involved in some way in the local movie business. In one issue alone, the *Bulletin* portrayed major player Harry Davis, who is portrayed looking grim in his bowler hat; "hustling exhibitor" W. H. Ketcham, whose portrait accompanies praise for transforming his nickelodeon "from a lemon to a gold nugget"; and Mike Ray, "head shipper for Max Herring's three-a-week proposition down the Ferry street way" who poses in his boxing attire, glaring at the camera.[28] The *Bulletin's* rhetoric and accompanying imagery of a shared communal life was at once both self-serving and limited in its inclusion. Virtually no references appeared, for example, to the movie theaters, owners, and personnel that catered specifically to Pittsburgh's African American community.[29] Despite these telling absences, it seems likely that Mayer's espousal of a local community, something not readily available on the pages of the national trades, was a significant factor in the *Bulletin's* ongoing success in attracting readers and advertisers.

Advertisers were critical to the journal's success because, unlike the national industry papers, the *Bulletin* did not charge a subscription fee. According to Mayer, "The *Bulletin* is not going to cost you a cent. It will be mailed to you every Wednesday free of charge. All we ask in return is that you read it over carefully, if you find it worthy, lay it aside for future reference, and patronize the advertisers therein." While *Moving Picture World* charged most of its readership a subscription fee of three to four dollars

OPERATORS, BEWARE!

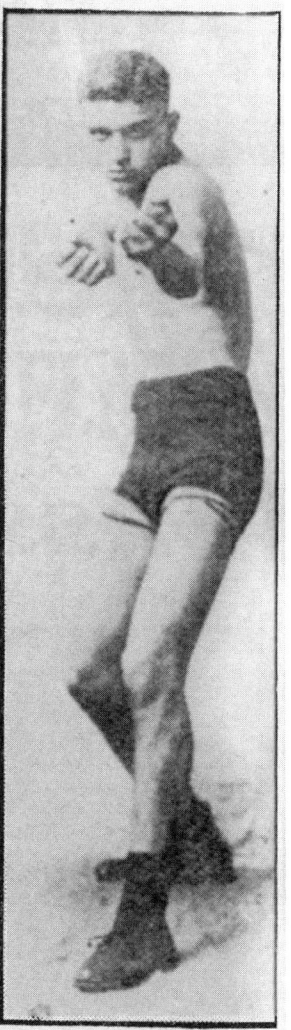

Look who's here! Blest if it isn't Mike Ray, the ray that shines as chief film hustler and poster man at Warner's feature exchange—in other words he's head shipper for Max Herring's three-a-week proposition down the Ferry street way.

And that pose! Sure Mike, it's the genuine article—"everything you see in the poster is shown on the screen"—no fake about Warner's even if the expression is extended to the people who earn their bread and butter thereat.

But, seriously speaking, Mike is some boxer. He's an ex-amateur champion, having won his laurels last year as the best mit mixer in the tournaments conducted by the Crafton Athletic Association. And, let me whisper to those obstreperous operators who persist in calling down the shipper when they think he is slow, Mike hasn't forgotten the use of his mits, and so—beware! He's in the 125-pound class, but if you happen to weigh about 150, don't let that encourage you to "sass" him, for we honestly believe he would not be afraid to tackle "Fatty" down at the Independent Display Company.

FIG. 4.2.
"Operators, Beware!" feature on Mike Ray of Warner Brothers.
Pittsburgh Moving Picture Bulletin, May 20, 1914, 8.

a year, Mayer was able to give his *Bulletin* away for free to local exhibitors and distributors by "cover[ing] the expenses of the publication" with advertising: "income derived from the film people and supply houses."[30] In his earliest years of publication, Mayer charged up to fifteen dollars for a full-page advertisement in the weekly *Bulletin*. Although a year into the venture he claimed that its "publication . . . has not been a howling success financially," many of the local film-related businesses kept their weekly ads running continuously throughout the known life of the paper.[31]

In an analysis of all issues of the *Bulletin* in its first three years of operation, 1914 to 1917, the trade journal averages around thirty pages in length. Of that, approximately half the total pages are "paid" advertisements divided between producers and exchanges (sixteen ads per week, almost equally split between half- and full-page ads); exhibitor supply houses (six ads per week, again equally divided among half and full); and poster distributors and printers (two or three ads per week, usually smaller sizes). Exhibitors rarely bought space from Mayer, although occasionally an advertisement was placed when a theater was up for sale. Most advertisers appeared to have signed long-term contracts with the *Bulletin*, which Mayer advertised as guaranteeing discounted fees. However, one-time ads were not unusual, as was the case for the half-page bought by the Denol Chemical Company to promote its Denol germicide, which when "sprayed throughout your house will kill all germs and at the same time impart a delicate perfume."[32] Virtually every regular advertiser received some additional promotional write-up within the body of the journal—either a direct commendation in the form of a brief filler paragraph, or more circumstantially through an interview or article about the "doings" of the owner or manager of the business in question—a common marketing practice that continues in many trade journals and popular magazines today.

Mayer also regularly used his column space to promote the *Bulletin* to its own advertisers: "When you place a want ad in *The Bulletin* you put the announcement before EVERY exhibitor in Western Pennsylvania. . . . That's what you pay for and that's the amount of publicity you get. Nothing more—nothing less. You get your announcement before the people who want to buy your goods—other people do not interest you."[33] Mayer's reference to "announcements" made to "other people" is likely a critique of the few exchanges who chose to advertise their services in Pittsburgh's daily city newspapers. This practice, which, according to Richard Abel, occurred in other cities as early as 1912, appears to have been an irregular and short-lived exercise by a few of Pittsburgh's smaller independent exchanges, who probably quickly realized that Mayer was correct about his journal being a much more direct device with which to hail their prospective customers.[34]

Advertisements by the exchanges on the pages of the *Bulletin* initially emulate the promotional methods of American corporations, which sold more consumer-oriented products such as Nabisco crackers and Crisco shortening. Branding—the packaging and trademarking of goods—was a relatively new phenomena but one that was increasingly recognized as a crucial marketing tool for any product manufactured on an industrial scale. According to cultural historian Susan Strasser: "Branding offered manufacturers a new kind of control when supported by effective advertising, by altering the balance of power in the traditional chain from manufacturer to wholesaler to retailer to customer. No longer were customers to rely on the grocer's opinion about the best soap; no longer could wholesalers choose among various manufacturers who might fulfill their orders. People asked for Ivory, which could only be obtained from Procter and Gamble."[35] For the majority of film manufacturers, whose one- and two-reel films were designed to fit within a daily program change of multiple movies, advertising any one particular film was practically impossible and financially fruitless. Branding allowed exhibitors and audiences to easily identify, and hopefully come to depend upon, the film's manufacturer. Equally important, like the well-established commercial equation, Ivory Soap = Purity, effective advertising by the manufacturers and/or exchanges that distributed their films could then work to connotatively fix a second-order signification such as Vitagraph = Quality or Keystone = Comedy. Additionally, as Strasser points out, branding had the added benefit for manufacturers and their exchanges of shifting power away from the exhibitors by creating a specific desire for a product *they* produced. As William W. Hodkinson, president of Paramount Pictures, wrote in a 1915 trade editorial, "To do this the mountain trade mark of Paramount must be popularized nationally.... A trade mark... in itself has only potential value. It becomes real value only so far as it becomes a trade mark in popular demand, and, therefore, represents large sales possibilities."[36]

As important as the brand and its associated meanings became to major studios like Paramount, Pittsburgh remained full of small-time and independent exchanges whose films were rarely ever associated with or promoted by their particular makers. The American Feature Company, which declared itself a "feature bargain house" advertised dozens of two-, three-, and a few four-reel "features" for five to ten dollars a film, none of which were new releases and none of which named their original producer.[37] The Western Film Company, whose slogan was "One or More a Day. One or More a Week," regularly bought a half-page ad in the *Bulletin* during these years. This exchange offered exhibitors the ability "to balance your program" at a rental price that will "Save You Money!"[38] Over three years, however, the ads never once actually listed either a film's title or production company, and often simply showed its own trademark, an image of a cowboy roping a steer. Western did not need to advertise specific titles of their films because their offerings belonged to a model of regular program cinema in which one film was as good as the next. That an exchange company could still, by the mid-1910s, successfully practice such a minimalist style of promotion emphasizes the continued saliency of this interchangeable exhibition format. Unlike Western, those producers and distributors whose business models focused on feature films, whether individually or as part of a program, needed to establish a promotional discourse based on differentiation. Surprisingly little has been made of this paradigmatic shift, except as it relates to the formal aesthetic and narrative aspects of the developing classical Hollywood cinema. The move from an institutional framework based on similarity to one of difference was, however, of profound and lasting consequence for both distributors' and exhibitors' attempts to advertise their shared product, particularly when that product was a feature.

According to Michael Quinn, "The term 'feature' derived initially from vaudeville, where the 'feature act' was the biggest and best on the program."[39] Biggest and best usually involves increased costs, and although expense (like length) was not necessarily the defining characteristic of the early feature, it was a significant determinant in the rise of film-specific advertising. Higher costs for the feature film, whether because of increased length, additional spectacle, or the involvement of known actors, required proportional increases in rental charges and so these films demanded additional work to "sell" them to exhibitors. The time and money that went into these more expensive or lengthier films also resulted by the early 1910s in a more predictable, if still diffuse, schedule and procedure for distribution. This meant that "feature" exchanges began to know not only when they would receive a particular film but also what elements of the film they could promote, including genre, stars, and plot. Mayer Silverman, for instance, utilized his "demonstration banquets" to market his newest films to the local exhibitors, a practice the *Bulletin*'s editors thought highly of, as it was "in line with the progressive policy which dominates the picture business at the present time. It will enable the exhibitor to see what he is to show—he will not be obliged to take some one else's word for the merits or demerits of a picture. He can judge for himself whether a subject will suit his particular class of patrons or not and can act accordingly."[40] Of course, Silverman and other local feature distributors could not solely rely on steaks and beer, or even the films themselves, to sell their product and so with greater and greater frequency feature films became the most prominent item advertised on the pages of the *Bulletin*.

While Mayer's editorial foregrounds a discourse of differentiation, the growing ranks of feature film producers did not completely refute "brand name" advertising as quickly or as decidedly as studio historians such as Staiger have suggested. As researched by scholar Kathy Fuller-Seeley, a Paramount campaign of the late 1910s and 1920s that ran broadly in trade papers, fan magazines, and the *Saturday Evening Post* continued to explicitly foreground their products' similarities over their individual differences: "The name of the play? Who cares? It's a Paramount . . . and that's saying we'll see foremost stars, superbly directed, in clean motion pictures."[41] In an era of growth and instability in which production companies quickly came and left, distribution deals coalesced and collapsed, and stars rapidly moved from studio to studio (for more and more money), organizations such as Paramount continued brand-based promotion in the hopes that it would create and maintain the public perception of a consistent corporate product that did not depend on any one particular determinant for its success.

Few production companies or exchanges had either the financial or cinematic resources that Paramount did, and smaller feature companies, particularly those who distributed through the state rights system and whose output of titles would never be "regular" enough to offer a true program service, found it much more efficient to advertise a single film. Although it may initially appear counterintuitive, the smaller the company, the more likely it was to place an ad announcing a single film in the *Bulletin*. Advertisements placed by well-funded, well-entrenched producers tended to either go without naming a specific feature title or, conversely, give minimal textual attention to as many as six different films. The ALCO Film Service, a short-lived national exchange that distributed state rights films, often took out half-page ads in the *Bulletin* to promote a single feature. Its advertisement for the five-reel melodrama *The Three of Us* (1914), a film by trumpeter-turned-producer B. A. Rolphe, is relatively typical for the less-established distributors of this period.[42] The only graphic element is a border with the distributor's name embedded in its design, and the ad's largest text is devoted to the film's title. A slightly smaller type is used to depict the name of the picture's lead actress, Mabel Taliaferro, promoted by the production company, Selig, as "the Sweetheart of American Movies," but described here in the ad only as "the dainty, yet forceful comedienne." No information appears regarding the film's story of gold mine rivalries in the mountains of Colorado, although a reader might (wrongly) assume that he was renting a comedy because of the description of Taliaferro. The advertisement does promote, albeit in its smallest and plainest type, the author of the film's scenario, Rachel Crothers, a respected Broadway playwright, in an attempt to associate the feature with its more culturally sanctioned

FIG. 4.3.
The Three of Us advertisement. *Pittsburgh Moving Picture Bulletin,* December 9, 1914, 6.

source material—an earlier "legitimate" stage production (1906) of the same name.[43]

At first glance, the ads placed by the Famous Players Film Service—which distributed the films of Famous Players, Jesse L. Lasky, and All-Star via the state rights system—look very similar to the unassuming layout of the ALCO ad.[44] Famous Players, a company with much greater resources, both human and capital, seems to purposefully understate its significant strengths in these advertisements. The relationship between information and text size is inverse to ALCO's ad, giving the biggest type to the corporate exchange name and the very smallest to the actual film titles. In the same small type, and without any other contextual information, appears the name "Mary Pickford." By 1914, there were no exhibitors, and very few citizens, left in Pittsburgh who did not know of "little Mary." According to the *Bulletin*'s editor, "The picture house which does not show a 'Little Mary Pickford' poster nowadays is something of a curiosity. In East Liberty three houses had posters out last Sunday announcing the little star in pictures for the week. One house is showing 'The Eagle's Mate,' the present-day Famous Players' production; another is showing the Universal re-issue and the third has the old Biograph re-issues. Still another house last Saturday ran a two-year-old-copy which has lain on the shelf of General Film Co. . . . for the past two years."[45]

Although recent scholarship has noted that production companies began to publicize individual actors as early as 1909, for reasons that are difficult to determine it was not until early 1915 that advertisers in the *Bulletin* began to shift their focus from selling films and their narratives to selling stars and their faces.[46] Distributors' decision to introduce stars into advertising also marks a dramatic shift in the use of illustration and photography on the pages of the *Bulletin*. Prior to the spring of 1915, very few of the producers' ads carried large amounts of illustration, and almost none used photography as a means of attracting the exhibitors' attentions. The reasons for this absence, and the concurrent late arrival of stars to the *Bulletin*'s pages, remain indiscernible. The *Bulletin*'s publishers were highly experienced printers with access to the necessary lithographic and printing technology, and photography and illustration was used relatively freely within the editorial text of the journal. Additionally, many of the larger equipment dealers regularly used ads with photos or drawings of projectors, pianos and electric fans. In April 1915, Famous Players placed an ad that included an image of Mary Pickford, becoming the first illustrated advertisement to appear in the *Bulletin*.[47] Stars and their iconic images were, by this time, another significant way in which producers could "standardize" their brand-name for advertising purposes while simultaneously differentiating their films from the literally hundreds of others being released every week.

The Universal "Nothing But Stars" ad of April 1915 clearly illustrates how the producers could use individual actors' images to achieve a company-wide standardization or branding effort. In this particular ad, the

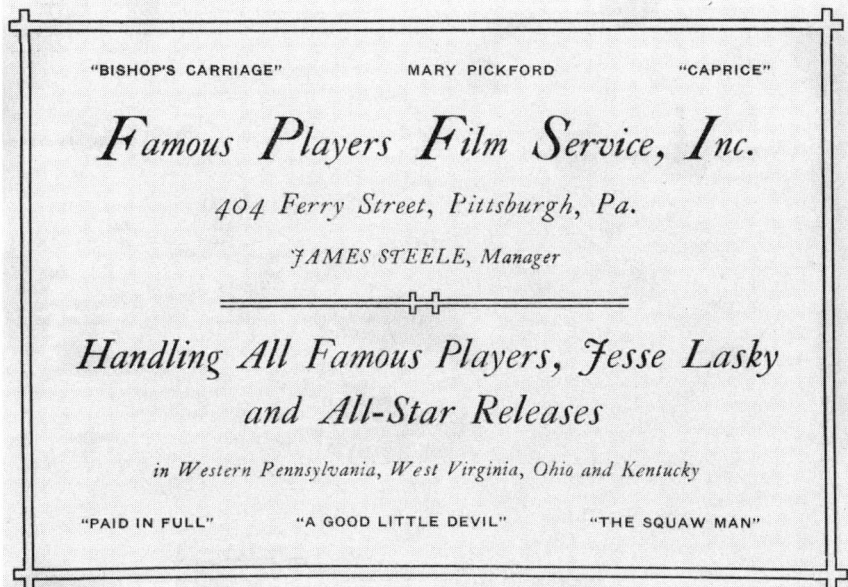

FIG. 4.4.
Famous Players Film Service advertisement. *Pittsburgh Moving Picture Bulletin*, December 9, 1914, 8.

star concept is the primary focus, but the actual images of the stars play a secondary role. The simply-bordered photos consist of "stills" of the actors from scenes in their individual films, and the busy backgrounds of the photos work to obscure rather than highlight the actors' visages. Below the photos, in which each contains a star "couple," the actual names of the actors, King Baggot and Jane Gales, appear in the smallest print of the entire advertisement. Baggot was one of the first publicized movie "stars" and, although his popularity has historiographically waned, in the 1910s his name and face were as recognizable as Pickford's or Chaplin's. This advertisement, then, uses the names and faces of the actors not to promote the actors themselves, but the fact that Universal films include (any) stars. The actors have become less themselves, and more icons of a successful

FIG. 4.5.

"Stars, Stars, Nothing But Stars," Independent Film Exchange advertisement for a Universal program. *Pittsburgh Moving Picture Bulletin*, April 28, 1915, back cover.

FIG. 4.6.
Mayer Publishing and Printing advertisement for "Chaplin Cuts."
Pittsburgh Moving Picture Bulletin, June 16, 1915, inside cover.

movie studio. Baggot was Florence Lawrence's leading man at Carl Laemmle's Independent Moving Picture Company (IMP) when Laemmle planted the story of her accidental death. And it was Baggot, "The Man Whose Face Is As Familiar As The Man In The Moon," who appeared at Lawrence's side when she made her first public appearance at Union Station in St. Louis after IMP "refuted" her death.[48]

The transformation of actors to icons occurred across an uneven and irregular terrain, and some actors moved across this visual geography much more quickly than others. Charlie Chaplin was one of the first to develop, and arguably collapse, his star persona into a set of highly recognizable visual codes, so it is not surprising that his image is one of the first to become photographically removed from a film's background and to literally stand on its own in the pages of the *Bulletin*. In fact, it is the owners of the

Bulletin, Mayer Publishing Company, that in June of 1915 suggested to local exhibitors they should make their "advertising effective by illustration through the purchase of Charlie Chaplin for seventy-five cents. They were selling a life-size photo-lithography cut-out of the already iconic image of Chaplin, designed to be backed with wood and stand outside the theaters owned by the city's "wide-awake exhibitors."[49]

While most exhibitors could manage the seventy-five cents necessary to purchase the paper Chaplin, stars made of flesh were an expense that not all film producers could afford. The cost of creating, promoting, and publicizing a star, as well as the increasing salaries of those actors who had already achieved stardom, kept all but the very largest producers from finding, developing, and keeping a stable of star-worthy actors. Ironically, however, the very iconic nature of the movie star allowed some of the more creative small-timers to steal the message from the messenger. Such was the case for Pincus, the Chaplin imitator, whose one-reel comedies were available for local rental from Mayer Silverman's Liberty Film. Pincus's appearance in the pages of the *Bulletin* highlight not only that Silverman spent the money to advertise him, but that film producers and distributors had made an early and relatively sophisticated recognition about the possibilities of the movie star.[50]

At once both sophisticated and silly, this star hijacking by the Ko-Ko Film Company, the obscure New York production company that created Pincus, and his promotion by Silverman's Liberty Film Company underscores the tumultuous industry atmosphere that continued to persist through much of the 1910s. Most scholars of this period emphasize the increasing standardization, integration, and consolidation of the industry's three branches, but Pincus, a marginal figure at best, disallows such a linear vision. Paradoxically, the structure of the film industry—the daily change, the "regular" program, the movie star— created the economic and cultural latitude for peripheral characters like Pincus to exist and potentially succeed.

In this freewheeling era, icons such as Chaplin's Tramp remained largely available for companies like Ko-Ko Film to capitalize on and profit from. How widely or successfully such a figure actually circulated is difficult to

FIG. 4.7.
Liberty Film Renting Company advertisement for Pincus, the Chaplin imitator. *Pittsburgh Moving Picture Bulletin,* October 20, 1915, inside cover.

presume, however, for Pincus does not appear on the pages of national trade journals like *Moving Picture World* or *Variety.* The national trade papers, which had begun publishing as early as 1907, had quickly become the standard method by which manufacturers and distributors addressed exhibitors and marketed their collective product. Although the *Bulletin* sought to provide a similar service at the local level, its real and discursive distance from the industry's central sites of development—Chicago, New York, and Los Angeles—reveal those businessmen who, like Pincus, existed on the outer edges of the institutional boundaries and did not have the resources to enter the mainstream. While big and small manufacturers and their exchanges chose to regularly address Pittsburgh's exhibitors through their ads in the *Bulletin*, those same exhibitors had to look for other, often less direct ways, to address their potential audiences.

The Exhibitor Sells the Show

In the fall and early winter of 1916, *Motion Picture News* ran a series of front-page articles and editorials debating how best to solicit and sell the movies to American audiences. Not surprisingly, there were many disagreements among the interested parties as to division of labor and methodology. An anonymous exhibitor wrote in December of that year: "I contend, and have clearly proven to my own complete satisfaction, that no newspaper advertising is necessary to a neighborhood and, as a matter of fact, I think a canvass of the entire country will show few who are doing it. . . . None of these houses can afford newspaper advertising, and as a rule they don't require it. The business-street house is all transient trade and the neighborhood house has its regular patronage."[51] Only a week later, a producer responded in his own article that exhibitors should "use the local newspapers for as much space as [they] could possibly afford."[52] Newspaper advertising by the film industry as a whole was infrequent and inconsistent for the movies' first decade of existence. In Pittsburgh, as Charles Musser has noted, the first fifteen years of exhibition included almost no theater advertising and relatively little mention of their activities in this city's popular press.[53]

While some newspapers in other parts of the country routinely carried advertisements for local nickelodeons, especially when they first opened, Pittsburgh's major papers carried none at all. William Mayer complained of this lack in his very first issue of the *Bulletin*, placing much of the blame for its absence on the frugality of the local exhibitors: "A daily paper is conducted for profit and a non-advertising institution stands a pretty slim chance of getting any publicity at the hands of a modern daily newspaper manager without paying for it. The moving picture men [of Pittsburgh] are not liberal advertisers."[54] But as exhibition conditions changed, some local theater owners became quite "liberal." In July 1914, the *Pittsburgh Dispatch*, the city's largest circulating paper at the time, hired George Downs Jr. as "photoplay" editor to begin a regular Sunday section on the moving pictures.[55] The initially small section, approximately three columns wide, shared the part of the paper belonging to the "Theatrical Reviews and News," and perhaps not coincidentally, commenced around the same time that the city's larger legitimate theaters took the initiative to show feature films during the traditional summer theatrical break. The *Pittsburgh Index*, a weekly social and cultural calendar conspicuously aimed at the region's elite, began its own coverage of photoplays later that same year. Reporting on the parties and polo matches of the city's wealthiest patrons, the paper introduced its movie news that fall by producing short synopses of the feature films its editors felt were the "grandest" and most "worthwhile" to play in the city; such as the eight-reel spectacular, *Anthony and Cleopatra*, which arrived in early October for a month-long engagement at the downtown Pitt Theater and which was presented with "a short prelude by a capable company of singers and dancers that lends atmosphere to the picture."[56]

The first year of movie advertising in Pittsburgh newspapers rarely contained photographs or other graphic illustrations. The *Press*, however, began to reproduce photographs of "Famous Movie Stars" in conjunction with its Sunday column, "Feature Photoplays to Be Seen in Pittsburg [*sic*] This Week."[57] These articles and their accompanying images of stars were a form of advertising—their introduction onto the page was a quid pro quo result of daily newspaper advertising by some of the biggest players in the local exhibition scene.[58] Mayer suggests such a mutual relationship when he asks his readers: "Are the newspapers in your town treating you right? Are you treating them right? Get together boys; get on good terms with all of the editors and advertising men. It pays."[59] Regardless of such cooperation, it is not until late in 1916 that the local exhibitors and the national producers began to regularly use photography and illustration in their newspaper-based attempts to attract Pittsburgh audiences.

It remains difficult to fully decipher the mediated economic relationships between exhibitors, distributors, and producers in regard to newspaper advertising of this period. As the 1916 debate in *Motion Picture News* makes clear, most exhibitors, particularly those who operated smaller neighborhood nickelodeons believed, probably rightly, that film-specific newspaper advertising was money best spent by producers. Producers, conversely, hoped that theater owners would "advertise individually every feature" and accept that "the chief advertising responsibility rests" with the exhibitor.[60] These differences aside, in many cases newspaper advertising appears to have been a mutually cooperative, if not always equally beneficial, enterprise. This association can most easily be seen in the newspaper advertisements introducing another relatively new innovation for the film industry, the episodic serial.

According to Shelley Stamp, the first major serial, *The Adventure of Kathlyn* (1913), produced by Chicago's Selig-Polyscope company, was created to coordinate with a weekly written installment of Kathlyn's adventures in the *Chicago Tribune*.[61] The popularity of the screen serialization significantly advanced the *Tribune*'s circulation, and encouraged the rest of the film industry to quickly follow Selig's example.[62] The manufacturer's enthusiasm for the serial was similar in form to its growing dependence on the star system—a reliance on the belief that it is much easier to sell a product whose likeness to its predecessor is greater than its difference. The key to the successful marketing of the serial was for the industry to attract consumers to their initial offering. In terms of newspaper advertising, this meant an unprecedented burst of collective address by all three industry branches, designed to convince the audience to seek out and commit themselves to a regular weekly adventure that might last four months or even longer. Exhibitors may have found themselves more willing to invest in newspaper advertising for this particular cinematic genre because, according to Stamp: "Newspaper and magazine tie-ins that almost always accompanied the serials targeted new kinds of cinema patrons, untapped by more traditional forms of motion picture publicity lie posters, heralds, and lobby displays that circulated at street level."[63]

Although other serials were exhibited in the city as early as 1912, on Sunday, October 8, 1916, the first full-page advertisement for a moving picture, in this case for the coming fifteen weeks of Pathé's "wonder" serial, *The Shielding Shadow,* appeared in Pittsburgh newspapers.[64] Pathé, which was the U.S. distributor for the series produced by the Astra Film Corporation, claimed a five-million-dollar budget for the fifteen episodes and a national audience of 25 million newspaper readers. In addition, in its trade advertisements, Pathé promised exhibitors a full range of "excellent quality paper" including lobby cards and one-, three- and six-sheet posters. In twenty of the largest cities, including Pittsburgh, the French company planned to rent billboards "designed with a space for the name of the theatres and the dates they will show the picture."[65] The newspaper advertisements for the serial, which appeared simultaneously in both the *Pittsburgh Press* and the *Chronicle,* are more strikingly graphic than any previous local print ad for the movies. In the first ad, the image of a helpless damsel suspended in horrifying freefall over the grasping tentacles of the octopus worked to symbolize the episodic, cliff-hanging structure of the serial narrative. Following Selig's well-established precedent, Pittsburgh's movie patrons could read in either of the papers the weekly adventures of the "mysterious avenger, Ravengar"—capable of hypnotic feats and the inventor of an invisibility cloak—and watch his exploits on many of the city's movie screens. One week later in another full-page spread, the octopus shared the spotlight with a group of strikingly different characters: all of the exhibitors who were presenting Pathé's weekly adventure at their Pittsburgh-area theaters. The well-groomed, if somewhat stern, visages of thirty-two regional exhibitors look out from the page, hailing their respective patrons and claiming their continued importance in the moving picture show.

Stamp, in her extensive work on this popular format, claims that the rise of the serial "coincided with a marked change in film advertising . . . [which in] large measure . . . can be attributed to the shift away from localized, exhibitor-base promotions towards nationally coordinated publicity campaigns engineered by film production companies."[66] However, Pathé's willingness to attach such Pittsburgh-specific imagery to their nationally advertised product reveals the significant position exhibitors retained as the literal face of the movies for their local audiences. The melding of these

FIG. 4.8.
The Shielding Shadow serial advertisement with images of Pittsburgh exhibitors. Reproduced in *Pittsburgh Moving Picture Bulletin*, October 25, 1916, 10.

two very different kinds of images can also be seen as a representation of the ongoing intricate negotiation of national and local allegiances that were seen by many as an integral component for institutional success.[67] As trade articles written by men like Sargent continued to emphasize, "[a]dvertising starts with the personality of the Exhibitor and the personality of his house." The *Shielding Shadow* serial was specifically designed to create a national audience but, as the ad's imagery registers, that audience was best introduced to its local consumers by a familiar and known entity. In an increasingly corporate cinema, the exhibitor's role remained that of a genial host who, according to Sargent, must intimately understand the needs of his (paying) guests: "The Exhibitor who holds his trade best is he who spends a great part of his time about the house. He is known to the greater portion of his clientele. . . . He knows their likes and dislikes; their preferences for certain stars. He knows what they desire and tries to procure it, but he does not promise what he knows he cannot. He listens attentively to complaints and either explains or corrects. He is primed with information as to the business and is looked upon as a well of information."[68]

According to one national survey done by *Motion Picture News* in 1916, the majority of exhibitors believed that what their patrons continued to desire was a daily change of program. Even the serial film, which ran over the course of many months, consisted of episodes typically played in each theater for a day or two.[69] Of those exhibitors that responded to the survey, only 3 percent answered that they ran their program an entire week (presumably those presenting "big" features in larger theaters), while 36 percent still changed reels six days a week. With such frequent changes, advertising one particular film continued to be of little value. In the same survey, fully one-quarter of exhibitors who responded said that the quality of any one individual film they showed was of *no* importance to their box office totals.[70] Although such rapid turnover diminished the economic import of any particular film to the overall program, the results of this survey may in part reflect exhibitors' attitude toward the growing power of the feature and its producers. Smaller neighborhood and business-district houses, which continued to be the majority of movie-exhibition sites in America, worried that manufacturers were "seeing too big . . . seeing only the big theatre, the big audience, the big production," at the expense of the kind of show they continued to see as critical to their own success and survival.[71] Exhibitors' answers to this trade survey represents a resistance to this mass-produced vision in that it refuses to grant significant status to a single movie and its increasingly large producers.

It's a Show

Advertisements placed by Pittsburgh's exhibitors in this period were still primarily designed to emphasize the *show* part of the moving picture show. The movie never stood alone, and the idea of the "show" incorporates the roles played by the exhibitor and their significant intertextual elements including music, songs, contests, and the overall environment of the theater, as well as less film-specific notions of pleasure, entertainment, and community. By 1914, a few of the city's most successful local exhibitors—some who owned a single large theater, such as Pete Antonopolis and his downtown Olympic, and some, like Clark and Rowland, who had control of a small chain of theaters spread across the city or region—were regularly promoting their weekly schedules in small newspaper ads, usually in the major papers' Sunday editions. Such ads, however, represent only about a dozen or so of the more than one hundred movie theaters found across the city. By the *Bulletin*'s account, most of Pittsburgh's exhibitors continued to rely on a combination of selling practices that closely followed the successful patterns established by the nineteenth-century showmen of the dime museum, vaudeville theater, circus, and carnival. These were a set of diverse practices that focused attention on the moviegoing environment and the pleasures associated with the entire show rather than the films themselves.

As Mintz and Sargent have collectively revealed, a specific vocabulary evolved around the selling of the moving picture show. Although certain terms do, over time, become attached to a specific set of procedures and/or a particular branch of the industry, the actual distinctions between schemes, stunts, advertising, promotion, publicity, exploitation, and others remains blurred at best even in the period of their initial invention and use. These indistinct boundaries are complicated by the elusive, ephemeral, and often purposefully undocumented nature of many of the subsequent practices, particularly those undertaken by individual exhibitors. Unlike the exercise of branding a product, which is intrinsically designed to call attention to itself, many of the exhibitors' selling strategies worked best when they were able to "divert the attention of the onlooker, expand or contract to fit the occasion, and take the shape of the forms at hand."[72] Like a good sleight-of-hand card trick, the well-performed stunt or scheme was designed to leave little or no reference to its methods, only its achievements.

In November 1914, the *Bulletin* published a small photograph of a massive throng of people stretched down the street as far as the eye could see, all apparently waiting and watching for something in front of a small neighborhood movie theater, the Beechwood. The crowd was intriguingly disproportionate to the size of the theater. The teasing caption asked: "What makes such a crowd in front of this new theater of Ernie Johnson's? Albert Cook had a plan to draw the crowd and it worked well."[73] However, no answer to the question was forthcoming. Cook was a salesman for a local company which sold theater supplies, but there is no way for the reader to know what his idea entailed, or how it worked—only that it worked well. The few references to specific promotional methods and behaviors of Pittsburgh's local exhibitors in the *Bulletin*, however, illuminate at least some of the individuals and the types of labor involved in such promotions.

Exhibitor-initiated selling strategies most often fell into the contemporary descriptive categories of "publicity" and "promotion," which might include the aforementioned stunts and schemes along with, but not limited to, snipes, handbills, window cards, banners, parades, posters, novelties, contests, tricks, and gimmicks. Often collectively described as "street work," an endless range of materials and practices were designed to draw the public into the semi-public space of the movie theater. As Leslie Midkiff DeBauche has noted, such "methods of salesmanship . . . had . . . a dual function: to sell seats in their theaters and to constitute a regular film going audience."[74] Additionally, and perhaps even more importantly, these public forms of advertising functioned within a larger discourse of community and worked to reinforce the position of the exhibitor and his theater within this sphere.

By the mid-1910s, exhibitors were able to engage in these methods of salesmanship with the help of a number of industry advice columnists who discussed issues of publicity and promotion on the pages of the national trade journals. As previously mentioned, the most well known of these arbiters of all things cinematic was Epes Winthrop Sargent. Sargent, a regular and influential contributor to *Moving Picture World*, compiled and published *Picture Theatre Advertising* in 1915, and a sequel, coauthored with John F. Barry in 1927, *Building Theatre Patronage*. The earlier of these how-to handbooks for theater owners and managers classified, analyzed, and prioritized a variety of selling tactics and strategies. According to Sargent, "there are many forms of advertising possible to the man who uses his brains and thinks. You must be a schemer to make the best success in this business."[75] Sargent's philosophy was that "advertising ... is not confined to one or two forms of announcement but ranges from the personality of the house owner to the condition of the broom with which the house is swept."[76] The thirty-two chapters of Sargent's advertising manual illustrate the practical application of this broad theory of selling, including: "The Lobby as an Advertisement," "Street Advertising," "Novelty Advertisements," "Prize and Contest Schemes," and "Rainy Day Advertising." On a local level, the infrequent but illuminating reports in Pittsburgh's *Bulletin* of the successful promotions by the city's exhibitors—such as Mintz and his dead flies—verify not only the reality but the practiced efficacy of many of Sargent's strategies.

"One of the best, cheapest and most direct forms of advertising to patrons whose favor you already enjoy is by means of the screen," begins a chapter entitled "Advertising on the Screen," which primarily focuses on a discussion of a theater's employment of magic lantern slides before and between reels. Such slides could be utilized as an advertising medium for the theater itself as well as for businessmen from the surrounding neighborhoods who would pay for the chance to connect with their customers.

Sargent warned exhibitors to resist the allure of additional revenue such ads could provide, as the patrons would resent being "anchored in a seat and then forced to . . . watch a seemingly endless projection of advertisements of trades people."[77]

Whether or not exhibitors took Sargent's advice is difficult to determine, but another, even more cinematic form of screen advertising was popular in Pittsburgh during this era, the moving picture "local view." Consisting of scenes of the city's neighborhoods, citizens, and local landmarks, such films were photographed by either the exhibitor himself or, more often, by local companies that specialized in such work. The Fort Pitt Film Company placed a *Bulletin* ad in early 1915 declaring, "WE MAKE MOTION PICTURES of Lawn Fetes, Picnics, Lodges, Churches, Private Homes and for Educational Purposes . . . Advertising Film and Lantern Slides a Specialty."[78] This company competed with, among others, a local cameraman named George Bates Jr., who offered the region's exhibitors "a plan whereby the burden of the cost of such a proposition falls on the merchants of the town, who obtain some exceptionally valuable advertising." Bates, who had already made a dozen of these local advertising films, suggested that exhibitors could make three to five hundred dollars while providing their patrons with an "extraordinary attraction."[79] In addition to profits, local films provided exhibitors with a vivid cinematic claim to proprietorship of the moving picture show and its audience.

Another innovation that took advantage of the theater's screen was the new and novel idea of the "trailer"—a short film prepared as an advertisement for a forthcoming movie. Although the term was widely used and accepted by the late 1910s, "trailer" first appeared in the *Bulletin* in the spring of 1914. Alexander Parke, an independent exchangeman specializing in state rights films—including exploitive titles like *Smashing the Vice Trust* and *The Drug Terror*—was credited in the pages of the *Bulletin* with "pulling off a good advertising stunt. . . . For several days in advance he shows a strip of film announcing the coming of the complete picture, thereby giving a very good idea of the offering. The scheme is proving effective."[80] According to Janet Staiger, by the early 1920s, a small national adjacent industry developed specifically to prepare these types of promotional films. In Pittsburgh, the idea of the trailer was initially pursued unevenly and inconsistently, primarily by the various feature exchanges as a means of directly advertising their wares to the public. At least a few local exhibitors, however, also entered the early trailer business. In March 1915, the Regent's managers were praised in the pages of the *Bulletin* for their creation of "Filmannouncements." Shot by another local production company, Photoplay Entertainment, the hundred-foot film presented the Regent's audience with the undercranked image (motion speeded up) of a bill poster climbing a ladder and hanging three sheets of the coming attractions for the week ahead. The theater promised its patrons different moving presenters every week, including a Méliès-like magician who would mysteriously cause the new posters to appear and disappear in a poster frame.[81]

In the years between 1910 and 1920, film production could best be described as excessive. According to *Motion Picture News*, in a single week of December 1915, 230 reels of pictures were released.[82] The prolific amount of footage available allowed local exhibitors to show and advertise more and more films for the same nickel price. In such a resulting competitive atmosphere, particularly in Pittsburgh neighborhoods with dense concentrations of movie theaters, the city's exhibitors soon began to offer additional incentives to their patrons. These "premiums" for admission included cash, dishes, and even livestock. At least one Pittsburgh theater advertised a "payday" on which each patron was "handed an envelope with their ticket . . . contain[ing] cash, from a penny to five dollars—no blanks."[83] Sargent devoted two chapters of his manual to these popular prize, contest, premium, and coupon schemes, but the *Bulletin*'s editors were often cautionary or derogatory in their discussion of these types of promotions: "While we sympathize with any manager who is so situated that he is obliged to give premiums in order to attract trade . . . the pictures should be strong enough. If they are not, the premium giving manager has made a mistake in picking his location, or has underestimated the strength of his opposition."[84] Such criticism, however, was relatively rare in the *Bulletin*. Conversely, the frequency with which the editors mentioned this type of promotion suggests that such practices were, in fact, an integral part of selling the movies in Pittsburgh.

It was never too early to start a contest, and in July 1914, G. D. Demas offered ten dollars to the person who suggested a name for his newly built three-hundred-seat North Side theater. Demas eventually chose to christen it the Court Theatre. This less than exciting name had been suggested by not one but by five patrons, allowing Demas to spread the wealth (and word of his new theater) among the group. It was, however, rare that exhibitors rewarded their patrons with actual cash; many schemes instead consisted of merchandise given away on well advertised "prize days." The *Bulletin* praised R. A. Jones, owner of the South Side theater called the American, in December 1915 for his clever prize contest tied to the approaching holidays, which resulted in increased admission prices for the Christmas Day show. Jones's "prize hunt" consisted of an employee dressed as Santa Claus passing out numbered tickets along Carson Street for the two weeks preceding the holiday show. When the audience members arrived on Christmas Day, after each paying ten cents instead of five, they were allowed to compare their tickets to a large list painted on the wall inside the theater; if their number matched they won "useful articles . . . consisting of sleds, skates, hosiery, suspenders, handkerchiefs, etc. . . . Some comedy was injected into the proceedings, such as presenting a pair of old corsets to a man . . . which pleased the audience immensely."[85]

Outside the House

In late 1915, the *Bulletin* reported that local poster entrepreneur S. Van Lewen "has an immense stock of paper suitable for most kinds of pictures. The range covers everything in the line of dramatic, military, Indian, repertoire, western, animals, as well as circus, carnival, and aeroplane illustrations. If you consider your front week [*sic*], call on Van Lewen and you are sure to be able to strengthen it . . . posters can be profitably used as stock subjects, and can be used indefinitely for pictures of certain styles. The writer's description of these wares was matched, not surprisingly, by Van Lewen's full-page ad in the same issue, in which he offered one million of these posters for five cents a sheet, in sizes ranging from three to twenty-eight sheets.[86]

Such "stock" posters were not originally intended for a specific film; they were generic in both form and content and designed to fit the widest range of potential subjects. Prolific in size and number, and cheap to produce and post, this type of promotional material underscores the relationship the movies continued to have with the traditions of the circus, carnival, and other traveling forms of commercial entertainment. The graphic imagery, particularly on the kind of "stock" paper that Van Lewen and many others offered, was heavily influenced by (and in fact sometimes was), from, and for the circus. According to historian Kathy Fuller, the Morgan Lithograph Company of Cleveland, Ohio, "was the most important supplier" of movie posters in the 1910s, but long before they began designing and making posters for movie manufacturers, their primary customers were the circuses of Bailey, Barnum, and Ringling Brothers.[87] The circus, however, was not exactly the cultural object that many in the film business wished to emulate. As DeBauche has noted: "A hierarchy was established with the circus at the bottom and the theatrical drama at the apex. Moving pictures were on a slide between the two, pulled by its proponents upward toward the theater, pushed by its crude, bright posters toward the circus."[88] In Pittsburgh, this "push" continued as late as 1928, when the Mayer Publishing Company offered "Circus Heralds" to movie exhibitors, which, according to the *Bulletin*'s owners, "make a flash where other types of paper fail."[89]

Such posters provided "flash" and spectacle, and were designed to attract patrons with bold colors and sometimes lurid subjects, but they were, by design, unable to move beyond a generic connection to what would actually appear on the theater's screen. The disassociative relationship that existed between poster and film worried many in the business, including Sargent, who wrote: "a clean story of rural life might be advertised by a river scene in which one man was throwing another from a bridge while a second pair engaged in a knife fight in the water, and in the foreground a black-bearded pirate playfully beat a golden haired heroine over the head with an oar.... More persons [see] the posters than ... the films and gradually the impression is created that films are vicious. After that censorship!"[90]

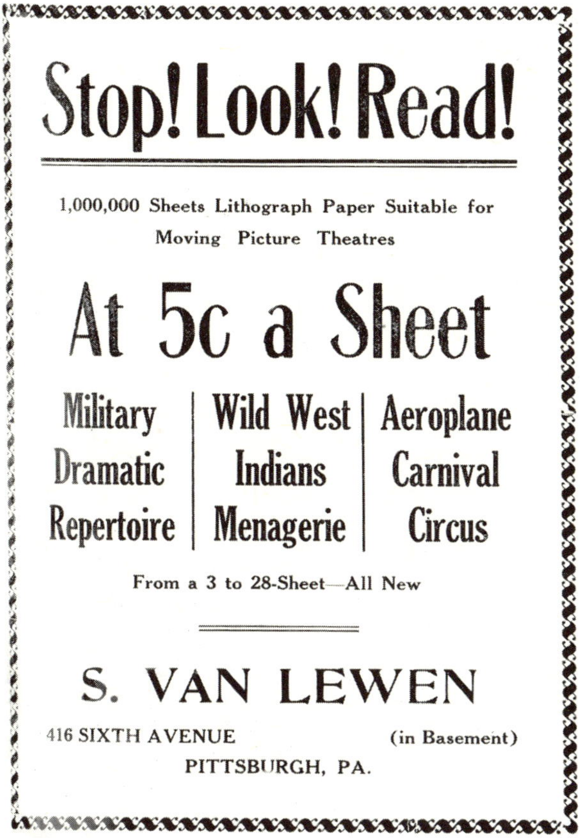

> **Stop! Look! Read!**
>
> 1,000,000 Sheets Lithograph Paper Suitable for Moving Picture Theatres
>
> **At 5c a Sheet**
>
> | Military | Wild West | Aeroplane |
> | Dramatic | Indians | Carnival |
> | Repertoire | Menagerie | Circus |
>
> From a 3 to 28-Sheet—All New
>
> **S. VAN LEWEN**
> 416 SIXTH AVENUE (in Basement)
> PITTSBURGH, PA.

FIG. 4.9.
S. Van Lewen advertisement for movie poster paper. *Pittsburgh Moving Picture Bulletin*, June 24, 1914, 17.

Whether or not movie censorship was a direct result of the overcharged symbolism of these stock images, poster censorship was a growing issue both within the business and for those outside who were seeking to gain control of the medium, including government officials in Pennsylvania, where a censorship board was passed into state law in the summer of 1914. The censors' initial work, in fact, included upholding a standard that required posters "and other advertising matter [to] follow the rules laid down for the pictures themselves."[91] This did little to please the *Bulletin*'s publishers, whose primary business relied on the printing of posters and programs for its financial success. The editors archly noted: "The State Board of Censors has announced that it will endeavor to prohibit the display of sensational posters in conjunction with moving-picture shows, and in this it will receive the co-operation of the local police. Posters showing the hero sinking a knife in the heart of the villain will not be tolerated."[92] Knives and posters were clearly a bad mix.

Edison Manufacturing Company began in early 1909 to market and produce posters tailored to each individual film as an attempt to more directly connect the two narratives, and to thereby maintain control over the product. Historians like Staiger and DeBauche have assumed that the use of film-specific "paper" (as posters of all sizes were called) produced by film manufacturers became the normative promotional model by the 1910s.[93] Exchanges, however, typically charged exhibitors a separate rental fee for posters, and many theater owners found it more economical to rely on "stock" papers to advertise their shows. After all, a generic Western poster could "be used indefinitely" for every Western film that the exhibitor showed.[94] With daily film changes still occurring in most theaters, the expense and time involved in switching paper rarely seemed worth the effort.

Stock papers remained in regular use throughout the period, particularly by smaller neighborhood and business-district theaters that maintained regular, short-reel-based programs. Feature theaters, however, increasingly came to rely on film-specific imagery to promote their shows. Pittsburgh had a number of companies that purchased posters from the film manufacturer's printing companies and then "mounted" them for renting to the local theaters.[95] These poster companies reported to the *Bulletin* the amount of sheets being produced for a particular film or theater, especially when a "significant" feature was coming to town. For instance, according to the Exhibitors' Display Company, the Schenley Theater in downtown Pittsburgh used five hundred one-sheets and two hundred three-sheets when it began its engagement of Metro's quarter-million-dollar spectacular *Romeo and Juliet*.[96] Posters were distributed throughout the areas of the city from which the exhibitor believed he could draw his audience. With over one hundred movie theaters in Pittsburgh in the 1910s, many neighborhoods had multiple theaters competing for their patrons' attention. The resulting competition had the possibility of turning into what was contemporarily described as a "poster war." These battles must have been a fairly regular event, as Sargent offered exhibitors a strategy: "If the opposition houses are not too close to your own it would be better to limit your posting to a point just inside the opposition territory. . . . On the other hand, if the other house is run along lines that cause dissatisfaction, it would be well to invade the territory and draw the patronage to your own house."[97] A good poster war did not end on the streets of the neighborhood but continued right up and onto the fronts of the theaters. In areas with a particularly high density of moving picture houses, putting on a "bold" front was understood to be of paramount importance in attracting a steady audience. The concentration of theaters on the North Side's Federal Street had the collective reputation of putting on the city's boldest fronts, which often included the construction of mechanical devices, large billboard-sized apparatuses that entertained audiences with eye-catching movement. After all, according to Sargent: "Motion more than doubles the value of an advertisement."[98] The *Bulletin* mentioned the Elite Theatre more than any other for use of mechanical fronts, and especially noted the device in September 1914 used to promote the imported Nordisk adventure feature *Atlantis* (1913): "It is the size of a nine-sheet poster and shows the ship rocking on the waves and a smaller boat being tossed about on the water. This effect is produced with the aid of a small motor attached to the back of the frame. The wireless effect will also be in evidence by sparking wires and the cracking sound helps to attract the attention of the passerby and 'pull 'em in.'"[99]

Because these types of fronts involved considerable time and effort to create, exhibitors employed them primarily to promote their feature films such as *Atlantis*. So-called "novelty" fronts—like the twenty-four-foot replica of a German U-boat that "was built by Manager Bonheyo" and hung above the ticket booth at the Elite where it "attracted much attention" for his feature *Deutschland*—were the product of the individual exhibitor's imagination and mechanical skill.[100] Such labor was significant in a number of ways. The creation and use of these handmade devices represented at least a partial rejection of the industry's regularizing elements of the feature film, which were the domain of the producer and distributor. Moreover, such labor signaled the exhibitors' refusal to concede their patrons' attentions and allegiances solely to the film itself. The exhibitor-constructed front was an aspect of the theater's personality, and, as such, provided an element of entertainment and pleasure that allowed the theater owner to maintain a measure of control over his show.

Obviously, not all exhibitors had either the skills or finances that such construction entailed, but there were a variety of other attention-grabbing stunts and schemes that designed to "pull 'em in" to the theater. Local theaters often incorporated street-side performances by live people in costumes into their promotions: "Frank Panopolis of the Lyric, McKeesport, used four real, live Indians to advertise his show *The Navajo Blanket*, last Monday and reports fine business."[101] In this instance, Panopolis had chosen to promote a two-reel "Indian" picture starring Mona Darkfeather and produced by Kalem Film Company, a film that typically would not be understood as a feature. Panopolis was promoting the "realness" of his Indian performers, but more often such roles were played in the Pittsburgh region by "local ballyhoo artist" Tex Arthur, who dressed in costume and "redface" to "build up business for theatres" exhibiting "Indian" pictures. In addition to standing outside of the theaters, Arthur regularly performed alongside the film, offering lectures on Indian tribes and performing the "famous 'Rain, tobacco and fire dance.'"[102] Other local ballyhoo "stars" included Major William McCloskey, "[t]he original drummer boy of Winchester," a Civil War veteran whose potential as a moving picture salesman was strong enough to even warrant notice on the national pages of the *Moving Picture World*.[103] Sargent offered a long list of other potential human "attractors" including: "awkward countrymen having trouble with a huge umbrella ... until he opens it to display a sign painted on it ... dressing men as children or children as men," and "the Goose Girl ... a pretty girl in costume who is seen driving her charges through the street ... each goose wearing a blanket with the name of the picture and the house."[104] Posters were not the only form of advertising derived from circus traditions, and

FIG. 4.10.
"Local ballyhoo artist" Tex Arthur. *Pittsburgh Moving Picture Bulletin*, January 13, 1923, 4.

FIG. 4.11.
Major William H. McCloskey as "the original drummer boy of Winchester." *Pittsburgh Moving Picture Bulletin*, December 16, 1914, 22.

many of the methods involving live advertising, like Sargent's Goose Girl, were designed to draw a crowd that began far from the theater and lead it through the neighborhood to the lobby of the picture house. The Belmar, in the Homewood neighborhood, worked such a "street stunt" for the first episode of the serial the *Crimson Stain Mystery* and, according to the *Bulletin*, got the pictures off to "a flying start" with a parade down Homewood Street consisting of six luxurious Overland touring cars and a sixteen-piece band.[105]

The serial lent itself to extensive and extended exhibitor stunts and schemes, many of which began in the weeks leading up to the first episode's exhibition. Patrons whose curiosity was piqued by these stunts could purchase "course tickets," prepaid printed cards that guaranteed admission to every episode of the serial shown at the theater. According to Sargent, it was critical that as soon as an exhibitor "learn of a serial that you intend to use . . . begin to snipe." Snipes, also sometimes called gutter snipes, were rolls of thin, cheap paper on which the title of the film, and sometimes the theater name, was imprinted. Exhibitors and exchanges paid workers to paste these short strips on any available surface around the neighborhood: "on boxes, barrels, dead walls, ash cans or even the curbs." These snipes, although they did not last long, were a kind of early form of saturation marketing, "useful in supplementing the permanent display by getting the title everywhere for a short time."[106] As the opening day for the first episode of the serial got closer, exhibitors often built large fronts dedicated to the film and introduced a variety of street stunts. H. F. Thomas, manager of the North Side's Casino Theater, was granted the title "live-wire exhibitor" by the *Bulletin* for his promotion of the fifteen-part circus serial *Peg o' the Ring* (1915), starring "serial queen" Grace Cunard and Francis Ford. Thomas's efforts included posting "four 24-sheets, six 6-sheets, six 3-sheets and twelve 1-sheets at promient [*sic*] places in town." The week before the show, Thomas employed a horse-drawn wagon "painted in true circus colors" to travel through the streets of the neighborhood accompanied by two clowns who passed out hundreds of heralds imprinted with the film's title and the theater's name.[107] Although the *Bulletin* credits Thomas with creating this successful campaign, it is very possible that at least some of his strategies were directly derived or adapted from exploitation advice provided from the film's producer, Carl Laemmle's Universal Company, which had grown out of the former IMP along with other movie companies.

The initial usage of the term "exploitation" and its accompanying occupational title, "exploiteer," is concurrent with the arrival in the 1910s of serial films like *Peg o' the Ring*. According to Sargent, who later reminisced about the practice in a 1931 *Variety* article, exploitation is any form of promotion, "but . . . the word is held more closely to stunts other than the use of newspapers, billboards and distributed handbills or throwaways."[108] At the time of its initial usage in the movie business, however, the term specifically referred to promotional actions taken by industry manufacturers or distributors. The exploiteer was typically a studio or distributor employee who specialized in promoting individual films. Although the exhibitor, as showman, had previously been the primary creative and initiative force behind most types of promotional "stunts," the establishment of the term exploitation represented the industry's attempt to appropriate and consolidate advertising power away from the individual exhibitor. The standardization of stunts and schemes as exploitation is visible in the increasing "advice" given to exhibitors by producers and distributors regarding the promotion of their collective product. A *Bulletin* article for the serial *The Yellow Menace* (1916) suggested that exhibitors "strive for *original* Oriental effects" (my emphasis), which included dressing the ushers in "Chinese costumes," burning incense during the film, and "hang[ing] a Chinese gong at each end of the stage . . . repeatedly striking them to produce an Oriental effect before you swing into the Oriental music *which you will of course use*" (my emphasis).[109] Advice of this nature appeared in "a special booklet" prepared by the Serial Film Company, "devoted to advertising and publicity stunts in connection" with the release of the serial and that would be "sent to any exhibitor upon application."

Professional exploiteers prepared such booklets for producers and manufacturers. As Gaines has written, Paramount was the first, in 1914, to have an exploitation department, and its "field men, working out of regional exchanges, were lent to local managers who booked feature pictures."[110] Although some exploiteers were independent and worked on a freelance basis offering their services to individual theaters, within a year or two, most major exchanges offered local exhibitors regular "help" from professional exploiteers. Pittsburgh's Universal exchange manager reported to the *Bulletin* that his men would offer specific promotional advice for most films they distributed over two reels in length.[111] Exhibitors, however, were often not eager to accept such help, and what Gaines and others have not written about is that the shift to a producer-based advertising structure was as much about power as it was about promotion. A series of articles in the *Bulletin* written in 1919 by William N. Robson, the exploiteer for the local Universal exchange, highlights the fact that many exhibitors continued to resist the loss of control represented by the professionalization of schemes and stunts. Robson stated: "There are many exhibitors who do not see the necessity of exploitation men or exploitation either. There are exhibitors who look on the exploitation man as a meddler, and then there are exhibitors . . . who are jealous of the . . . exploitation man, even half wishing he will not get results so they can point to the better work they do . . . all this means lack of cooperation for the exploitation man.[112]

Robson's obvious frustration with uncooperative exhibitors contradicts the idea of a standardized and industrialized studio-based cinema solidly in place by the mid-1910s; still, the majority of exhibitors' stunts and schemes were slowly being transformed into a more nationalized producer-centered publicity.[113] From the very beginning, the *Bulletin* had sought to turn local exhibitors away from one-armed violinists and other "old style" methods of promotion, and its editors welcomed the trend toward a professionalized workforce for marketing movies: "Exploitation is rapidly becoming an important feature in connection with the presentation of picture plays. In Pittsburgh we have a number of experts in this line . . . effective lobby displays are an essential factor in the conduct of a modern picture house—not the old time ballyhoo style of display but something artistic yet forceful; modest yet striking."[114]

The battle for control between "modern" and "old time" promotion of the moving picture show lasted longer than is usually described. Its beginnings can be seen on the pages of the *Bulletin* as early as the fall of 1915,

FIG. 4.12.
Universal Moviegame advertisement. *Pittsburgh Moving Picture Bulletin,* September 29, 1915, 19.

when Universal began its own contest, "The Wonderful Universal Moviegame." Because this contest was national in scope and boasted over five thousand dollars in prizes, not even the most successful of Pittsburgh's filmmen could hope to compete. Universal's promotions in the *Bulletin* suggested as much: "The plan is backed by the mighty resources and entire organization of the UNIVERSAL. You perhaps understand and appreciate what that means. If you don't understand it, it's time you found out."[115] The advertisement's rhetoric of an "engulfing wave of success" that "is destined to sweep the country like wild fire" underscored that the promotion was both economically overwhelming and nationally irresistible.

It is tempting, in the face of Harry Mintz's dead flies, to agree with the power of these words and the finances behind them, and certainly the trajectory of history proved them to be largely self-fulfilling. But it is important not to dismiss out of hand the model of salesmanship that Sargent put forth and that Mintz and others regularly applied to their neighborhood theaters throughout the 1910s and beyond. In the same issue of the *Bulletin* as Universal's full-page Moviegame ad is a positive report of a local theater giving away loaves of bread to its patrons, distributed by the new neighborhood bakery.[116] Most of Sargent's promotional offerings, and the examples of showmanship made visible on the pages of the *Bulletin*, were designed to create the idea of the movie theater as an integral and welcome part of a neighborhood or community. From the auto parades to local war veterans banging drums, to fresh bread and even children with bags of dead flies heading to the theater, exhibitor-based advertising actively worked to hail new and returning patrons to the theater through the reinforcement of its place within the community—often with the films themselves being tangential to the promotion that surrounded it.

5

THE MORALS OF THE MOVIES

In many ways, it was just another stunt—an attempt by one minor independent production company to grab the spotlight and call attention to itself. The difference this time, however, was the publicity seekers were not looking to ballyhoo a theater, star, or particular film. Rather, on June 3, 1916, Vim Comedies, a short-lived but prolific studio specializing in one- and two-reel slapsticks, ran a brief ad in a number of New York City morning papers:

LYNCHING

That varmint, Censorship, has been maraudin' round too long—an' we're goin' to get him Friday night at the Garden an' string him up. All law-abidin' citizens invited to be present at the obsequies.

Those curious few that made the trip that evening to Madison Square Garden, as well as any number of passers-by, looked up to the arc-lit rooftop.

As the "show" began up on this high perch, three of Vim's stock performers dressed in clown costumes were seen minding their own movie-making business, only to be dramatically set upon and viciously attacked by an unprovoked "Western desperado," aka "Mr. Censorship." Word of this brutal act upon these good citizens was carried to the "Vim Comedy Sheriff," who, not a moment too soon, arrived on the scene (with his own posse of deputized clowns) to bring the marauder to swift comedic justice. After "an exciting chase in which toy pistols were pitted against the big 'forty-five' of the desperado, Mr. Censorship was captured and strung up in approved western style." According to *Motion Picture News*, which ran a positive account of the evening's events, after the lynching the "corpse" was cut down, sealed in a coffin with a scoop of quicklime, and sent to one Louis J. Breitinger, Esquire, otherwise known as chief censor of the Pennsylvania State Board of Censors.[1]

While there is no evidence that Mr. Breitinger ever received his funereal package, Vim's attempt at raising public awareness of censorship brings to light a set of practices and personalities engaged with censorship of the movies during the 1910s. In this decade marked by rising movie attendance across a widening spectrum of the populace, attendance statistics suggest that by the end of World War I, Americans participated in moviegoing more than any other leisure activity. This growing national access to local audiences thrilled most in the film industry. It troubled others, however, particularly those groups and individuals seeking to keep some form of local control over a mass medium that had become, as they perceived it, an increasingly dangerous part of the fabric of daily life. Censorship would not be the only tool employed by those looking to control the movies, but it would be their most explicit method toward this end. Its effects were also the most severe, at least for the film industry, which is why Vim Comedies chose a poorly paid Pennsylvania civil servant to symbolize the most dangerous threat to the movies.

If a small-time, New York–based production company found the Pennsylvania State Board of Censors worthy of such vilification, what were its effects on Pittsburgh's exchanges and exhibitors, shows and audiences? Pittsburgh exhibitors encountered considerable bureaucratic intervention at the municipal level in this period, including theater visits by undercover policewomen, weekly "safety" checks by the Bureau of Building Inspection, and attempts at cinetextual control by the city-funded Morals Efficiency Commission. The state and its censors, however, came to wield the most pervasive and influential power confronting the Pittsburgh moving picture show.

Groundbreaking studies of American movie censorship written beginning in the 1960s, including Richard Randall's *Censorship of the Movies* and Ira Carmen's *Movies, Censorship, and the Law*, have been joined in the last two decades by new scholarship, such as Lee Grieveson's *Policing Cinema*, an essential work on the role that early censorship struggles and practices played in the broader "definition and shaping of cinema" from 1905 to the mid-1910s.[2] In accord with Grieveson, I understand the formation of Pennsylvania's censorship bureaucracy, like the admission prices and the dead flies discussed previously, to belong to the contested and highly uneven process of a culture (and industry) determining, defining, and regulating what the movies should and could mean—what Grieveson rightly describes as the "fabrication" of cinema.[3] The specific evolution and codification of censorship behaviors, here the legal and civil procedures of Pennsylvania state government, must be situated within a broader and much more diffuse discourse of power and social anxiety as they emerged within the transformative landscape of urban industrialized capitalism. The machinations of ideologues, reformers, politicians, and showmen intersected at the site of state-operated censorship. Pittsburgh's relationship to this censorship, particularly in the 1910s, was unique in a number of ways, as the city became home to battles, both real and ideological, in which Progressive reformers, politicians, civil servants, social scientists, and, of course, the film industry itself struggled over the movies and their audiences. At the same time, it is important, if obvious, to note that the Pennsylvania State Board of Censors was a statewide entity, affecting movie and picture men and their audiences across the Commonwealth. As such, this chapter remains particularly attentive to Pittsburgh in relation to its place in the state and to those other places and people across Pennsylvania that impacted the censorship board and its work.

The First State Censorship Board—and the Worst

Despite the recent interest and productive scholarship that situates censorship as central to American cinema's determinative matrix, surprisingly little has been done to understand the role played by state censorship boards in its development. In 1911, Pennsylvania was the first in the country to legislate the state censoring of motion pictures, but it was quickly joined by Ohio in 1912, Kansas in 1913, Maryland in 1916, Virginia in 1921, and New York in 1922.[4] These six states controlled over one-third of the nation's total theater seats and thus collectively exercised a disproportionate influence over what movie attendees across the country might see.[5] Pennsylvania's board, within the industry, had "the distinction of supporting the most arbitrary and severe board of censors. . . . No censor board in the country can compete with the Pennsylvanians. Movies that go untouched in every other state in the union are hacked and retitled in Pennsylvania."[6] The state board's power to cut up and retitle movies was confirmed by the U.S. Supreme Court in 1915. In perhaps the most influential legal decision regarding the role of movies in American culture, the Court unanimously ruled in favor of a state's right to decide what its citizens might watch, determining: "the argument is wrong or strained which extends the guaranties of free opinion and speech to the multitudinous shows which are advertised on the billboards of our cities and towns, and which . . . bring motion pictures and other spectacle into practical and legal similitude to a free press and liberty of opinion."[7] The resulting state authority, both legal and economic, over such a wide audience had a profound and lasting impact on how producers, distributors, and exhibitors thought and went about their business and led directly to the organized politicization of the film industry. Although external censorship of the movies has traditionally been understood as a detrimental force—bad for creativity, intellectual freedom, and the economic bottom line—state censorship, and Pennsylvania's version in particular, helped to clarify and strengthen the industry's developing power hierarchy. Ultimately, battles with the state board contributed to the film industry's ability to achieve and maintain cultural and fiscal authority over its product. At the same time, state-organized censorship became, in its influence on motion pictures and audiences, the most effective, powerful, and longest lasting form of localized control in the history of American cinema.

Film historians have achieved an indispensable knowledge of the film industry's earlier failed attempts to prevent formal structures of censorship through accommodation and cooperation with (primarily) New York–based politicians and reformers. What largely remains missing is a narrative of the industry's later endeavors in the face of successful state-sponsored and bureaucratically-organized censorship of the movies. These battles and their outcomes resulted in the industry's successful efforts at containing censorship through a system of production-based self-regulation, which was eventually formalized in the Production Code and the formation of the Motion Picture Producers and Distributors of America (MPPDA).[8] The history of motion picture censorship is ultimately about power. As the movie industry quickly expanded its place within American culture in the 1910s, individuals and institutions at all levels of society and government sought its associative power—from women and church groups to fire and police departments to local and state legislators to the federal courts and Congress—each hoping to gain some control over what could or could not be shown and seen.

Although the movies had been a popular form of entertainment since the 1890s, it did not become an object of wide public scrutiny until about 1906, when the success of the nickelodeon rapidly spread across America. A diverse set of individuals and groups representing multiple branches of Progressive society, including women's organizations hoping to educate and assimilate immigrants into a crowded social milieu, technocrats and bureaucrat needing to standardize and sanitize a chaotic urban industrial geography, and politicians seeking to consolidate and control their shifting sphere(s) of power, all undertook this scrutiny, which was simultaneously driven by fear and fascination. When New York City's mayor, George B. McClellan, first raised the specter of formal censorship by shutting down all of his city's motion picture houses on Christmas Eve of 1908, exhibitors and film producers alike realized that, if their business was to continue its exponential growth, some form of accommodation was imperative.[9]

In the spring of 1909, this accommodation took the form of the Board of Programs of Motion Picture Shows (soon renamed the National Board of Censorship); a collaborative vision of Edison's Motion Picture Patents Company and the People's Institute, a New York–based civic reform group composed of social-minded Progressive professionals and their wealthy patrons.[10] The board belonged to a sector of Progressive society that saw moving pictures as a popular medium that could, if properly developed, offer both entertainment and education, and thereby help blunt potential social conflict. According to board member Mary Gray Peck: "Motion Pictures are going to save our civilization . . . they provide what every previous civilization lacked—namely a means of relief, happiness and mental inspiration to the people at the bottom. Without happiness and inspiration being accessible to those upon whom the social burden rests most heavily, there can be no stable social system."[11] Progressives like Peck saw the movies as a double-edged sword: a potential instrument for education that might promote human freedom as an aspect of communal responsibility, and a necessary tool for assimilation of the ethnic other; or, conversely, and much more dangerously, a seductive weapon of indoctrination, able to move fragile viewers to debauchery, crime, anarchy, and even socialism. If censorship ran counter to a reformer's rhetoric of man's enlightenment, it was a required (if less metaphysical) need for the Progressive state to control that very same man.

The MPCC and, eventually, most of the independents were less interested in such lofty goals and less convinced about their collective products' dangers. More practically, these producers hoped that by supporting the National Board, they might thwart, or at least limit, the crippling creation of multiple municipal and state censorship boards. The board and its project of cinematic uplift carried the imprimatur of an advisory committee consisting of nearly sixty public figures as diverse as Lyman Abbott, Andrew Carnegie, Samuel Gompers, Jacob Reiss, and Stephen S. Wise, but the actual review of individual films was the responsibility of the Censoring Committee, a subgroup of the National Board of Censorship composed of lesser-known and unpaid volunteers. The censors, who worked in offices paid for by the MPCC, reviewed films on an ad hoc basis according to what the board defined as "empirical standards."[12] The board occasionally refused to approve a film (as in the case of the 1907 Pathé film *Rat Catching*), but it rarely took such measures, passing as acceptable over 95 percent of all films it reviewed from 1909 to 1914.[13] More often, the committee suggested specific eliminations or changes. For example, under the rubric of "if children see it they will do it," the committee requested the elimination of shots from Lubin's *Mama's Angel* of a young boy throwing a banana peel on the pavement, and the Katzenjammer Kids were not allowed to get away with sawing the legs of a chair in half.[14] Board members and film manufacturers agreed that the appearance of the official line, "Approved by the National Board of Censorship" on a film's title card should be advertised as a way to promote "morally" acceptable movies and gradually "uplift" public tastes.[15] "Uplift" was a word that powerfully resonated for both Progressive groups and the industry, and it became the primary rhetorical password for transforming moving picture shows into cleaner, safer social centers and for encouraging the production of "quality" entertainment that might appeal to audiences of a more refined (and better paying) nature.

Hegemony is hard work, and although Justice Joseph McKenna wrote in his opinion on state censorship that "general terms ... of what is educational, moral, amusing, or harmless ... get precision from the sense and experience of men," in practice, the reality was often sharp disagreement, even among otherwise likeminded Progressive reformers, over the meanings of such terms as they related to the movies.[16] As a result, "narrow minded club-women and bigoted reformers," as they were called by some film industry insiders, argued that the National Board of Censorship and its decisions were complicit with a morally bankrupt industry and actively sought out alternative sources to provide what Robert Fisher has called "censorship with teeth in it."[17] Ironically, but perhaps not surprisingly, animosity toward the board was heightened by the industry's attempt at cooperating with the National Board and its goals; critics interpreted this as clear evidence of the board's inability to operate as an independent, autonomous body. Reformers from places other than New York regarded the board as too "Eastern," that is, too lenient and liberal in its tastes and standards for the movies, which other reformers believed did not accurately reflect their local (and better) moral codes and cultures.[18]

Based on this desire for such localized control, municipal governments and various groups quickly sought to delimit their own regional values. As is already well documented, "the work of censoring pictures in this country began in the local community [where] . . . Chicago was the pioneer, the experience of that city with the subject having begun in 1907."[19] Historian Moya Luckett has hypothesized that because Chicago was second only to New York as a hub for both film manufacturers and distributors, "it is possible that its censors hoped that their standards, not New York's, would set the example that the rest of the nation might follow."[20] In the end, of course, Chicago could no more answer for "other parts," whether Pittsburgh or anywhere else, than New York could, and although its well-publicized work received considerable national attention, as a municipal system, its influence remained fairly limited. Not surprisingly, many other towns and cities of differing sizes attempted to follow Chicago's example, including: Seattle; Dallas; Camden, New Jersey; Joplin, Missouri; and Portland, Oregon, whose mayor wrote to Chicago's board seeking advice on how to best create a local form of motion picture control.[21]

Pittsburgh Seeks Control

Pittsburgh and its large immigrant working-class populace offered the movies an audience that in many ways symbolized the dialectic of perils and possibilities that the modern medium represented to Progressive society. A site of the "success" of American industrialization, Pittsburgh was also tightly bound to the poverty, racial, and ethnic strife, urban decay, and labor unrest that resulted from such success. For at least some, the movies offered an experience that could smooth over the worst of those disturbing byproducts, but it just as easily could inflame them. Pittsburgh's Progressives recognized this, and in the years before state regulation went into effect, a number of local, city-based attempts were made to control the representational power of the movies. Ad hoc undertakings to ban specific films occurred in Pittsburgh at least as early as 1907, but one of the first formal municipal endeavors, the Morals Efficiency Commission, began in 1912 to officially associate the movies with the city's other "social" problems and urban ills. The commission, as its name suggests, believed in both the centrality of morality to public order and the use of "scientific" practices to effect this morality. The commission was, however, just an advisory panel, granted only the power to recommend to the police, the city council, and the mayor, "such measures and activities . . . as shall tend to improve the public morals of the city."[22] Funded through the city budget, with members consisting of up to a dozen local doctors, academics, and religious leaders, the commission began its work by studying the economic, social, and moral costs of prostitution in the city, particularly the spread of venereal disease, which, according to the report, infected up to ten thousand Pittsburghers on any given day.[23]

Pittsburgh's new civic commission was part of a wider trend of municipalities conducting inquiries into vice. Most, according to Shelley Stamp, "tended to regard prostitution less as an expression of individual female perversity than as a collective enterprise where women's activities supported largely male-run networks of pimps, procurers, and saloon owners."[24] Such was the case in Pittsburgh, but in addition to directing police to close local brothels and recommending that "confirmed criminals and degenerates should be sterilized," the city's commission also actively pursued: "[b]etter censorship of moving picture shows and supervision of their frequenters. Besides the nickelodeons, some of the cheaper vaudeville theaters, all of the so-called burlesque shows, and some of the high-priced revues and musical comedies ought to be censored and many of them suppressed. The vulgar . . . shows are patronized by many young boys, who there are schooled in viciousness and have their minds filled with filth."[25] How the group of reformers actually planned to supervise the city's movie patrons is unknown, but the commission appears to have regularly offered the city administration advice on the banning of specific films from local screens in the years leading up to official state censorship. Until the summer of 1914, the job of policing the movies in Pittsburgh was, like in many places, left literally in the hands of law enforcement, in this case either the superintendent of police or the director of the department of public safety. Extant records show that for a number of years either one or both of these men often accompanied members of the Morals Efficiency Commission to the screening of potentially troublesome films.[26]

The most problematic movies for city leaders in this era were the now well-known "white slave" pictures. As Shelley Stamp and Ben Singer have extensively discussed, the early and mid-1910s saw a brief surge in popularity for this exploitive genre that "capitalized upon widely circulating tales of innocent victims forcibly abducted and sold into prostitution."[27] These films, which promised a voyeuristic experience with titles such as *The Inside of the White Slave Traffic* and *The Exposure of the White Slave Traffic*, tended to be dismissed by both film critics and Progressive reformers as "smutty" entertainment cloaked in the guise of educational warnings. However, at least initially, according to *Moving Picture World*, many of these films drew substantial audiences of both men and women.[28] The Pittsburgh Morals Efficiency Commission, with a declared interest in the "social evil" of prostitution, took a particularly dim view of these films; both of the films named above were banned from being shown by the city's movie theaters. *The Wages of Sin*, another white slave film, was also banned by the city after the police superintendent previewed it along with "Rabbi Rudolph I. Coffee and Dr. Frederic Rhodes of the Morals Efficiency Commission . . . [who] decided not to allow the film because there is no moral lesson in it. . . . The picture is one of immorality and not calculated to have a good effect on the mind of any girl. No man would permit his daughter to see it."[29]

In May 1914, two weeks before the state censorship act was to take effect, and knowing that "few photo-plays dealing with 'white slavery' or drugs" could earn the state board's approval, Alexander Parke successfully booked a copy of *Smashing the Vice Trust* into a number of the city's theaters. Parke, a local state rights exchangeman, timed the release of this prostitute-fighting six-reel film to circumvent the arrival of state censorship, as well as bypass the commission's less than favorable opinion of the slavery films, but he was unwilling to risk entirely ignoring local "moral" opinion. He arranged a personal screening for M. L. Hubbard, director of the city's department of public safety. Hubbard expressed his willingness for the film to be exhibited in Pittsburgh and even gave Mr. Parke a strong letter of endorsement in which he wrote, "as a whole, the picture teaches a moral lesson, and should have the approval of the police as it is a great advertisement of police activity."[30] The film had a brief, successful run, which Parke promoted by reprinting Hubbard's letter in a number of the local papers, but three weeks later, along with *The Drug Terror* (another state rights film that Parke distributed in Pittsburgh), *Smashing the Vice Trust* became one of the first films to be condemned by the newly activated state board.[31]

Many pro-censorship parties argued that state or, even better, federal control of the movies was the best solution in the face of such local variances. In the words of one of Pennsylvania's first censors: "[the] conditions under which films are changed daily, with movement at all possible speed from place to place, go far to preclude the development of any local system of supervision. . . . The territorial unit is too small. It is to the interest of the industry, as well as for the advantage of municipal authorities that censorship over a large central area shall be established . . . and we look to the state as the jurisdiction in which control may become practicable and efficient."[32]

As proponents of censorship moved to control a larger "territorial unit," they shifted the focus away from the site of exhibition, arguing that municipal boards were ill-equipped to deal with the film industry's increasingly advanced and fast-paced system of distribution. They claimed that moral control of a mass-produced product like the movies required its own form of "efficiency" in order to be successful—and the state agreed. On June 19, 1911, the Pennsylvania General Assembly (the state legislature), in reaction to what it saw as a failure by the National Board of Censorship to provide the "necessary moral authority," and local commissions' inability to be broadly effective, voted to become the first state to legislate motion picture censorship.

The State Gains Control

The new law, signed by newly appointed Republican governor John K. Tener, created the Pennsylvania State Board of Censors, "which will endeavor to establish standards on Progressive lines and will attempt to keep motion pictures attuned to public opinion and not necessarily in harmony with productions of the stage or newspapers, but rather to restrict the motion pictures to such as would afford clean entertainment or amusement and to eliminate everything which would tend to debase or inflame the mind to improper adventures or false standards of conduct."[33]

Like many on the national board, Pennsylvania lawmakers recognized motion pictures to be a powerful cultural force, separated by its ephemeral and mass-consumed textual nature from other forms of popular entertainment, and containing various potentials—whether as educator, assimilator, or instigator—that lay in the hands of whoever controlled its powerful representations. In its first iteration (there would soon be others), the Pennsylvania edict required that this power belong to two primary members, a man, the chief censor, and a woman, his assistant. Although the man and woman were not literally intended to be a couple, the statutory requirements for this bureaucratic marriage required that each "be duly qualified by education and experience" and collectively required them "to [jointly] examine all moving-picture films, or reels, and stereopticon views, to approve such as shall be moral, and to withhold approval from such as shall tend to debase or corrupt the morals."[34]

The specific legislation of a male/female pairing highlights just how tightly gender roles and their cinematic representations had become linked in the time period. Morality as an ideal was discursively and socially marked as belonging within the domain of the woman, particularly the figure of the wife and/or mother.[35] At the same time, the continued shifting of roles of and for women in the public sphere, and the rapid transformation of that sphere in modern industrial life, allowed and even required the deployment of gender as part of the work for this kind of explicit regulation to occur. This shift occurred primarily only for women of wealth and the growing, but still statistically small, middle class.[36] The industrialization of the American economy before the Civil War and the dramatic move to corporate capitalism around the turn of the century resulted in consumption overtaking production in the private sphere of the middle classes. As Christine Stansell has shown, this shift to a labor of consumption caused the women in this strata to focus their work and resulting discourses on an increasingly ideological goal, to define a moral "American" culture.[37] Writing seventy-five years earlier, Harriet McClintock expressed such a goal in an editorial to her local Pennsylvania paper: "It is with great pleasure . . . that I notice that one of the censors is a woman; for I believe that women understand better than most men what constitutes a really demoralizing picture."[38] Indeed, this new civil servant post of assistant motion picture censor was a kind of ideal job for the New Woman, a productive occupation for a Progressive female of a certain means and ideas. This kind of work allowed the woman censor to inscribe herself and her gendered labor within the public sphere while—through the process of eliminating the "dangerous" and "immoral" of the movies—safely limiting the representation of womanhood to the more traditional bounds of the private.[39]

Pennsylvania's first assistant censor was Katherine Anne Niver of Charleroi, Pennsylvania, or, rather Mrs. E. C. Niver, as she was addressed in virtually all published accounts of her public life as a censor. Governor Tener named Louis J. Breitinger to the position of chief censor. The original state edict gave the duo broad, if somewhat ill-defined, powers to "inquire into, and investigate [all] moving-picture films, or reels, or stereopticon views, which are intended to be displayed in the state." *Rules and Standards*, publicly released as a pamphlet for members of the film industry, delineated a set of fifteen directives of the Pennsylvania legislature for the state board to follow. No records exist detailing the specific parties involved in the drafting of these first censorship tenets, but their rather accommodating tone and rhetoric point toward the influence of industry participants (or their lawyers). Rule Five of the state edict, for example, was designed to limit moving picture "vulgarity," but according to the actual language of the law, "Unless the vulgarity closely borders on immorality or indecency the Board may ignore it." Even something as potentially problematic as Rule Six, "prolonged passionate love scenes," were allowed to remain on Pennsylvania's screens as long as such "experiences are treated truthfully, sympathetically, and artistically . . . [and] provided that they not be cheapened to the extent of losing their significance." The last standard, Rule Fifteen, was an overall summary (and reminder) of this philosophy of general censorship restraint, and its wording foreshadowed the guidelines that the MPPDA would eventually employ prior to the creation of the Production Code Administration in 1934:

PICTURES WILL BE JUDGED AS A WHOLE

Pictures will be judged as a whole with a view to the final total effect they have upon the audiences, and will not be condemned because of some little incident in them if it becomes merely tributary to the principal idea which may be good, and not one of the features of the story to be remembered and emulated.[40]

Neither reformers nor industry participants had a chance to react to these rules, because the entire law was immediately neutralized through the lobbying efforts of a powerful group of attorneys, whose work was financed and organized by the Universal and Mutual production companies.[41] Although the lobbyists for these studios were unsuccessful in their repeated attempts at entirely killing off the censor bill, their legal maneuverings within the halls of the State Capitol in Harrisburg removed the appropriations necessary to fund the act, leaving the board hamstrung and unable to actually censor anything. The result was a law without a budget, a fiscal purgatory that remained in place for the next three years. Further legal tactics led held up the enforcement of the bill's standards until June 1914.

This extended period of legal maneuvering allowed members of the state's film industry to begin to organize and cooperate in ways they had been incapable of prior to this legislative threat. Organization by the industry, at the local, state, and national levels, however, remained difficult to achieve due to a number of issues that included regional rivalry and antagonism. In Pennsylvania, local exhibitor competition, particularly between Philadelphia and Pittsburgh, and ongoing differences between the industry's three branches were the major obstacles to cooperation efforts to stop state-based censorship.

Prior to the bill's target enforcement date of June 1914, Pennsylvania's various regional "exhibitors' leagues" often were at odds with each other as to how best to tackle "the difficult censorship question." However, the passage of the board's budget by the state senate in January 1914 and its impending implementation led to the formation of the first statewide organization of motion picture exhibitors "born in a three-day convention [where] . . . harmony among the members and a spirit of cooperation were the keynotes of the gathering. . . . All the past differences were forgotten. Both the Pittsburgh and Philadelphia delegations were glad to let it be an open meeting."[42] It is probably not a coincidence that the first elected president of this new organization was showman Ben H. Zerr of Reading, a smaller city in the central (neutral) part of the state. With the years of regional east–west acrimony that existed prior to the convention it is doubtful that "all the past differences" were truly swept aside, but the end result was that when the state censorship legislation finally became enforceable on June 15, Pennsylvania's exhibitors cohesively mobilized alongside national and local representatives of the major producers and distributors. The industry, acting in "harmony," immediately sought a temporary injunction against the board in the Pennsylvania Supreme Court, claiming that the new state law was unconstitutional because: it unfairly burdened interstate commerce (films distributed by Pittsburgh exchanges were also intended to be shown in Ohio and West Virginia); it was based on imprecise and unenforceable language; and it violated the right of free speech guaranteed by the state constitution.[43] Additionally, the suit argued that it was "a physical impossibility for the censors to fulfill the provisions of the act in respect to examining all reels before they are exhibited."[44] According to the appellants, who claimed they were renting 465 films per week at the time, the censors, watching 1 film every fifteen minutes, working ten hours every day, "without intermission," could only examine 240 of the films needed to be released that week. The suit claimed that the resulting backlog of films would thus cause undue economic hardship to the industry and result in many of the state's distributors and exhibitors being forced out of business.[45] When the injunction was initially denied by the judge, the industry arranged for a Philadelphia exchange to willfully disregard the new law and to be quickly charged in order to obtain an immediate test case against the legal standing of the board.[46]

While the film industry organized, parties and politicians in favor of the state board did not stand idly by. Both those for and against state censorship recognized that the 1911 law as written was "inadequate and defective" and likely to eventually fall under judicial appeal, as it suffered both from a lack of specificity and the absence of a legal appeal process for the distributor of a film condemned by the board.[47] The 1911 standards, which "disapprove[d] of a good woman doing what would be considered a bad thing," cut too broad and vague a swath, even for many of the reformers. For the industry, these intervening years afforded the time and cooperation required to produce its own serviceable structures to fight the state and its well-developed bureaucracies. For the state and its Progressive backers, however, this period provided time to write a tighter, more enforceable code that addressed many of its initial legal flaws. The result was that state legislators passed a new, more enforceable law (see this chapter's appendix), which went into effect on June 15, 1915, and thus nullified the language of the earlier code.[48]

Now lengthier (totaling twenty-four rules and standards), more specific, and less accommodating in terms of what could be viewed, the new act left less to the imaginations of both the filmmakers and the censors. If the initial set of rules allowed for films with "prolonged passionate love scenes" as long as they were portrayed "truthfully, sympathetically, and artistically," the new standards simply refused the presentation of such bodily images regardless of their narrative underpinning: "Sensual kissing and love making scenes, men and women in bed together and indelicate sexual situations, whether in comedies or pictures of other classes, will be disapproved. Bathing scenes, which pass the limits of propriety, lewd and immodest dancing, the needless exhibition of women in their night dresses or underclothing, will be disapproved."[49]

To match these latest standards, the board itself was also newly fashioned, requiring a panel of "three residents and citizens of Pennsylvania, two males and one female."[50] In May, one month before the law was to go into effect, a new Republican governor, Martin G. Brumbaugh, formally appointed the state's first active censorship board, with members including: J. Louis Breitinger, chairman; Katherine A. Niver, vice chairman; and Dr. Ellis P. Oberholtzer, secretary.[51]

Of the three, Breitinger, a Philadelphia-based attorney and former Pennsylvania legislator, had the most experience in both state government and the moving picture industry. Records and newspaper accounts from the period show that Breitinger was a well-connected "Penrose man," a politician whose his career and allegiance were aligned with U.S. Senator Boise Penrose (1860–1921). Penrose, a larger-than-life figure, was at the turn of the century arguably the most powerful Republican not just in the state but in the country. According to one of the senator's contemporary biographers, Penrose was "never greatly interested in nor impressed by social legislation, 'moral movements,' and reform groups."[52] It is fairly clear that Breitinger got the job as chief censor because the Penrose machine wanted him to have it. Correspondence also shows that prior to his appointment, Breitinger had close professional ties to then State Attorney General Francis S. Brown, another Penrose "appointee."[53] This relationship with Brown was critical since one of Breitinger's major duties as chairman was appearing for the state as the board's legal spokesman in any judicial appeals brought by the film industry.

According to *Variety* articles from January 1914, prior to becoming chief censor, Breitinger was employed by the Pennsylvania Exhibitors League as its lead counselor; he resigned his position only upon taking his new job as chairman.[54] While neither the *Bulletin* nor any other trade journal from the period explains this significant relationship, the censorship board and Breitinger, a former advocate for the state's exhibitors, were potentially less strange bedfellows than they might initially appear. As cultural historian

Francis Couvares has previously noted, in regard to state-sponsored censorship, exhibitors were often "understood by all to be the least reliable link in the chain of industry solidarity."[55] Many exhibitors rejected state and municipal censorship because it infringed on their rights of expression and potentially impacted their businesses, and perhaps equally importantly because it diminished the value of their experience, knowledge, and talents to program the kind of show they believed most appealed to their audience. Exhibitors took pride in their ability to measure the "moral temperature" of their potential patrons and to program and exhibit their films accordingly. As the consolidation of booking practices by producers and their exchanges removed much of the daily programming from the exhibitors' direct control, theater managers and owners found themselves in the difficult position of defending material and images they had not necessarily selected. Whether some exhibitors actually felt ideologically aligned with reformers in their distaste for salacious images on their screens, whether they simply were acceding to the political reality of the situation, or whether they were frustrated by the sense that producers and their exchanges were requiring local exhibitors to fight battles caused by their (national) products, the result was that an unknown percentage of exhibitors accepted, if in some cases even vocally endorsed, some forms of local and state control. In nearby Ohio, for instance, M. A. Neff the president of Ohio's Exhibitor's League, actively worked for passage of the state's censorship law and then, upon its legislative approval, accepted a position on its subsequent board.[56]

Mrs. E. C. Niver, like Breitinger, held connections that may have influenced her appointment to the censorship board. Mother to a son in the army and wife to Edward Cyrus Niver, owner and editor-in-chief of the *Charleroi Daily Mail*, Kathryn Niver played a significant role in the social life of her small, prosperous western Pennsylvania town thirty miles south of Pittsburgh. Mrs. Niver, along with her husband, was recognized in this coal and glass community as a "leader in numerous movements for the public uplift."[57] Records show that prior to her invitation to become a state censor, Mrs. Niver had proven herself to be the very model of Progressive womanhood, actively involved in a multitude of local reformist and cultural improvement organizations that included: The Athene Club, a literary group whose "principal object [was] to bring together more closely women interested in Art, Literature and Science"; the Charleroi Marketing Club, launched in 1912 to educate "every woman to be a market woman" so as to effectively respond to the "high cost of living and the danger of high living"; and the Women's Auxiliary of the County Juvenile Court Association, "instrumental in looking after several small children that needed homes and attention."[58] The chairwoman of this last association happened to be Mrs. J. K. Tener, wife of Pennsylvania's governor. In addition to their mutual participation in the life of their hometown, newspaper reports show that Mrs. Niver and Mrs. Tener were regular social companions, often traveling together "in the Governor's motorcar."

The new board's final member was also known within the state but was primarily hired to lend an air of refinement to the proceedings, based on his previous education and experience. Dr. Ellis Paxson Oberholtzer, a Philadelphia native, described himself to be an "individualist" and an "ordinary" man who was "tolerably well educated at American and European colleges," and held a PhD in literature from the University of Pennsylvania. His earlier experiences as a newspaper dramatic critic, secondary school teacher, and director of "two large historical pageants" qualified him, he later stated, for the "social welfare work" required of a state censor.[59] As the board's secretary, Oberholtzer's primary official job was to author the censors' annual report to Governor Brumbaugh, a man with whom Oberholtzer claimed a "warm friendship." Although Oberholtzer was prone to hyperbole, it is entirely possible that this relationship was real, as Brumbaugh had once served as the superintendent for the Philadelphia school system in which Oberholtzer was employed. Oberholtzer was also a fairly successful published author, a historian who had written multiple works of nonfiction, including a literary history of Philadelphia, and a five-volume treatise on the history of the country since the Civil War.[60]

Pennsylvania's censorship board, as represented by these three individuals —the lawyer, the mother, and the teacher—can be understood as strictly constructed along Progressive lines. Mr. Breitinger embodied the legal and bureaucratic structures of the state. Mrs. Niver personified the female engendered code of morality's role in public life. Finally, Mr. Oberholtzer stood in as the literary agent of pedagogical enlightenment.

The Fight

The film industry had no intention of ceding all the potential Progressive power of the movies to the censors. Although the film *Sealed Life* (1914) was chosen by the industry as the object of their legal test case in Pennsylvania, another film, *John Barleycorn* (1914), a movie with its own self-proclaimed Progressive merits, became the first case the industry attempted to try in the court of public opinion. *Barleycorn* was an adaptation of Jack London's semi-fictional biography of the same name that had been successfully published in serialized form the year before in the *Saturday Evening Post*. The film opens aboard Jack London's yacht, where the grown author chronicles his lifelong struggle with alcoholism, which began at the young age of five when, as a young farm boy, he slyly drank from a beer pail intended for his father. He recounts his juvenile adventures as a newsboy, "oyster pirate," and seal hunter, and how his need for drink intensified as he grew older. Throughout his youthful travails with the addictive "John Barleycorn," it is his (African American) nursemaid who remains his staunchest ally until, eventually, he meets the beautiful and brave Haydee at a Salvation Army meeting. Ultimately they, of course, marry, and with her unswerving help he overcomes his addiction.[61]

The story's theme of alcoholism and its redemption belongs to a tradition of temperance narratives dating back at least to the 1850s, and of temperance films dating almost to the beginning of the medium. The earliest American production companies, such as Edison, Lubin, and Biograph, made a number of temperance-themed shorts, including: *The Kansas Saloon Smashers* (1901, Edison); *Carrie Nation Smashing a Saloon* (1901, Biograph); and *Mrs. Nation and Her Hatchet Brigade* (1901, Lubin). All three of those particular pictures focused on the real-life adventures of Carry A. Nation, a well-known, eccentric temperance crusader whose axe-swinging, bar-breaking antics caught the imagination of the press and the public.[62] These films about Nation and her destructive ways could be understood as both a form of re-created actualité footage and/or as violent comic spectacle. *John Barleycorn*, on the other hand, represented the later, more staid, Progressive-themed feature-length films, in which the film industry actively sought to pursue a middle-class female audience. By producing and distributing films supporting temperance and demonizing the dangers of alcohol, the filmmakers hoped to appear ideologically aligned with reformers and thus gain the status and stature necessary to help separate their entertainment from other, less wholesome sites of leisure—particularly the neighborhood saloon.

There already was little love lost between bar and movie theater owners. Although the subject remains virtually unresearched, local taverns, according to some scholars, were likely a popular site for early movie exhibition, offering an added inducement to stop, stay, and drink on the way home from the mill, but the practice tapered off with the rise of the nickelodeon. By the 1910s, neighborhood movie theater attendance directly impacted the profits of nearby saloons, and vice versa.[63] When West Virginia voted for state prohibition in 1914, five years prior to federal prohibition, the *Bulletin*'s editors claimed that the movies "have done more to draw men from drink than all the temperance sermons that have ever been preached. If prohibition . . . will prohibit drinking . . . then the people will have more money to spend and the moving picture houses will get their share."[64]

The liquor industry clearly feared the results the *Bulletin* predicted. Lobbyists for the state's brewers, distillers, distributors, and barmen are reported to have offered *John Barleycorn*'s independent producer, Hobart Bosworth, $25,000 to permanently shelve or at least delay the film until after certain crucial state elections were held on "whether to stay wet or go dry."[65] Bosworth, who had set up his company specifically to produce films based on Jack London's works, publicly declined this supposed offer, but there is the distinct possibility that this "bribe" was never tendered, and was rather a clever attempt by Bosworth, known as the "Dean of Hollywood," to gain publicity and establish the film's moral constitution. In July 1914, the film was released by its distributor, Famous Players Film Service, just a month after the Pennsylvania State Board of Censors began its work.[66] According to reports in both the national trade journals and the Pittsburgh *Bulletin*, the film was submitted to the board by William E. Smith, head of the Philadelphia branch of Famous Players, fourteen days in advance of the film's release date, as required by the board's newly redesigned rules and standards. This two-week buffer was designed to give the censors enough time to do their work without disrupting an exchange's program schedule, but Smith, upon attempting to retrieve the film for distribution, found that the Pennsylvania board had refused to pass the film, demanding that "nearly every scene in which booze is shown in its hideous features shall be eliminated or softened and that an extra 500 feet of pleasant domestic life be added at the end, showing the man's true reformation."[67] The board, among other changes, wanted a happier ending.

Contemporary newspaper accounts represent Breitinger as particularly volatile in his dislike for *Barleycorn*, and report that he even supposedly threatened Smith, the exchange owner, with prison if he dared exhibit the film in Pennsylvania. Again, it is possible that the story of the threat came from Smith himself, as a way of increasing publicity; regardless, the exchange owner was not going to back down. Instead, utilizing a loophole in the new law, Smith quickly set out to undermine the cultural authority of the board and the state by providing free exhibition of the film to influential political and public figures in both Philadelphia and Pittsburgh. Breitinger and the board could not legally stop such shows (or the free publicity that came along with them) because the state law, in order to not infringe on the exhibitor's First Amendment rights, allowed for "private exhibitions of a film to a chartered association without the approval of the board of censors."[68] In Philadelphia, Smith publicized his exhibition of the film to a full house of "leading temperance advocates, ministers and members of the W.C.T.U. (Women's Christian Temperance Union)"; and in Pittsburgh, marshalling a citywide parade of respectability, Smith received endorsements for *John Barleycorn* from "representatives of the Anti-saloon League, the W.C.T.U. and a group of clergymen," who screened the film in the auditorium of the Young Men's Christian Association.[69] At the end of each show, Smith collected reviews from the "assembled dignitaries . . . who pronounced the film a strong moral lesson." He then designed a series of press and poster advertisements that foregrounded these testimonials, placing the ads in numerous Pennsylvania newspapers and industry trade journals.[70] At the same time, in a coordinated plan by the industry lobby, the exchangeman began a succession of interviews with journalists sympathetic to the movies, in which Smith raised damaging questions about Breitinger's relationship with "liquor interests," which were then repeated in the popular press: "The *Evening Bulletin* has the largest circulation of any daily paper in Philadelphia and has always ranged itself on the side of the films, and in previous editorials has proven its friendship for the industry. Several of the other papers which favor local options have attacked Mr. Breitinger personally because of his connection with the liquor interests."[71]

These interests were, however, rather limited. Archival evidence shows that Breitinger, on taking his position on the board, remained a partner of Breitinger and Breitinger, a small private law practice he ran with his brother in Philadelphia. Both prior to and during his tenure as chief censor, Breitinger appeared as a private attorney in the Court of Quarter Sessions (Philadelphia's municipal court), representing local brewers and saloon owners in the process of renewing their liquor license applications.[72] Whether this ongoing financial relationship in some way influenced Breitinger's position on the film is indeterminable, but Smith and the state's film industry employed the appearance of bias to their best public advantage, turning the rather staid legal facts into an intense, and ultimately effective, attack on Breitinger's credibility as chief censor: "We told Mr. Breitinger that he could not possibly have any reason for suppressing this film, as it has been approved as a strong temperance argument by ministers and church workers throughout the land. But . . . he did not care a rap for them because all those . . . people 'are biased, anyway, against the other side.' This 'other side' that Mr. Breitinger talks about is, of course, the rum side, and that seems to be the only side Mr. Breitinger is considering."[73]

Smith's statements to the press were well timed, as Breitinger was out of the state on business; upon returning he found himself in the middle of a controversy that had become front-page news across Pennsylvania. The *Pittsburgh Press*, a newspaper that had previously editorialized against the formation of the censorship board, reported: "When Mr. Breitinger returned [to Philadelphia] yesterday he denied published statements that his withholding of approval was, because of the fact that he is an attorney for liquor interests, and said that during his temporary absence the impression had been given out that the Board of Censorship had definitely passed on the film. 'The film has neither been approved nor rejected by the board.... The false impression created in connection with the film indicates that the parties interested desire to create a fictitious sentiment for advertising purposes.'"[74]

Breitinger, who had once been employed by the state's exhibitors, was correct. Hobart Bosworth had managed to generate considerable interest across the state for *John Barleycorn* without incurring the costs of traditional advertising.[75] As the editors of the *Bulletin* extolled in their announcement of the film's impending Pittsburgh release; "[t]his film has gotten so much advertising in the daily press lately ... and when it is released it should prove one of the biggest money makers on the market."[76]

This form of journalistic publicity, explained by Sargent in his *Picture Theatre Advertising* chapter on "Doing Press Work," offered filmmen enormous value, "not because it is free, but because it is accepted as news and is read as news by those who take little or no interest in frank advertisements."[77] Because the film industry understood and often employed this form of discursive power, censorship battles such as the one over *Barleycorn* are problematic, if not impossible, to historically unravel. Underlying social and ideological issues have been tightly, and in many cases purposefully, woven around the potential of these films for political, promotional, and economic gain. Not surprisingly, but even more troubling, is the additional advice proffered by Sargent "that [n]ow and then a story may be manufactured. This takes ... experience and it is necessary to work with care. If you send out a story of how your box office was broken into by a burglar with a brick, you cannot very well show the burglar, but you can offer the broken glass and a brick in evidence. The glass may have been broken in getting out the lobby signs, but no one but yourself and the doorman know this."[78]

Perhaps Smith and the wider industry saw Breitinger and his board as metaphorical burglars attempting to steal their movies (and money), for Smith, along with C. H. Pierce of Bosworth Film, Inc., continued to produce their own "evidence" against the censors. Stepping up the fight in well-advertised defiance of the new state laws, and "to emphasize [the board's] attitude toward censorial dictation," the film's producer and distributor announced that they had rented the Garrick Theatre, a large, prominent (and independently owned) movie theater in Philadelphia's downtown main entertainment district, to publicly show *Barleycorn* for a twelve-hour period on Monday, August 3.[79] According to later reports, the exhibitors were warned that they would be apprehended if they proceeded with the commercial exhibition, and so "Pierce and Smith patiently waited all day for the threatened arrest and fine, which failed to materialize."[80] One might expect relief at their fortune to escape jail time, but the two film promoters were, in fact, disappointed, because Pierce and Smith had paid a cameraman from the nearby Lubin studios to stand guard with them, camera and stock in hand, in hopes of obtaining footage of their arrests, a scene that would have "proven a great crowd getter." Luckily, all was not wasted, as the "camera man took several hundred feet of film showing the exterior of the Garrick and the crowds entering the theatre. This will be used in boosting the show after it starts around the circuit."[81]

At this point, Breitinger offered Bosworth and his distributor a compromise: in return for Pierce submitting himself voluntarily for arrest and paying a fifty-dollar fine for the public exhibition, the board's chairman agreed to drop his most serious objections to the film. Having obtained their desired publicity, and unwilling to pay the increasing fines that would have come with continuing their offensive, the filmmen agreed "to [a few] nominal cut outs" and the feature was approved by Breitinger and the board, albeit missing the film's original images of a childhood London drinking from his father's beer pail.[82] The film's ensuing release was deemed wildly

FIG. 5.1.
John Barleycorn at the Garrick Theatre, Philadelphia, "in defiance of the censors."
Motion Picture News, August 15, 1914, 19.

successful, both in the rest of Pennsylvania and in the country at large, and Famous Players continued throughout its run to market the battle with the censors as a victory for Progressive ideals—prominently advertising their triumph over "the rum interests" in many of their newspaper and national trade ads.[83] In many ways, Smith and Pierce's marketing achievement for *Barleycorn*—which operated not despite the strictures of censorship but rather because of them—became a model for decades of independent producers who sought to distribute and promote a film by simultaneously appealing to its public notoriety and maintaining the context of moral authority and cultural significance.

By the end of the *Barleycorn* release, Pennsylvania's filmmen were efficiently organized and ready for a fight, having created their own group of lobbyists, the Moving Picture Protective Association, with its headquarters in Pittsburgh. The new association was funded both by the studios and membership fees from state exchangemen and exhibitors. With tacit backing from the Penrose machine, it immediately sought passage of a new bill that would nullify the 1914 law creating the censor board. In the spring of the following year, however, the United States Supreme Court ruled in *Mutual Film Corporation v. Industrial Commission of Ohio* that the motion pictures were a "a business pure and simple, originated and conducted for profit, like other spectacles, not to be regarded . . . as part of the press of the country or as organs of public opinion."[84] Not surprisingly, only a few months later, deferring to the new precedent set by the federal court, the Pennsylvania Supreme Court affirmed the constitutionality of the board's authority to censor the exhibition of movies, noting that it was "an exercise of the police power of the state enacted to conserve the morals and manners of the public."[85]

With these rulings in place, it quickly became apparent that the state board would seek primary control over not just the film industry and its product, but also over any local bureaucracy that continued to attempt to influence the movies shown in Pennsylvania. In October 1915, Judge J. Reid of the Allegheny County Court of Common Pleas ruled, in a suit brought by the state attorney general against the city of Pittsburgh, that the state board's powers superseded those of Pittsburgh authorities, and that the city no longer had the right to prevent the local exhibition of a film approved by the state board. The test case in this matter was D. W. Griffith's famous racist epic, *The Birth of a Nation*. The judge noted in his ruling that the board, as a legal state entity, was "entitled to respect," and that its rulings were binding regardless of potential "differences in moral temperament" that might exist between city and state authorities. Judge Reid, while legally bowing to the decisions of the state board, could not resist weighing in with his own review of Griffith's production: "To a great extent, present scenes are undoubtedly historical, and many of them are uplifting. Where they depart from the accuracy of history, or depict scenes that might excite race prejudice in some people who do not know our country's history or realize its meaning, it is to be regretted; but the fact that such are presented does not warrant this Court in interfering [*sic*]."[86] This ruling, which allowed Pittsburgh's Harry Davis to present *Birth of a Nation* for an extended run at top prices in the city's largest legitimate theater, the Nixon, was to be one of the few victories for the city's showmen, in that they had resisted local control, albeit at the cost of submitting to state control.

It was a Pyrrhic win at best for the moviemen. Fearing what now seemed inevitable, and hoping that proximity would allow some degree of influence or control, the General Film Corporation offered to furnish the Pennsylvania Board with a projection room, operators, and the salary for an additional censor if they would agree to do their (hopefully limited) work away from the state capital and instead within the environs of (Penrose-controlled) Philadelphia. This arrangement was similar to the Trust's earlier practice of contributing space and equipment to the National Board of Review in New York.[87] The Pennsylvania board agreed to locate its main offices in Philadelphia, in part because that city was recognized as the geographic focus of the state's film industry. Within two months, the board also opened a branch office in Harrisburg, the state capital, for its bureaucratic centrality and for the regular publication of all board-related materials, and finally, one more in Pittsburgh, to keep a closer eye on an increasing source of exchange and exhibition troublemaking in the state.

The Labor of Censorship

The arrival of the Pennsylvania board coincided with what was probably the most prolific period of film production, in terms of both number of reels and movies released, by the international film industry—the board estimated an average of four hundred reels of film produced each week.[88] In 1916, its first full year of continuous operation, the three-member board met in its Philadelphia projection hall, a converted church auditorium on the northwest corner of Eighteenth and Filbert Streets, six days a week (Sundays off, of course), viewing approximately a million and a half feet of film a month. From December 1, 1915, to November 30, 1916 (the fiscal year for the state at that time), the board examined 17,020 reels, or approximately 17 million feet of film. The hall was set up with six projectors lined up side by side for the most efficient presentation—truly silent, without even a piano for accompaniment.[89] The censors watched a lot of movies.

The owners of the exchanges were responsible for preparing and submitting a formal application for a film they wished to distribute commercially anywhere in the state. As seen in the representative sample provided by the board, the "Facsimile of Application Properly Filled Out," the ideal application included a producer who would "Domuch" to further educate the unknowing, and an exchange that would promote only the "Popular" —as in the sense of Progressively moral, and a movie that offered its potential audience a positive "lesson or moral to be taught." In the vast majority of extant applications, this last blank remained unanswered by the exchanges. The applicant typically sent the completed form, along with the film's reels, and the application fee of $2.50 a reel (and a dollar for each duplicate print) to the board's closest office, although the majority of films were actually viewed in Philadelphia. No later than three days before the film's intended release date, the censor in charge watched the film, marking an official "scorecard" that offered categorical evaluation of the film's "Educational, Artistic, Entertainment Values" and "Moral Effect," along with any eliminations or suggestions for necessary changes that the individual censor required.[90] Of course, the censor could also entirely ban a film from state commercial exhibition.

18

Facsimile of Application Properly Filled Out.
(Typewriter to be used.)

Form No. 21.

PENNSYLVANIA STATE BOARD OF CENSORS

No.........................   Date, September 1, 1915

APPLICATION FOR EXAMINATION

PROJECTION ROOM N. W. COR. EIGHTEENTH AND FILBERT STS., PHILADELPHIA
All checks must be certified and made payable to State Treasurer of Pennsylvania.
Mail all checks and applications to Projection Rooms one week before release date.

TITLE	THE EYES OF GENIUS.				
MANUFACTURER	Domuch Film Co.	Length	4,000 feet.	Extra Number of Duplicates or Prints	*See below.
EXCHANGE	Popular Film Co.	Parts	4		
DESCRIPTION	Seward, a sculptor, finding his eyesight failing leaves his model Lucile (who is in love with him) for the country, where the gypsy Magda poses for him. He becomes blind after the work is completed, and is attended by Lucile. Magda with her gypsy friends try to steal the famous statue, but are thwarted by Lucile, who realizes once more that she has regained Seward's love, when he destroys the statue of Magda.				
STYLE (Comedy, Drama, &c.)	Drama.		Date Manufactured	(If known).	
			Date to be Released	September 10, 1915.	
LESSON OR MORAL TO BE TAUGHT	The love everlasting.				
NAMES OF LEADING CHARACTERS	Male John Andrews. Arthur Brown.		Female Ida May, Sarah Winters.		

It is agreed that the duplicates applied for are exact copies of the original film as submitted for examination, and that all eliminations or changes required by the Board in the original have been or will be made in the duplicates before released in Pennsylvania.

POPULAR FILM CO.
Signed, JOHN SMITH, Manager.

The above to be filled in by Applicant. Below to be filled in by "The Board"

DATE APPLICATION RECEIVED BY BOARD		Date and Place Examined	
DATE OF APPROVAL OR DISAPPROVAL		Examined by	
ELIMINATIONS			
COMMENTS			

*If no additional sets are desired mark "none." If any additional sets are to be shown in Pennsylvania, mark number desired.

FIG. 5.2.
Application for examination, Pennsylvania State Board of Censors, circa 1915.

On completion of the examination, the censor sent the application with the board's determination—usually consisting of an attached list of required recommendations—back to the owner of the exchange via messenger. If the film's distributor agreed to the alterations, he then received the reels to be edited, along with the board's official approval, consisting of the state's logo on approximately four feet of film attached as a leader to the picture's title.[91] If the distributor disagreed with the decision, he was permitted, within ten days, to file a request for reexamination, whereby the movie would be reviewed in his presence by at least two members of the board who would discuss the alterations "with a view of carrying out the intent of the act and to properly portray the story." If, after this review, the exchangeman remained unwilling to concede to the changes, the law allowed him to file an immediate appeal with the appropriate municipal Court of Common Pleas. The addition of this legal appeals process to the 1914 statute was initially seen as a major victory for the motion picture interests, but in practice it offered little hope to the film industry. In each of the eight times in 1916 when Pennsylvania distributors chose to appeal to the court, the Pennsylvania State Board of Censors was sustained on every count.[92]

On a weekly basis, the board published its own "bulletin" which listed the pictures condemned outright as well as descriptive listings of the necessary "cut outs" required for other films to be released in the state. The censors saw this publication as educational for those in the industry. It reminded exchanges of their legal duty, taught producers to recognize what would be judged as inappropriate, and informed exhibitors what was illicit and what was approved. Additionally, these detailed records enabled the board's cadre of local inspectors—men and women whose work it was to see that the censors' collective vision was being carried out—to confirm that their efforts were not undermined by unscrupulous exchanges or exhibitors. By law, inspectors were granted free entrance to any Pennsylvania picture show—a source of never-ending aggravation to the state's theater owners, who complained that inspectors routinely gave passes to friends and relatives for casual moviegoing. When an inspector came across a film "without

FIG. 5.3.
Seal of approval, Pennsylvania State Board of Censors, circa 1915.

eliminations having been previously made as ordered by the Board of Censors," he or she completed another official form swearing out a criminal complaint for the responsible exchange. The grievance resulted in a letter of inquiry being sent to the exchange owner, such as this one:

> Dear Sir:
>
> Beg to advise you that our inspector, Leah Cobb Marion reports that eliminations of "2-A" and "2-C" as ordered by the Board in your picture "Slaves of Beauty" were not made when exhibited at the State Theatre, Harrisburg, on June 29th, 1927. Kindly let me have a report on the above violation.
> Yours very truly,
> Chief Inspector[93]

The exchange owner had to reply in writing (within seven days), explaining the reasons for the violation and his plan to remove the offensive material. In the particular example above, the Fox Exchange of Pittsburgh admitted to "inadvertently" forgetting to remove "views of girl lying on table with legs bare all the way up . . ." and "views of upper part of girl's body when she is shimmying" and reluctantly agreed to pay a fairly standard fine of fifty dollars plus costs.[94]

In addition to its official inspectors, the board also actively pursued help from municipal law enforcement, providing, in one case, the "chiefs of police of over six hundred cities and towns throughout the commonwealth" with a list of the titles of seventy-eight films that they deemed most offensive and that had previously been condemned by the board.[95] Further, the censors regularly sent copies of the condemned list as well as its weekly bulletin of eliminations to municipal libraries, women's clubs, and "to individuals who may express a willingness to aid in the enforcement of the law," thereby offering every state resident the power to police the movies.[96] It appears that this call to cinematic arms was productive, for numerous telegrams from private citizens of this era direct the board's attention to the local exhibitions of improperly censored or uncensored films.

One Pennsylvanian, James M. Farr of Wilkes-Barre, wrote to complain about the illegal employment of the name "Elinor Glyn" in local newspaper advertising for the five-reel feature *Three Weeks* (1915), directed by Perry Vekroff for the Reliable Feature Film Corporation. Glyn was the infamous author of the novel from which this film was adapted. Farr complained not only about the local exhibitor who had published her name but also generally about the content of the film:

> I object to the film "Three Weeks" as one which seems to have absolutely nothing redeeming in character or outcome, which relies on the coarse and immoral and to whose case the phrase "tending to corrupt the morals" seems to be applicable. . . . With regards to the advertising, I enclose the ad from the front page of the Wilkes-Barre Record on Washington's Birthday, showing the name of the author as well as the story of the book is claimed for the production. I congratulate you on the many exercises [*sic*] and condemnations which you report, I hope it may not be long be-

fore film manufacturers learn that it is unprofitable to produce photoplays of a criminal or degenerate tendency.[97]

Farr included a clipping from an ad for the Savoy Theater that prominently displayed Glyn's name in promoting the state rights film as "the only authorized adaptation of the famous novel."[98] The film tells a somewhat convoluted tale of royal intrigue and adulterous romance, highlighted by a three-week courtship between an exotic but unhappy queen and an Adonis-like English aristocrat. The 1907 novel, on which the film was based, eventually sold more than five million copies and helped establish the purple-prosed author as an international figure of both sexual desire and knowledge. Glyn's book, unlike the film, was filled with baroque descriptions of lovemaking, the most intense of which was located on a tiger-skin rug.[99] The success made both the novel and its author objects of popular culture, even worthy of poetic adulation:

> Would you like to sin
> with Elinor Glyn
> on a tiger skin?
> Or would you prefer
> to err with her
> On some other fur?[100]

But unlike her infamous appearance in the better-known 1927 cinematic adaptation of her later novel, *It*, Glyn does not have a on-screen role in *Three Weeks*, and, according to reviews not written by Mr. Farr, the film's scenes of sinning were minimal. After a few minor eliminations, primarily involving intertitles alluding to the character's (procreative) honeymoon activities, the film was given the Pennsylvania censors' seal of approval. However, attached to this official endorsement was the major proviso that Glyn's name not be visible in the promotion of the film in any shape or form. Significantly, at least in this case, the board was less concerned with the actual images on screen than how they would be "read" by audiences through the extratextual lens of promotion surrounding them.[101]

FIG. 5.4.
Savoy Theater advertisement for *Three Weeks,* March 1915. *State Archives, Harrisburg, Pennsylvania.*

```
┌─────────────────────────────────┐
│           SAVOY                 │
│     TO-DAY AND TO-MORROW        │
│         ELINOR GLYN'S           │
│  Sensational drama of thrilling │
│  love, embodying all the excit- │
│  ing adventures that made the   │
│  novel the most universally     │
│  popular romance of the century—│
│         "THREE WEEKS"           │
│  280 SCENES    FIVE BIG ACTS    │
│    The only authorized adaptation│
│  of the famous novel, featuring │
│  Madeline Traverse as the queen.│
│         ADDED ATTRACTION        │
│           PEARL WHITE           │
│      In the Ninth Episode of    │
│         "THE EXPLOITS           │
│           OF ELAINE"            │
└─────────────────────────────────┘
```

For the board, censorship was not simply about what would be seen, but also how it would be seen. As is made most visible in the case of *John Barleycorn,* however, the promotion of a state rights film was often designed with, and in fact often required, such extratextual context to ensure box-office success. In an increasingly competitive feature market, the publicity for *Three Weeks* primarily came in the typographic form of Glyn's hypersexual star persona. This indefinable but valuable excess of sexuality attributed to the author and her novel was something the film's producers had no doubt paid for, at least indirectly, in buying the adaptation rights to her popular book, and had then sold down the line to distributors buying the film's state rights and the exhibitors showing the film. The Specialty Film Company, which distributed the film in the Pittsburgh region, obeyed the censors in

FIG. 5.5.
Specialty Film Company advertisement for *Three Weeks*. *Pittsburgh Moving Picture Bulletin*, May 17, 1915, 23.

its *Bulletin* advertisement for the film by leaving Glyn's name out of its promotion, but many of the state's exhibitors felt they could not give up this crucial context. As a result, in a letter dated March 8, 1915, Breitinger informed the film's Pennsylvania owners: "The film . . . was approved subject . . . upon the agreement that the use of Elinor Glynn's [*sic*] name was not to be used on any banners, posters, or any advertising matter in connection with this subject. This has been repeatedly violated and the film is, therefore, not approved. Any writing or certificate to this effect is hereby revoked."[102]

Revoking a film's approval was an unusual step for the censors to take, but in the fall of 1917, the board was forced to confront the possibility of recalling an entire genre of movies that they had not only approved but which had previously been exhibited statewide. Once again, the board was required to respond and take issue not so much with the actual films but rather the larger context in which the audience would potentially derive meaning from those images. In this case, the context, World War I, was far beyond their means to control. The war had been in progress since the summer of 1914 and American response to the fighting, and to the possibility of joining that fight, was, to say the least, conflicted. By 1914, over a third of American citizens were either foreign-born or the children of immigrants, and the horrific images and stories of combat in many of their nations of birth produced a broad range of responses. Antiwar protests had begun almost as soon as the conflict itself; President Wilson's call for neutrality, to be "impartial in thought as well as action," and his reelection in 1916, had initially helped strengthen the development of a number of American pacifist organizations.[103] But the outcry for U.S. military involvement also began with the death of Archduke Ferdinand, and it intensified with the sinking of the *Lusitania* in 1915, resulting in the federal government shifting much of its active resources to preparation for war.

This lack of national consensus around entering the war posed a number of potential problems for the collective film industry. Although scholar Leslie Midkiff DeBauche has stated that "World War I facilitated . . . a greater sense of national community . . . providing the film industry with the opportunity to play a central role in this new community," by going "over the top in helping the government," the period leading up to the American entrance into the war found the film industry no more in agreement than the heterogeneous population it sought to entertain.[104] While some filmmakers and studios may have gone "over the top" in producing films "which enhanced citizen support for the war effort," a number of successful feature films instead advanced the causes of pacifism in their narratives, including: *War Brides* (1916); the Italian imported series *Patria* (1916); and Thomas Ince's epic *Civilization* (1916), a film that the national Democratic Party had skillfully employed in the reelection of President Wilson that year.[105] All of these films were initially accepted by the state's board of censors, with varying number of eliminations required, and each had been released in Pennsylvania by their individual owners and/or distributors prior to America's entry into the war. While the three films can best be understood under the generic rubric of "war" pictures, and all were variously promoted as such in both local newspapers and the national trades, they all displace the geography and politics of the European conflict with safer landscapes of imaginary kingdoms and mythical, far-off lands. And although both *Civilization* and *War Brides* contain spectacular scenes of battle, their narratives are driven not by men at war but by powerful female protagonists who undertake the ultimate fight, that of delivering the world to peace.

In *War Brides*, exotic stage star Ali Nazimova, in her first cinematic role, delivers the film's strongly pacifist message. The film, designed by producer Lewis J. Selznick as a launching pad for Nazimova's film career, is an adaptation of a one-act dramatic sketch the actress had performed the year before in her successful debut American vaudeville tour. The eight-reel feature, directed by Herbert Brenon, tells the tale of Joan, the pregnant wife of one of four brothers who all die fighting a great battle for their (imaginary) king and kingdom. When the king's government decides that unmarried women, such as the newly widowed Joan, will be compelled to wed soldiers departing for battle so as to provide a new generation of soldier boys, she balks and rises up to become a peace activist. Eventually, in the final reel of the film, Nazimova's Joan leads a contingent of like-minded women to confront the king and his warlike ways, boldly proclaiming: "I call upon your Majesty to stop this cruel war, or we will stop giving you children." Upon his patriarchal reply, "Impossible. War—of course, we will always have war," Joan declares, "I am the symbol of all womanhood. For life, not death—for peace, not war we give our children. NO MORE CHILDREN FOR WAR," and then shoots herself. The film ends with the female brigade of pacifists raising her martyred corpse above the crowd, her body becoming a symbol for their continued struggle.[106]

The better known *Civilization*, although similarly themed, tells a somewhat different tale of war's gendered relationships: in Ince's epic, the female peace activist Katheryn Haldemann (played by Enid Markey) is able to convince the previously war-loving Count Ferdinand (played by Howard

FIG. 5.6.
Selznick Pictures advertisement for *War Brides*. *Motion Picture News*, October 14, 1916.

Hickman) of the evil of battle and persuade him to join her noble cause. The result of his conversion is that during battle, Ferdinand purposefully sinks his powerful, enemy-destroying submarine and gives his own sacrificial body to the sea—only to return to life, resurrected with the soul of Christ, whereby he convinces the imaginary kingdom and its monarch of the need to pursue world peace. *Civilization* appears to have passed through the board's hands relatively unscathed, but *War Brides*, with its brazen text and images of an unmarried (if suitably widowed) pregnant woman proclaiming her ability to withhold procreation and/or birth as a weapon of peace, was in flagrant violation of at least two of the board's standards: "(3) Prenatal and childbed scenes, and subtitles describing them, will be disapproved," and "(8) Pictures, and parts of pictures, dealing with abortion and malpractice, will be disapproved. These will include themes and incidents having to do with eugenics, 'birth control,' 'race suicide' and similar subjects" (see this chapter's appendix for the full list of standards).

The Pennsylvania branch of Louis Selznick's exchange was ordered by the board to remove from the film's story any signs of Joan's pregnancy including "that portion of a scene of Joan in bed where she is pressing and rubbing her abdomen with the palm of her hands and apparent anguish indicating that she is *enceinte*." Even more problematic than the prenatal images for the censors were three brief intertitles in the film's fifth reel that provocatively declared:

> "I Will Not Be a Breeding Machine."
> "Food for the Next Generation's Cannon."
> "War Brides! Brood Mares!"[107]

All three intertitles were duly eliminated from the picture for exhibition in Pennsylvania. The cinematic representation of a woman "enceinte," whether in words or images, was not a matter taken lightly by the board; according to Oberholtzer's summation in the annual report of trends later that same year: "Pre-natal and childbed scenes, and explanations of these scenes in subtitles, constitute one of the great present offenses in American film . . . such material is . . . cut out of pictures in Pennsylvania, because it is profoundly offensive to womanhood, as well as to right-thinking men."[108] But *War Brides*, perhaps because of its strong pacifist message at a time when the country was attempting to remain isolationist in attitude, if not in actual military preparations, was not condemned *in toto* by the board, and after a month-long series of negotiations back and forth with Selznick and his local exchange over the film's images and intertitles, the board granted *War Brides* its official seal and approved it for general Pennsylvania exhibition in December 1916.[109] The United States entered the "Great War" on April 13, 1917. Even before the United States declared its intentions to join the battle, however, angry citizens of Pennsylvania sent telegrams about *War Brides*, *Civilization*, and *Patria* to the board's offices.

As soon the United States entered the war, Pittsburgh's Department of Public Safety and Military Authority sent a series of cables to the state attorney general. The cables, written in the name of Colonel Griffith, the department's director, urged that an "Emergency ruling be procured by the Board . . . by which war films approved prior to declaration of war between United States Germany be subject to recall or review *Patria Civilization War Brides* tabooed by Authorities here but Authorities would prefer state to handle this emergency."[110] Colonel Griffith wielded broad powers over every aspect of Pittsburgh as it related to the war effort, including banning or censoring films already passed by the state board, but apparently he hoped that the state would support such a decision rather than allow municipal leaders to contradict the state board's legal authority and political supremacy in such matters. The state, perhaps wary of creating a precedent for ceding such power to the city, was willing "to handle this emergency" for Colonel Griffith. State Attorney General Francis Shunk Brown, wrote to Frank R. Shattuck, who had replaced Breitinger in late 1915 as chief censor: "the exhibition of these films tends to discourage enlistment and is contrary to the spirit which should exist in this Country in its present crisis. . . . Whilst strictly technically you would have no right to disapprove or recall your approval of a film, yet if public conditions so changed that that which was formerly unobjectionable afterward became objectionable you would, in my judgment, have a right to recall such an approval. . . . I await such communication and any further advice from you."[111]

FIG. 5.7.
Telegram from H. J. Ruthven to Dr. Ellis Oberholtzer of the State Board of Censors, April 11, 1916. *State Archives, Harrisburg, Pennsylvania.*

Although there is no indication that *Civilization* was ever recalled by the board, the seal of approval for *War Brides* was permanently revoked by the board in late fall of that year; the weekly censors' bulletin announced its new "NOT APPROVED" status along with the following explanation: "This is a picture to be shown in Germany or Austria, not America. The propaganda is in the interest of these countries. It is pacifist in its main points, and certainly not in the interest of America. It advocates the doing of things because of the edicts of the 'all powerful' Kaiser and such things border on the indecent."[112]

This group of films was clearly viewed as dangerous to the state not only for their pacifist discourse but also for the way in which they narrativized and made visual the gendered reorganization of the cultural and psychic space of Progressive America. In their stories of women actively participating in, and seeking to dramatically alter, the public sphere through socially sanctioned roles as moral sustainers and delimiters, these films replicated the blurring and shifting of traditional gender roles that was occurring with women's increasing engagement and involvement in mass culture. According to a review of *War Brides* in *Motion Picture News*, the picture "has as its very basis the demand of women for equal voting rights in national government whereby they can approve or veto the plunging of their country into war."[113]

Although the board may have struggled over how to approach such politically sensitive issues, it had little trouble financially. From its second year of operation, the Pennsylvania State Board of Censors was able to generate enough revenue to support its own operating costs as well as annually submit a surplus income to the state treasury.[114] It collected this income from two major sources: fees for application and fines levied on the state's distributors and exhibitors for failing to comply with the censorship act. In the first three years of the act's statewide enforcement, Pittsburgh's distributors and exhibitors provided a disproportionate percentage of the fines by breaking both of the two fineable offenses. The first, relatively minor, infraction (resulting in a five-dollar fine) involved exhibiting an approved film without the accompanying four-foot long piece of celluloid that carried the state's official seal of approval. The most likely reason an approved film would be shown without its official seal was that a local exchange was trying to save money, as it cost a dollar to add the footage with the seal to each duplicate print of an approved film. Often, although the exchange was responsible for the seal's absence, the state inspector levied the fine on the exhibitor, or worse, confiscated the film while the theater owner was still in the process of screening it. This typically caused friction between exhibitors and exchanges. The second, much more serious, finable offense involved showing and/or distributing a film in which some or all of the board's required eliminations had not been made, or, worse, the exhibiting of a film either never seen by the board, or one that it had previously rejected entirely. Such blatant rebellion cost the (caught) offender the egregious amount of twenty-five dollars a reel.[115] This was no slap on the wrist; if caught showing an unapproved six-reel film, for example, an exhibitor was subject to a fine of $150—a large loss to make up at a nickel or dime a patron. My sense, however, from examining the extant lists of fines paid to the state, is that the majority of films that were shown without approval were one- or two-reelers, and overwhelmingly comedies. At a time when feature films were beginning to be promoted in the newspapers, but multi-reel programs of short subjects were still in popular abundance, it makes sense that exhibitors and distributors would find short films a much better risk for this illicit practice.[116] Of the 63 Pennsylvania exhibitors or exchanges caught attempting such feats and fined in the first six months of the act's enforcement, 32 were from Pittsburgh. In comparison, Philadelphia's filmmen were only cited 16 times during the same period. The following year, Pittsburgh provided 52 of the 203 statewide infractions.[117] The censors' Pittsburgh-based inspectors, situated in a local downtown office near many of the larger exchanges, were fiscally democratic in their prosecutions; administering fines to the smaller nickelodeon neighborhood theaters as well as the new photoplay theaters in the larger entertainment districts and the wealthier suburbs. Both the three-hundred-seat Lawrenceville Eagle and the nine-hundred-seat East Liberty Regent paid sizable penalties during this period.

Although *Moving Picture World* describes Pennsylvania's censors' exceptional attention to Pittsburgh as a "crusade," there is nothing in the board's existing files to suggest why the city's film industry would be cited in such a disproportionate way.[118] Geography, bureaucracy, and politics all likely played roles in the censors' pursuit. Pittsburgh, as the second largest city in the state and a major distribution center with its own board of inspectors, obviously faced closer and more intense scrutiny than the state's many smaller cities and towns. Yet Philadelphia, the state's largest city (and the country's second largest) and the recognized center of Pennsylvania's film industry, did not garner a similarly high percentage of violations and fines. With the board actually headquartered in Philadelphia, that city's exhibitors and distributors were closely monitored, and recognizing this, were unwilling or unable to attempt to easily circumvent the censorship laws. Pittsburgh's filmmen doubtlessly felt, and probably were, less constrained by the law's reach. An article in *Motion Picture News* from the period, reporting on methods used by Pennsylvania exchanges to undermine the state censors, supports this thesis:

> [some] submitting films for the approval of the censors have been in the habit, first of making four or five sets of duplicate films, and have been sending these duplicates out without eliminations, after some parts have been ordered removed by the board. The parts ordered removed . . . are cut out of the original film and the film thus emasculated is shown in Philadelphia . . . where the film is most likely to come under the eyes of a censor. . . . The duplicate films, with the censored features still in, are then sold throughout the state and placed on exhibition.[119]

Presumably, a high percentage of these uncensored films made their way to Pittsburgh, where exhibitors and distributors were becoming increasingly organized. Due to issues of social control, including state and local censorship, a heavy federal war tax levied on commercial amusements, and the looming fear of a new, much stricter, citywide building code for theaters, Pittsburgh's filmmen desired the kind of power that is only available in group form, as one notice illustrated: "Have you sent in your application for membership in the Pittsburgh Moving Picture Protective Association? If not do so at once. The money is needed for the protection of your own business as well as that of your brother exhibitor."[120]

In addition to the growing ranks of the Protective Association, the Pittsburgh Screen Club was formed in November 1914, and over 150 local exhibitors and exchangemen paid membership dues at the club's inaugural banquet. Along with raising admission prices, one of Mayer's primary objectives in starting the *Bulletin* "was to help . . . combat legislation affecting the industry."[121] Mayer had a vested economic interest in fighting state censorship when his larger livelihood as a printer was jeopardized: "The State Board of Censors . . . announced that it will endeavor to prohibit the display of sensational posters in conjunction with moving-picture shows, and in this it will also receive the co-operation of the local police. Posters showing the hero sinking a knife in the heart of a villain will not be tolerated, while pictures of bank robberies, hold-ups, suicide and any scene likely to excite youth, will not be found adorning the front of the moving picture theatres hereafter."[122]

The combined result of this organizational zeal was a propensity for the city's film professionals to engage in struggle with the state board, an engagement that Mayer supported, as well as instigated, in his weekly *Bulletin* editorials: "Live-wire exhibitors can do much against censorship if only they make up their minds to do so . . . open [your] eyes to the injustice of the injury being done to the picture business."[123]

Pittsburgh's exhibitors and distributors used their expertise and skills as showmen to gain support from the community and to open their collective patrons' eyes to the censors' otherwise unseen work. Because censorship resulted in the absence of shots and scenes prior to exhibition, the local exhibitors had to be creative in the ways they went about making the missing visible to their audiences. A series of rebellious acts that accomplished this project for Pittsburgh exhibitors focused on the use of magic lantern slides to inform theatergoers of the role censorship was taking in their picture show, while another involved the Screen Club parading an "advertising wagon" around the city with banners proclaiming censorship as un-American. Using imagery including Lady Liberty blindfolded by Pennsylvania censorship, "Father Penn" in the stockade, a lawyer's foppish top hat, the schoolmarm's prudish bonnet, and the preacher's chaste headgear, the distributors sought to frame the state censors as elitist, Victorian-minded reformers whose actions were simultaneously anti-American and anti-populist. A related local campaign, which was so successful it was instituted statewide by exhibitors, involved the production and exhibition of "Liberty Bell" slides, which when projected before a censored show provided an image of the state symbol of revolutionary freedom alongside the words: "It proclaimed liberty to all the people. Censorship put the crack in it."[124]

Pittsburgh exchanges often provided their exhibitors with an additional type of slide, which called attention to specific eliminations made by the censors. Depending on the film, and the exchange, the distributors either produced short intertitle synopses of the action eliminated by the censors, or slides warning to the audience that footage was missing courtesy of the state board. Mayer and other trade journalists urged exhibitors to project these slides in places where the film had been aggressively cut. In cases where "the cuts were too numerous" for slides or intertitles to bridge a film's disrupted narrative, Mayer offered exhibitors "cards or a circular that could be handed to patrons as they enter the theatre. They would thus

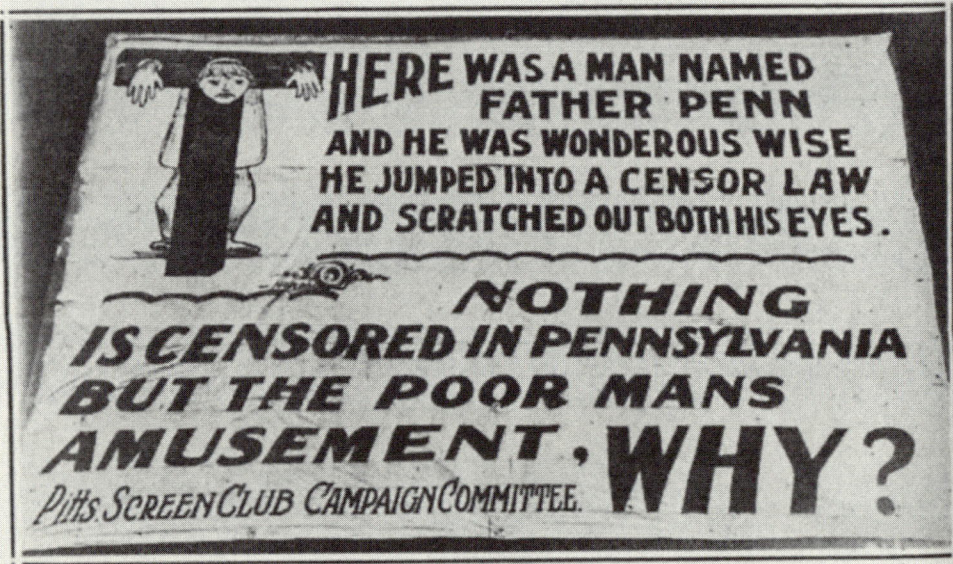

FIG. 5.8.
Anti-censorship banners, Pittsburgh Screen Club.
Pittsburgh Moving Picture Bulletin, May 24, 1916, 8.

be enabled to follow the story more readily and at the same time the fallacy of censorship would be brought home to the people."[125] The owners of the large downtown Pitt Theater took this process a dramatic step further by hiring a troupe of actors who stepped out from behind the screen at a point where the film had required cutting and "frequently enact eliminated portions of the film on the stage." The success and/or popular reception of these unusually hybrid theater and cinema performances, along with the less kinetic slide shows and printed summaries, is, unfortunately, impossible to directly measure. A strong indication of their impact on the censors, however, appears in the board's legislative retort, which in 1917 pressed for, and received, an amendment by the state legislature to the censorship act to outlaw any activity that would "by act, publication or utterance . . . reproduce any eliminated portion" of a censored film.[126]

Because the film exchanges were legally responsible for submitting their films to the board, it was the city's distributors who were most likely to find themselves on the wrong side of the law in the fight over censorship. Accordingly, distributors were most often jailed for their outright refusal to obey the board's orders. Examining the rhetoric of the *Bulletin* writers, its indignant but cavalier attitude towards such behavior suggests that these arrests were a relatively common occurrence: "Mayer Silverman of the Liberty Film Renting Co., who was arrested last week by the Board of Censors on charges of neglecting to make some eliminations, says the experience is not such an awful thing after all. This is the first time Mayer has been caught in the censor's dragnet and he says he didn't mind it a bit. Experience is a great teacher, he says."[127]

The economic result of this organized rebelliousness was, according to Oberholtzer, "money in the pot" for the state board as Pittsburgh exhibitors and exchangemen paid their fines.[128] While the city's movie interests continued to struggle with the board well into the late 1920s, in the following decades developments both inside and outside of the industry slowly altered the state's ultimate role in censoring the movies.

Once the Supreme Court had ruled in legal favor of the practice in *Mutual v. Ohio*, a surge of interest in this form of motion picture control developed in legislatures across the country. Pennsylvania's first board members actively supported and lobbied other states to join with them in defending the morals of the movies. The National Board of Review, which now found itself in the ironic position of developing into an anti-censorship lobby, distributed an article in 1921 by William A. Nealey, union president of the Massachusetts branch of the American Federation of Labor (AFL), which complained about: "a gentleman who apparently spends a large part of the time for which he receives pay as a censor of motion pictures traveling around in the non-censorship states and trying to induce groups of reformers to establish boards like the Pennsylvania board. This person, Dr. Oberholtzer by name, visited Massachusetts and . . . under [his] inspiration . . . a bill has been introduced in Massachusetts which its sponsors claim possesses all the virtues of Pennsylvania censorship."[129] When this state-led movement reached its peak during 1921, Massachusetts was joined by thirty-one other states in the introduction of their own motion picture censorship bills, not including the five—Pennsylvania, Ohio, Kentucky, Maryland, and Virginia—in which boards were already operating. At the same time, the film industry, particularly the major producers and exchanges, had increased their political influence to the extent that in 1916, President Wilson was the guest of honor at a dinner held by the Motion Picture Board of Trade: "The honor which is conferred upon this industry by being granted the privilege of entertaining the nation's Chief Executive as its official guest is one which should make every exhibitor, exchangeman and manufacturer proud of the industry's record and alive to its dignity, its influence and its future."[130] As a result of the industry's growing "influence," both state-based and national organizations, including the National Association of the Motion Picture Industry and the Motion Picture Exhibitors League (along with their well-financed lobbyists), were highly versed in the persuasive and political arguments against such regulatory control. With the help of labor organizations like the AFL, and reform-minded groups unwilling to endorse official censorship such as the Federation of Women's Clubs, the industry was able to defeat the legislation in thirty-one states. New York gained the distinction, in 1922, of instituting the last state motion picture censorship board.

Not surprisingly, the same argument used to promote state censorship over municipal boards was advanced in the name of an omnipotent board of censorship based in the federal government. Supporters of such a federal body claimed that final authority must rest with the national government and that the continuing trend of state censorship would lead to forty-eight versions of a film, inevitably resulting in chaos for the industry. Various committees introduced bills to promote a federally mandated board in 1914, 1916, 1920, and in 1921—but the industry was able to apply the required political pressure so that each bill was defeated with relative ease.

The movie manufacturers were less adept at controlling activities within their own sphere. A series of media-driven scandals that resulted from the death of Virginia Rappe at Fatty Arbuckle's party in late 1921 and the murder of William Desmond Taylor in February 1922 were the final incentives needed by the industry to promote the establishment of a self-regulatory body.[131] Pittsburgh exhibitors met in September 1921 "determined to force the producers and stars to clean house," collectively agreeing to "cancel bookings on any picture in which the star or any other player might do anything that will cast a reflection on the picture industry in general."[132] The wider industry reaction was the formation of the Motion Picture Producers and Distributors of America the following year, with Will Hays, ex-chair of the Republican Party, at its helm. The MPPDA was explicitly created to raise and promote the highest moral standards for the movies and implicitly meant to shut down further attempts at government regulation of the industry, thereby protecting its expanding political interests. The creation of the MPPDA, the hiring of Hays, and the association's policy of forming relationships with a broad range of reform, religious, and educational organizations so as to make them "friendly rather than hostile critic[s] of pictures" were the resulting summation of knowledge gained in the failure of the National Board of Censorship and the industry's struggles with municipal- and state-based censorship.[133]

Hays banned Arbuckle from the movie screen, which initially helped to establish the association's moral credentials with many reformers. The MPPDA voluntary adopted thirteen points of self-regulation in 1922 and a set of stricter rules known as the "Don'ts and Be Carefuls" in 1927, which were designed to limit potentially objectionable images and actions from appearing on screen. Through these steps, the MPPDA succeeded in preventing any new state or federal legislation in the following years. Even as late as 1930, however, when the industry formalized and widely implemented its Production Code, the Pennsylvania State Board of Censors refused to yield its now firmly entrenched, state-based power over the movies: "Pennsylvania has the distinction . . . of supporting the most arbitrary and severe board of censors. . . . No censor board in the country can compete with the Pennsylvanians. Movies that go untouched in every other state in the union are hacked and retitled in Pennsylvania . . . resulting in enormous expense for movie companies. . . . No political power or pressure from the Hays office has served to break down the severity of this state board."[134]

While "pressure from the Hays office" never stopped Pennsylvania's board from regulating the content of movies exhibited in their state, the Production Code's resulting mechanisms of restraint left the state censors with considerably less material with which to work. By the time a series of Supreme Court rulings in the 1950s and early 1960s removed the constitutional underpinnings for state-controlled censorship, films that were being cut or condemned by the board were primarily of foreign origin.[135] The Pennsylvania State Board of Censors, the longest active government censorship body in America history, stopped work in 1958 and was legally disbanded in 1962. At the beginning of the twentieth century, movies, with their seeming potential for universal access, had both thrilled and scared a Progressive society looking for ways to communicate both the possibilities and pitfalls of their rapidly changing industrialized culture. Pennsylvania's state censorship, as part of a larger movement, had been the bureaucratic articulation of the desire to control such potent representations of culture —but it had come to an end.

APPENDIX

Standards of the Pennsylvania Board (1914)[136]

(1) The Board will condemn pictures, and parts of pictures dealing with "white slavery." The procuration and prostitution in all forms, of girls, and their confinement for immoral purposes may not be shown upon the screen, and will be disapproved. Views of prostitutes and houses of ill-fame will be disapproved.

(2) Pictures and parts of pictures, which deal with the seduction of women, particularly the betrayal of young girls, and assaults upon women, with immoral intent, will be disapproved.

(3) Prenatal and childbed scenes, and subtitles describing them, will be disapproved.

(4) Pictures and parts of pictures dealing with the drug habit; e.g., the use of opium, morphine, cocaine, etc., will be disapproved. The traffic in habit-forming drugs is forbidden and visualized scenes of their use will be disapproved.

(5) Scenes showing the modus operandi of criminals which are suggestive and incite to evil action, such as murder, poisoning, house-breaking, safe-robbery, pocket-picking, the lighting and throwing of bombs, the use of ether, chloroform, etc., to render men and women unconscious, binding and gagging, will be disapproved.

(6) Gruesome and unduly distressing scenes will be disapproved. These include shooting, stabbing, profuse bleeding, prolonged views of men dying and of corpses, lashing and whipping, and other torture scenes, hangings, lynchings, electrocutions, surgical operations, and views of persons in delirium or insane.

(7) Studio and other scenes, in which the human form is shown in the nude, or the body is unduly exposed will be disapproved.

(8) Pictures, and parts of pictures, dealing with abortion and malpractice, will be disapproved. These will include themes and incidents having to do with eugenics, "birth control," "race suicide" and similar subjects.

(9) Pictures which deal with counterfeiting, will be disapproved.

(10) Stories, or scenes holding up to ridicule and reproach races, classes or other social groups, as well as the irreverent and sacrilegious treatment

of religious bodies or other things held to be sacred will be disapproved. The materialization of the figure of Christ may be disapproved.

(11) Scenes showing men and women living together without marriage, and in adultery, will be disapproved. Discussion of the question of the consummation of marriage, in pictures, will be disapproved.

(12) The brutal treatment of children and of animals may lead to the disapproval of the theme, or of incidents in film stories.

(13) The use of profane and objectionable language in subtitles will be disapproved.

(14) Objectionable titles, as well as subtitles of pictures, will be disapproved.

(15) Views of incendiarism, burning, wrecking and the destruction of property, which may put like action into the minds of those of evil instincts, or may degrade the morals of the young, will be disapproved.

(16) Gross and offensive drunkenness, especially if women have a part in the scenes, will be disapproved.

(17) Pictures which deal at length with gun play, and the use of knives, and are set in the underworld, will be disapproved. When the whole theme is crime, unrelieved by other scenes, the film will be disapproved. Prolonged fighting scenes will be shortened, and brutal fights will be wholly disapproved.

(18) Vulgarities of a gross kind, such as often appear in slapstick and other screen comedies, will be disapproved. Comedy which burlesques morgues, funerals, hospitals, insane asylums, the lying-in of women and houses of ill-fame, will be disapproved.

(19) Sensual kissing and love making scenes, men and women in bed together and indelicate sexual situations, whether in comedies or pictures of other classes, will be disapproved. Bathing scenes, which pass the limits of propriety, lewd and immodest dancing, the needless exhibition of women in their night dresses or underclothing, will be disapproved.

(20) Views of women smoking will not be disapproved as such, but when women are shown in suggestive positions or their manner of smoking is suggestive or degrading, such scenes will be disapproved.

(21) Pictures or parts of pictures which deal with venereal disease, of any kind, will be disapproved.

(22) That the theme of story of a picture is adapted from a publication, whether classical or not; or that portions of a picture follow paintings

or other illustrations, is not a sufficient reason for the approval of a picture or portions of a picture.

(23) Themes or incidents in picture stories, which are designed to inflame the mind of improper adventures, or to establish false standards of conduct, coming under the foregoing classes, or of other kinds, will be disapproved. Pictures will be judged as a whole, with a view to their final total effect; those portraying evil in any form which may be easily remembered or emulated, will be disapproved.

(24) Banners, posters or other advertising matter, concerning motion pictures, must follow the rules laid down for the pictures themselves. That which may not be used upon the screen, must not be used to announce and direct public attention to the picture, in the lobby, on the street, or in any other form.

6

THE LOCAL VIEW

> The Waynesburg Lodge of Elks gave a home talent minstrel show one night last week and we understand they got one off on one of our exhibitor friends down there. One of the end men asked what the commotion was at the back of the house, when the reply came back that it was only Charlie Silveus breaking a dollar bill!
>
> "The Tattler," *Pittsburgh Movie Picture Bulletin*, April 4, 1920

A<small>PPARENTLY, C<small>HARLIE WAS CHEAP</small></small>. Charlie Silveus was the owner and operator of the Eclipse Moving Picture Theater in Waynesburg Pennsylvania, a town of four thousand residents some fifty miles south of Pittsburgh, not far from the West Virginia border. In the (re)telling of this comedic routine, we are reminded that Pittsburgh was at once both a city *and* a region. To delineate Pittsburgh, to determine where its moving picture history begins and where it ends, is not simply a matter of topography. The minstrel's humor is local; those in the Waynesburg audience that laughed that night did so because they knew Charlie and his thrift. But the readers of the *Pittsburgh Moving Picture Bulletin* also knew of Charlie's cheapness. Charlie's life, like most, was shaped by his relationship to more than one community.

Begun by the *Bulletin* in the fall of 1919, "The Tattler" was a weekly gossip column devoted to "live sayings about exhibitors from everywhere," in which "everywhere" meant those theaters serviced by the Pittsburgh exchanges—a tri-state territory of almost 2,500 square miles, roughly bounded by Altoona, Pennsylvania, slightly to the east, Erie, Pennsylvania, directly to the north, Wheeling, West Virginia, to the south, and East Liverpool, Ohio, out to the west. Written in a breezy, familiar style, "The Tattler" was a mix of rumors regarding the region's various theaters and movie-related businesses, tongue-in-cheek flatteries passed on from "the girls . . . at the film exchanges," and a wealth of lighthearted wisecracks of the type aimed at Charlie Silveus in the April 4 edition.[1] While on occasion the columnist covered Pittsburgh's urban exhibitors, more often he focused on the multitude of showmen located in the surrounding towns and smaller cities of the region. This attention to the outlying areas was likely paid at the behest of the *Bulletin*'s editors, and perhaps was even the motivation for the column's origination. The city's exchanges depended on the many exhibitors based in this territory for their survival and success, and in turn Silveus, and the hundreds of other area exhibitors, relied on the Pittsburgh exchanges to supply them with a consistent program of films. The *Bulletin*, of course, needed them both—the exchanges as their primary advertisers, and the exhibitors as their regular readers. "The Tattler" became one of many ways in which the weekly journal created a shared discursive landscape for a community of exhibitors who were spread across a wide economic, cultural, and geographic territory.

Initially, the *Bulletin*'s editors kept the identity of the author of "The Tattler" a mystery to their subscribers, but his name fairly quickly became something of an open secret. By the end of the year the journal revealed its columnist to be one A. J. Burgun, a well-liked "roadman" for Pittsburgh's Universal Exchange.[2] In his day job, Burgun was employed by the studio to promote and sell the Universal program to the region's theaters. In a career best suited for the garrulous, Burgun was good at his job. His column often reflected the conversations he had and the stories he was told while out working hard to sell his identical films to different people in different places.

Until very recently, the concept of "local" cinema has referred to these different people and places, but not the actual films. Local was not so much the text but the context, the specific conditions in which films made else-

FIG. 6.1.
Roadmen for Pittsburgh's Universal Exchange (A. J. Burgun, sixth from left).
Pittsburgh Moving Picture Bulletin, June 5, 1920, 6.

where by others about others were exhibited and experienced— where the movies were watched, not where they were made. Charlie Silveus, cheap or not, offers a strikingly different model of local cinema, because he was both an exhibitor *and* a filmmaker, making pictures that required no roadman to arrive in town. Instead, the people of Waynesburg were both the subject and audience of the films he made and showed. Beginning in December 1914, Silveus engaged in the regular production and exhibition of short, nonfiction films that focused their collective attentions on the people, places, and events of his hometown of Waynesburg. His films, some of which survive today, present a parochial range of events, both natural and social (parades, picnics, fires, and floods) as well as scenes of everyday life (children playing, people working), all laid out in a landscape of local fields, farms, streets, storefronts, backyards, and mill-yards. The organizing principle of these films, and much of their considerable power, lay in this everyday specificity. The result was a cinema of self-recognition, even self-definition, that addresses a limited populace living within in a limited landscape. It is, by its own design, by, for, and about the local.

Overwhelmingly, film scholars who have focused on the 1910s and 1920s have concentrated their energies on the stylistic and narrative evolution of the feature film, its structures of meaning, and its methods and modes of production, exhibition, and reception. Notions of the feature film's dominance have become tempered in the last decade by a number of scholars working with both short fiction and nonfiction films.[3] Additionally, these years, particularly the early 1910s, are increasingly marked by historians of early cinema as "transitional," a useful recognition of the many ways in which fiction film had yet to fully inscribe itself within the "classical" paradigm. While productively lengthening and complicating the developmental journey from "early" (in all its scholarly sobriquets) to "narrative" cinema, the existing history remains still (too) tightly bound to the industrial studio system and its fiction films. The local view, at least at first glance, appears to reject much about the advancing homogeneous industrialization of American studio cinema. Requiring no complex chain of industrial operations in order to reach its screen, local films defy the developing institutional oligopoly in which power and control were increasingly sought and gained by national studio manufacturers. Offering an explicitly local experience highly dependent on extradiegetic knowledge for pleasure and comprehension—the same kinds of knowledge required to have a laugh over Charlie's cheapness—the local view could also be said to resist the evolving "classical" formation of the self-explanatory and self-contained fictional narrative.

Whether or not one wishes to read these seeming contradictions and incongruities as necessarily oppositional or resistant probably has as much to do with the historian as with the history. Certainly aspects of the local view reflect the larger debates of the period over what the cinema was, who it was for, and what it should become. The local view can, in at least some ways, be seen as the visual manifestation of the very real struggles that were occurring over and between increasingly centralized production and distribution companies and locally situated exhibitors. If we were to accept scholar Miriam Hansen's description of the nickelodeon as an "alternative public sphere," one that is "self-regulated, locally and socially specific," then the local view offers historians a seductively parallel visual text to go along with this early exhibition space.[4] However, the local view can be best understood, at least at the level of exhibition and reception, as less of an alternative cinema than a complementary one. The local view is critical to include in film's wider history because it was an exhibitor's genre, but it was never meant to supplant or surpass the studio's own offerings, rather to provide the kind of images and experience that a roadman like Burgun could never offer an exhibitor like Silveus.

While Silveus's local films are literally exceptional, individual, irreplaceable traces of the past bound to a unique place and space in time, his practice of local filmmaking is neither isolated nor unusual. Rather, it is increasingly clear that Silveus and his movies belong to a well-established, if sorely under-historicized, tradition of local filmmaking practices that can be found throughout the world and across cinema's history. In their widespread popular reach local films disrupt many traditional ideas about both mass and local culture. We often tend to imagine "localness" as characterized by its uniqueness to a specific location or region, something we often positively situate in opposition to the "mass" or the national. As we will see, however, the production and exhibition of local views by Silveus and many others in the Pittsburgh region was neither organic nor accidental, but instead highly institutionalized and efficient. The local view was the regular practice of multiple communities, both real and imagined. A study of Silveus's films and their exhibition, offers us the potential to understand, as historiographer E. H. Carr put it, "what is general in the unique."

Cheap Charlie Makes Movies

By the time "The Tattler" came along, making movies was nothing new to Charlie Silveus, who appears to have first begun his career as a local filmmaker in the winter of 1914. According to the premiere report in the *Waynesburg Republican*, the town's weekly newspaper: "The local pictures shown last night attracted a large crowd and the theater was crowded until a late hour. Manager Silveus . . . expects to make some more local views soon and with the experience gained in the making of the first expects to be able to show better pictures."[5] Despite whatever shortcomings the newspaper hints at, and although this particular footage no longer exists, we know from the survival of many of Silveus's other films that he did go on "to make some more local views." Charlie Silveus, in fact, went on filming his hometown for another thirteen years, exhibiting images of Waynesburg, its citizens, and their lives up to the beginning of the sound era in 1927. About an hour and a half of footage survives to this day, providing us with a rare and moving document of this town's metaphysical highs and lows. Such films demand inclusion within the broader historiography of American cinema.

At the most fundamental level, Silveus's work contradicts the prevailing belief that (by very definition) exhibitors show movies but do not make them. Scholars like Charles Musser have explored the role that film's earliest exhibitors played in the creation of cinematic meaning through their use of off-screen supplements—particularly lectures, as well as the common practice of reediting films that producers supplied.[6] Yet little has been done to understand exhibitors as filmmakers, at least as they relate to American practices. The discovery and extensive research into the films of the British company Mitchell and Kenyon have revealed the widespread role that local films played in the United Kingdom in the late nineteenth and early twentieth century, but the broad use of these types of nonfiction films during the studio era have remained largely unexamined. However, it is not just the existence of Silveus's local films that marks them as significant. Our fascination with early film is tied to our sense of its dynamic possibilities, the idiosyncratic experimentation that was possible in an era before the industry instituted its narrative axioms and presentation techniques as the overriding mode of cinematic experience. When "early" cinema ended is a matter of continued debate, but scholars largely agree that over time, audiences' options and behaviors were curtailed, fiction films gained dominance, and the industry's notion of the "local" became flattened and homogenized. Yet in the very period in which cinematic potential is thought to have become more limited, Silveus took up the tools of production to expand the role of the exhibitor and the images available to his local constituency. This opening up is the result of narrowing the camera's and screen's field of vision to the immediate and shared life of the filmmaker and his audience, which challenges our current sense of the ways in which commercial movies were produced, consumed, and circulated in this era.

Silveus's labor and its results belong to an overlapping but diverse sphere of commercial production and presentation practices linked by heightened and purposeful attention to the "local." The resulting genre included movies produced by a broad range of professional, semiprofessional, and amateur filmmakers, including urban filmmakers "specializing in local scenes for moving picture houses," itinerant cameramen making and exhibiting local pictures as they traveled from town to town, and exhibitor-filmmakers much like Silveus. The ensuing films could offer the nonfiction "local view" or dramatic stories with titles like *Kidnappers' Foil* and *Metamorphosis of a Freshman* that mimicked studio-based films but replaced Hollywood stars with townspeople and back-lots with main streets. Although the majority were shorts—typically a reel or two—feature-length films were not uncommon.[7] Silveus began his filmmaking efforts in the 1910s and ended in the late 1920s, but good evidence suggests that local pictures were made in other parts of the country as late as the 1950s. Such an eclectic set of generically diverse films that span urban and rural, silent and sound, fiction and actualité were produced and deployed under varying conditions with varying economic, social, and ideological imperatives underlying their particular sensibilities of the local. Collectively, they suggest a history of American moviegoing and moviemaking that must attend to the persistence of difference and the extended importance of locality in order to acknowledge the complex ways in which the movies have embedded themselves in everyday life. Additionally, such films disrupt the conventional hierarchy of producer and consumer that are central to traditional thinking about American movie culture. In the local view, the consumer and the community are the objects of exposure and so, literally (pre)figure what will be produced and exhibited on-screen. At the same time, the political and social economies driving these various local films should not be assumed identical, and crucial distinctions of representation and purpose must be made and historicized between films produced *in* a community, by an individual like an exhibitor living within that community, and those made *of* a community, by someone from somewhere else.

As a set of production and exhibition practices, the "local view's" origins were as still images in a proto-cinematic magic lantern show. Research by scholars like Musser and Robert Allen has shown that the moving picture variety of the local view virtually begins with the movies' invention and was one of the initial ways that both foreign and domestic companies promoted their nascent entertainment technology in America. In many ways, the local view offered an ideal subject matter for what at the time required a highly individualized system of labor, presentation, and technology. In the pre-1900 period of development, companies like Biograph, Edison, and Lumière often had to rely on a few men intimate with an entire range of cinematic skills and knowledges—the fabrication and maintenance of the camera, the production and processing of the images, and, finally, the projection of the moving pictures.[8] Initially, vaudeville's established programming structure demanded that these men and their machines travel from city to city, often for months on end, and as one result, the local view genre offered an efficient way for the companies to continue to produce new images while keeping their critical personnel and equipment profitably employed on the road.

The act of producing a local view could also offer significant promotion for the manufacturers, for, as many historians of moviegoing have shown, "in the earliest years of exhibition the cinema itself was an attraction."[9] The motion picture apparatus itself drew a crowd, as much as or more so than the film it was designed to exhibit. Typically, historians refer to the projector as the primary technological attraction—this device is most closely associated with the site of exhibition and so comes in nearest physical proximity to the audience. The projector's physical requirements, however, dictate that it remain primarily hidden from view while in the midst of a performance—up high, in the back of a dimly lit darkened theater (and later, enclosed in a fireproof box). As Kathryn Fuller's work reveals, many early advertisements for motion pictures foreground the projecting device even over the specific films and their subject matters, but unless accommodations were made to exhibit the projector prior to the show few audience members ever clearly saw these new mechanical wonders close up.[10] The camera, on the other hand, particularly when involved in the production of a local view in broad daylight, created a highly accessible, visual spectacle. Local views then, from their very beginning, became a productive way of capturing the attentions of the public life of the community. This notice could then be successfully drawn into the theater and onto the screen. Early film historians tend to agree that these local views were a regular and important aspect of film programming as late as 1900.

As motion pictures increasingly became a standardized "turn" in the vaudeville program, owners of the major theaters and vaudeville circuits struck deals with the major manufacturers for the purchase or lease of projectors that could be permanently housed in their theaters. Such deals also required the film companies to provide a consistent flow of new film titles. The subjects of these films needed to be popular with audiences at all the theaters in the circuit, not just the towns in which they were initially shot. Although some films designed for local consumption were exhibited elsewhere, particularly if the subject was of national significance, local views usually had limited appeal to audiences from outside the immediate area. Fiction films had, on the other hand, at least the potential for wider appeal, and these films, made in a centralized location (mostly New York and New Jersey) with access to facilities for producing multiple prints of the subject, became the most efficient industrial structure through which to provide service to theaters across the country.[11] The result was that while projectors stayed, the multitalented traveling operators left—often to take on the more specialized role of studio cameramen—and were replaced by a local projectionists who typically had neither the training nor the equipment to continue photographing local views. This line of reasoning does not solely account for the rise in fiction filmmaking, but does suggest one industrial reason for why the production and exhibition of local views declined in the early 1900s.

At the turn of the century, those entrepreneurs, inventors, and investors seeking to enter the motion picture business found that while cameras remained difficult to buy, manufacture, or even use, projectors were relatively easy. Although the mechanics involved are nearly identical, creating a moving photograph is a more exacting task than projecting one, and so not surprisingly, beginning in late 1896, "an astoundingly large number of firms made projectors" while relatively few new companies entered the camera or production market.[12] Additionally, the fear of expensive and timely patent litigation meant that even the more established film-related companies tended to stay away from camera manufacturing. Cameras had become the mechanical loci of Edison's constant barrage of suits aimed at monopolizing the industry. It was much easier, cheaper, and safer for those interested in entering the field to purchase (and eventually rent) films made by Edison and others.

But by 1912, when Charlie Silveus decided to take the profits from his family's successful restaurant business and open the Eclipse Theatre, conditions had significantly changed.[13] The film industry had rapidly grown over the past decade, and the maturing of its business, along with its accompanying growing pains, had a significant effect on the moviegoing experience, whether it was in Pittsburgh or Waynesburg. In 1912, one could still attend a legitimate or vaudeville theater and see a moving picture, but more typically moviegoing involved an act unto itself—going to a theater where the film(s) played a central role, not just a turn on a larger bill. As previously discussed, developments within industrial practices helped regulate the production and, just as importantly, the distribution, of these films and allowed exhibitors to come to expect and depend upon a regular and predictable supply of subjects for their theaters.

However, the standardized dependability of production and distribution did not necessarily lead to the homogenization of exhibition. In fact, arguably the opposite is true. The national trade press and exhibitor how-to manuals of the 1910s stressed that patronage of a particular theater was dependent not simply on a high-quality feature service but also on the theater owner's ability to create a distinct "personality for his house."[14] As the moving picture product produced by the various studios became more generic in style, form, and content, many exhibitors believed it necessary to distinguish their theaters and presentations from those of their nearby competitors. As a result, particularly for urban exhibitors, live and local aspects of exhibition continued to significantly contribute to the motion picture experience of the 1910s and 1920s. Whether through the mediation of the studio film through lecturers, lantern slides, and sound effects, or events directly involving theater patrons such as sing-alongs and audience-based participatory promotions, the exhibitor who maintained these types of showman-like practices was understood to be positively "building up" the "personality" of his theater and show.[15] In part then, the local view as an exhibitor's genre should be read as a desire to create and sustain a distinct house personality. The production and exhibition of local views provided Silveus and his theater with a truly cinematic method of achieving such distinction.

Not nearly as sumptuous in its design or accoutrements as the East Liberty Regent, Silveus's Eclipse, initially with five hundred seats, was part of the national proliferation of midsize movie-only venues during this time period. In a 1916 survey of exhibitors compiled by *Motion Picture News*, the average seating capacity for an American motion picture theater was 502, and 32 percent of those surveyed had house seating for between 350 and 650 patrons.[16] If the Eclipse had been located in a city like Pittsburgh, it would have qualified in both its style and size as a rather typical neighborhood "house." But Silveus opened his theater in town with a single, relatively small downtown business district—there were no theaters outside of the town's center—and it was, from the very beginning, proudly designated by the local newspaper as "the Waynesburg Eclipse."[17] The Eclipse would provide a significant departure in how this town's populace had come to experience the movies.

Prior to Silveus's investment, moving pictures were exhibited in Waynesburg in two distinctly different venues: storefront nickelodeons and the town's Opera House, built initially as an Odd Fellows and Masons meeting house in the 1870s and remodeled as a large mixed-use theater in 1901.[18] Waynesburg, the county seat of Greene County, had a relatively stable economy built mainly on surrounding agriculture, nearby open-pit coal mining, and significant natural gas fields, and residents were able to support a typical, if eclectic, range of late-nineteenth- and early-twentieth-century commercial entertainments. These included: traveling acrobatic troupes, vaudeville

FIG. 6.2.
Eclipse Theatre advertisement.
Waynesburg Republican, January 9, 1919, 4.

FIG. 6.3.
Pittsburgh Commercial Motion Picture Company advertisement.
Pittsburgh Moving Picture Bulletin, May 20, 1914, 9.

performers, and stock theater companies; public lectures by personalities like William Jennings Bryan; and local talent shows, including the minstrel performance reported in "The Tattler" and *The Jollies of 1921*, presented by the same Elks Club. In addition, by the turn of the century, the Opera House was an exhibition site for a variety of motion picture–related events, including annual visits from travel lecture impresario Lyman H. Howe.[19]

The Eclipse, although built just across the street from the Opera House, was not designed to directly compete for its audience with Waynesburg's cultural centerpiece. Silveus, in fact, eventually managed the Opera House for its owners, while still running the Eclipse. In the 1910s, when Silveus first began operations, the Opera House typically presented motion pictures only about once every other week.[20] In opening the Eclipse, he sought to create a site where the town's residents could attend the movies, on a weekly, if not daily, basis. Just because they could regularly attend the movies, however, did not necessarily mean they would, and, as in much of the rest of the country, social and religious concerns about the morality of the movies meant that this attendance was not guaranteed. Only a year before the Eclipse's opening, the management of the Opera House had come under local fire for showing the film *The Monte Carlo Girls*, which was described by the newspaper's editors as "a disgrace to decent society," with "vile stories and innuendos . . . a disgraceful performance . . . beyond the limit of both law and decency."[21] Silveus knew he would have to be more careful.

As part of industry discourse on developing a theater's proper "personality," trade articles suggested that exhibitors, in addition to cautiously selecting and monitoring what appeared on their screens, should positively engage their community outside of their theaters. This required, at least according to Sargent, that the theater owner "have an influence extending beyond the confines of his house" and that he "should seek to make himself a man of mark in the community." To best attain this position of authority, Sargent proposed that the exhibitor should participate in local business organizations (but never seek to run them, lest he appear overly ambitious) and to designate his place of business as a space available for public welfare and community service: "If there is a movement to collect a fund, let him not only be a contributor to the fund. He should aid to influence others. He should let his house be designated as a depository. He should give a benefit matinee. He should make his theatre a rallying point."[22]

As the successful owner of a small-town restaurant, Silveus didn't need to be told about the importance of local good will. In fact, Silveus presented his first community-related benefit at the Eclipse less than a week after first opening, not during the less-profitable matinee slot recommended by Sargent, but on a busy Friday night: "The high school Athletic Association will have charge of the Eclipse Theatre [tomorrow] night. An exceptionally good picture has been secured . . . it is a thriller and one that is sure to please. The high school boys have been short of funds and have adopted this method of raising money."[23]

In a period in which Progressive discourse located the dangers of the movies within the picture house as much as within the picture itself, and in which the state's censors publicly railed against "the devastations which the theatre has made in the habits and manners of our boys and girls," exhibitors had to be extremely careful in how they sought a (profitable) youthful audience.[24] From the very start, Silveus appears to have expertly traversed this delicate geography by establishing his theater proprietorship as simultaneously commercial and altruistic in its goals. Silveus allowed many other local groups to use the Eclipse for their benefit, including a Sunday school class of the town's First Baptist Church, which used the proceeds of ticket sales for their building funds.[25] This particular program was held on a Sunday, following an exhibitor tradition of promoting the showing of movies on Sunday although it was frowned upon by religious organizations if not often outright banned by municipal or state "blue law" ordinances. The rhetoric of the town's newspaper, in which the high school "boys" take "charge of the Eclipse," illustrates how Silveus engaged in a set of exhibition and promotional practices that allowed his theater to function not as a site of potential danger but instead as a public vessel for good, in which the town's habitants were welcome to provide its contents. Two years later, in 1914, they literally became those contents, as Silveus began regularly filming and exhibiting his own local views.

As a set of films and practices, the local view enabled exhibitors like Silveus to create a particularly powerful and compelling way of visually marking their place within the larger community. Like the student and church groups to which Silveus opened his theater, the local view helped actuate a discourse of civic acceptance for the exhibitor and his show by transferring to his business the social and cultural aura associated with the events and people appearing on his screen. After all, the town could not help but identify with these images of its own collective life—even the most Progressive-minded critic would find it very hard to fault the subject matter of a film when that subject was himself. Although film scholarship generally attributes the formation of a middle-class audience for the movies to the rise of the picture palace, to the production of feature films based on more "legitimate" subjects, and to the effect of regulation and reform on the moral acceptability of the movies, local pictures also played a role in providing a cinema that literally reflected the views of its audience.

The report of one theater owner from Pittsburgh evidences such a belief in the local view's bourgeois power. After exhibiting footage of a neighborhood Easter parade, the owner of the Gem Theatre (whose name is unknown), happily testified in the *Bulletin* that "many church members who had come to see the pictures ended up becoming regular patrons." Operating a theater in a city the size of Pittsburgh, he had hired a cameraman named George Bates Jr., one of the resident professionals who specialized in industrial films and "local scenes that give your house prestige and profit."[26] Waynesburg, on the other hand, could not support a full-time filmmaker, let alone the three or four working in Pittsburgh at the time. Although Silveus could have easily hired one of these men to travel the short distance to his town and produce his local views for him, he decided instead to make his own movies.

In the 1890s and early 1900s, it was close to impossible for an exhibitor like Silveus to gain access to the equipment or the knowledge necessary to become a filmmaker, since the few companies that made cameras were extremely proprietary. Additionally, with the exception of the Cinématographe, the earliest motion picture cameras were extremely cumbersome and typically were powered by either temperamental and dangerous direct current or massive sets of short-lived wet-cell batteries.[27] Even as cameras became commercially available (between 1903 and 1904) and slightly more compact, in the first decade of the 1900s, the cost and difficulty of operation meant that production remained in the hands of a relatively small group of professional cameramen. Such men sometimes shot local views, either for a particular manufacturer or on a freelance basis, but the considerable expense to the individual theater owner precluded regular production and exhibition of local films during this period.

By the time Silveus decided to invest in his own moviemaking equipment, sometime in early 1914, a number of lightweight, hand-cranked 35mm cameras, manufactured both in America and abroad, had become available.[28] While the best new cameras, such as the Bell and Howell 2709, which cost approximately two thousand dollars when first released in 1912, remained prohibitively expensive for most independent cameramen, affordable used cameras were advertised for sale in many of the national trade papers as well as the *Bulletin*.[29] In *Moving Picture World*, the Bass Camera Company of Chicago offered to mail potential customers a "monthly bargain bulletin" for both new and used motion picture equipment, including the "Pittman Professional camera complete with lens for only $85.00."[30] Better known (and in all likelihood better made) cameras, such as the popular Pathé Studio Model, "perfect with lens, case and four magazines" were also available used for $350.00. While the widespread availability of relatively inexpensive lightweight camera equipment did not necessarily directly result in the widespread production of local filmmaking, its attainability made it possible for small-town exhibitors to also become filmmakers in the way that Silveus did.

There is some indication that Charlie Silveus, prior to entering the movie business, was an amateur still photographer of local repute, and so he may have already possessed knowledge of the mechanics and chemistry needed to create moving images.[31] Beginning in spring 1916, others who wanted to become local filmmakers could seek out the expertise and advice of "The Camera," a new weekly department in *Motion Picture News*. The

> # A Few Camera Bargains
>
> Prices Smashed, in Conformity with Bass Policy to sell at low prices—
> MOVE GOODS QUICK.
> GENUINE PRESTWICH M. P., London, made complete, with Tessar F:3.5 lens. Only.................$220
> PATHE Outside Magazine Studio Model —late type. Perfect, with lens, case and four magazines. Only.........$350
> UNIVERSAL—late model, with lens. Only....................$195
> PITTMAN PROFESSIONAL—complete with F:3.5 lens. Only... $85
> Tripods, Northern Lights, etc., at special prices.
> All goods guaranteed.
> Other Special Reductions in used and new Moving Picture Cameras offered in BASS MONTHLY BARGAIN BULLETIN, mailed FREE. Write for it TODAY.
> **BASS CAMERA CO.**
> 111 N. Dearborn St., Dept. 7, Chicago

FIG. 6.4.
Bass Camera Company advertisement. *Moving Picture World,* July 6, 1917, 117.

column was "prepared expressly for the exhibitor ... who shall learn how to choose and properly operate a camera in order that he may successfully take local event films."[32]

The exhibitor was, in this way, being marked by wider industry discourse as a legitimate producer of screen content. This institutional acceptance is particularly significant because it came at a time when studio manufacturers were far from being short of content, but were, rather, releasing a sustained flow of new films. This prolific output resulted in part from the increased specialization of motion picture labor within the studio system.[33] Accompanying this structural expansion and definition of labor boundaries came a discourse of increasing professionalization: "When an industry has reached such a magnitude that many people are employed in its work," one 1915 writer wrote of filmmaking, "some employees will develop greater ability in some lines than in others, and the lines of activity become so divergent that they are best cared for separately. As in any manufacturing industry, the manufacturer of motion picture films for exhibition in a modern factory has its division of labor, and a film picture is the joint product of the various departments and specialists who in turn take it and perfect it with their skill."[34]

"The Camera" column, counter to such rhetoric, actively rejected the need for such singular expertise and ability. By explicitly demystifying the "many secrets" of motion picture photography "supposed to be known only to the professional," the column presented theater owners with the material knowledge with which an exhibitor could become a producer. The intersection of technological, industrial, and historical conditions visible in the column offered a viable environment for the success of the local view filmmaker. Despite rising interests in local filmmaking practices, it is difficult to gauge how extensive and pervasive exhibitor filmmakers were in this era, but the language and subject matter of "The Camera" indicates that Silveus was not the only one with the desire to make his own movies:

> The wide-awake exhibitors in all parts of the country are manifesting great interest nowadays in making local pictures. Formerly when an exhibitor desired a local event filmed a cameraman was secured from the nearest large city at great inconvenience and expense.
>
> The cameraman's services cost a young fortune and, in addition, the developing and printing, generally taken care of by the cameraman, was charged for at a pretty stiff rate.
>
> Conditions in this respect are different now and greatly in the exhibitor's favor. The makers of cameras and apparatus have foreseen his wants and there are now on the market a large number of moderate priced cameras which are simple of operation and yield dependable results.
>
> The value of the well produced local picture is recognized by all exhibitors . . . [and] we propose . . . to help the exhibitor make a success of the purely mechanical end, the successful photographing of the various events or scenes which he wishes to portray.[35]

The column's help came most often in the form of material knowledge and advice regarding technical issues such as raw stock selection, lens and shutter calibration, exposure effects, and "recipes" for negative and positive print developing including effects such as tinting and toning.[36] The column, as well as other industry-related texts from the period, urge exhibitors to put any misgivings aside about developing their own footage and to know that "it is by no means so difficult as it appears at first and the rudiments of the process may be grasped readily by a person of average intelligence."[37] Exhibitors were able to purchase the materials required for developing and printing their footage from motion picture supply houses that typically could be found in any city with a large regional film exchange business. In Pittsburgh, Calcium, Light and Film Company, among others, sold the necessary chemicals and various types of printing apparatus. An exhibitor could also build a film processing laboratory from scratch by fashioning the necessary trays, racks, and tanks out of "hard close-grained wood . . . obtained from almost any lumber yard or mill" and then following the detailed construction schematics found in various technical manuals.[38] Having built a lab, the processing formula for "negative reversing" offered by "The Camera" would have been particularly tempting for the exhibitor filmmaker because it eliminated the need and expense of separate positive print, allowing the exhibitor to project his camera original. Such cost-effective measures were particularly useful in the production of local views, which were typically shown for a very short time in a single theater and required of the exhibitor a considerable financial commitment. Pre-made reversal film stock would become a commercial mainstay of amateur 16mm- and 8mm-gauge film production beginning in the 1920s. The column's author, however, designates his exhibitor readers as "professional" and, having once described the reversal process, warns against the technique's use, fretting that with the added savings the exhibitor might "start exposing film promiscuously on subjects of no consequence."[39] Although the column exhibited a belief in the competence and professionalism of the exhibitor-filmmaker throughout its five-year run, it is also clear that its author worried about an exhibitor's troubling potential to produce too much or the wrong kind of film. From the outset, the column's author cautions the exhibitor to focus solely on nonfiction local subjects and not get "the idea that he can lay out a feature or single-reel drama or comedy with an hope of its having a commercial value."[40] This threat of failure, if the local filmmaker attempts to replicate studio activities and products, discursively functions to both locate and contain the exhibitor at the bottom of the moving picture hierarchy. While the column regularly discourages the exhibitor from producing fiction content for their screens—something that Dan Streible has found that least some local filmmakers appear to have ignored—it is much more ambivalent, and occasionally even enthusiastic, about the exhibitors' potential to create footage of "value" as a subject for a national newsreel.[41]

Even as the multi-reel feature film proliferated and began to dominate American movie culture in the mid-1910s, the nonfiction short film endured and even flourished in the form of the national weekly newsreel. By the end of the silent era, this genre was produced or distributed by more than six different sources and had taken up a standardized position in the exhibition program, typically as a prelude to a longer program or feature film. One of the principal grounds "The Camera" writers offered for the local view's popular success was "the public's love for illustrated news, like that provided by the national newsreel."[42] Mass-produced newsreels were distributed weekly or biweekly and so constantly required fresh subjects and news every week. Because competition was stiff between the various newsreel companies, and because "newsworthy" events rarely happened on schedule in a particular place, the editors of the various national newsreels, in part, relied on unsolicited footage provided by hundreds of freelance cameramen working across the country. Many of these cameramen belonged to the recent profession of the motion picture newshound, dashing off with their camera to scoop other "stringers" for the payoff of, in 1916, "sixty cents to one dollar a foot." Exhibitors who made movies could also seek this remuneration, as "The Camera" explained in at least one column—the exhibitor who already had made the investment in equipment for producing local views could "put himself in the way of making extra money by becoming a contributor to the Weekly news film."[43] But, at the same time, the column cautioned, the types of local subjects that were of the most interest in an exhibitor's own theater—parades, county fairs, fires, amateur sporting events—were of little "news value" and unlikely to be accepted and paid for by the national editors. Additionally, *Motion Picture News* warned exhibitors that local participants were "generally very self conscious before the camera" and such reflexive acknowledgement was "not favoured by editors of News Weeklies."[44] "The Camera" also suggested that the very formal structure of the local view, which depended on extradiegetic knowledge for viewer comprehension—images that insisted local knowledge of local people, places, and events—was largely unfathomable to an outside audience.

Silveus's Cinema of Recognition

Silveus's films, for a viewer removed from the community—whether by geography or time—are typically indexical. In one extended sequence within the Waynesburg films, we are presented with three sets of images: first, a parade of townspeople, many bearing banners which include the phrase "W over G"; then the same people waving and laughing in the background as a young man with a megaphone moves toward and into the extreme foreground, engaging the cameraman and his lens with an antic smile; and, finally, multiple shots of other young men participating in an athletic event involving an oval-shaped ball. Although an outside viewer versed in American culture can easily "read" this film as representing various aspects of a football game, the footage alone affords little contextual information signifying the events' specificities, potential meanings, or values. Silveus's local, contemporary audience would have produced a much richer context, seeing: a parade in celebration of the 1921 victory by the Waynesburg (W) high school football team over the town's nearby perennial rival, "Greensburg" (G); the high school's head "yell leader" (whose name we do not know but whose name would have been known to the film's original audience) taking delight in Silveus's attention; and highlights from the game itself, including the winning touchdown in the final minute of the game by the team's star player (name also unknown).[45]

The young male cheerleader's self-produced and self-aware close-up can be understood to represent the local view and its multiplicity of visions. Here, unlike other commercial cinematic forms, the boy's look is not simply a gaze of anonymous acknowledgment to an unknown and unseen audience, but rather a look of receptive recognition. This look creates a cinema of recognition, as the gaze is not projected outward toward a disembodied spectator, but inward to a known and very corporeal audience. The young cheerleader looks at Silveus and his camera and, understanding both their roles within the community, recognizes that his look will soon be received and returned by a theater filled with his friends, his family, and most likely, even himself. Silveus's films, like other local films, are structured around these kinds of knowing looks that rely upon the immediate sensation of recognition for their pleasures and comprehension. With local films, where the text ends and the context begins is impossible to say.

Counter to this open diegesis, spread across the moments and spaces of production and exhibition, the authors of "The Camera" offer, "it is easy to define a good [national] news film subject. Such a subject is one which tells its own story and does not need a lot of lengthy explanatory titles to 'get itself over.'"[46] In its definition of a film "which tells its own story," the successful newsreel subject required the exhibitor to work within a formal system of aesthetics and meaning production that appears dialogically opposed to the existing Waynesburg films.

Collectively, Silveus's films can best be described as providing the pleasures of a "quotidian spectacle." That is, he produced and presented images displaying the familiar and the well known but that through their cinematic form and presentation could both fascinate and please his local audience. In describing this "quotidian spectacle," I am invoking, or rather opposing, Tom Gunning's pivotal "attractions" model that provided earlier audiences with "an exciting spectacle."[47] Like the films of the 1890s and early 1900s that Gunning situates within a "cinema of attractions," Silveus's movies engage in a visual poetics of display whose viewing logic does not depend upon a cohesive diegetic narrative. While it is apparent that Silveus took care in composing his images and choosing his shots, it is also clear from the repeated acknowledgment of the camera and cameraman by his subjects that this genre of local filmmaking, or at least this cameraman's interpretation of it, does not require an effacement of the camera's presence for its representational power. Although Gunning initially marked the dominant dissipation of this type of exhibitionist cinema around 1906, more recently his work that specifically focuses on nonfiction films has led him to extend its prevalence into and beyond the 1910s. While Gunning does not specifically refer to the production or exhibition of local films, he writes of an overarching "view" aesthetic as the "[ur]form of early nonfiction film" characterized by the way such films "mime the act of looking and observing." Gunning's definitional observation of the "view" is, for lack of a better term, a global one, in which the "camera literally acts as a tourist," providing the audience with a "surrogate" vision of spaces and places that they could otherwise not see for themselves.[48] That is, the excitement of the "exciting spectacle" in the generic form of the (non-local) view is in large part predicated upon seeing something new and unknown, something to which direct optic access is difficult or impossible. Whether travelogue, ethnography, industrial film, or even a national newsreel, the filmmaker's assumption is that the spectator is seeing a film made somewhere else about someone or something else.

The "local view," however, provides visual evidence of the easily and already accessible. The gratification and power of these films was derived, at least in part, from the pleasures of looking at the familiar in an unfamiliar way. In contrast to a wider cinema's representational and voyeuristic depictions of the exotic, the fantastic, or the foreign, the local view's visual impulse is exhibitionist, its appeal the prosaic and the quotidian. Additionally, the register of looks and gazes associated with the practice of these films is multivalent and diachronic, pointing to the ways in which the term "local view" is not fixed by a single relationship or moment. In these views, who is viewing whom? Local views have the potential to be experiential—to promote the activity of looking—for their consumers both at the site of exhibition *and* production. The Waynesburg films are Charlie Silveus's local views, but Silveus is rarely alone. Much of what he portrays in his films, at least in those that survive, are images of local people responding to, looking at, and interacting with Silveus himself. The townspeople greet his appearance: women shyly smile, men politely doff their hats, children energetically wave. His presence is marked time and again by locals looking directly at him as he looks at them, turning the crank and exposing the film. Of course, on-screen we never see Silveus at work. Typically, in mapping out the visual geography of a look toward the camera, historians and theorists analytically bypass the cameraman and head directly to the image and/or its audience. Film scholars habitually disembody the apparatus and its "taking" lens from its human operator when discussing the evolution of filmmaking in the silent era (or any era for that matter). We write of "acknowledgement of the camera's presence" and of a "world presented to the camera, and therefore to the spectator" but almost nothing to historicize or theorize the real dynamics of presentation and representation, of performer and filmmaker, that occurs at the site of production.[49] For the local view, reimagining this peopled locus is a definitional imperative.

Such films (and their filmmakers) actively engage in producing localness as much as they reflect it. Their work involves defining both the core and boundaries of what local is and is not. Localness, as I view it, is primarily comparative and contextual rather than scalar or spatial. It is a complex phenomenological quality based more on human actions than natural endowments. It is a function of a sense of social immediacy and the relativity of the environment. Who makes the local view matters. Issues of identity and authorship cannot be separated from the relationship between the filmmaker and those who are filmed. The production of localness is, in no small part, a function of the film, which helps to define not just the subject but the producer as well. Whether a local film is produced by a person who comes to town or who lives in town makes a difference, although how such differences might play out formally within the films is difficult to explicate. The ways in which people perform, what images are chosen, and how shots are composed are all complex actions informed by the local phenomenology of the film's participants on both sides of the camera.

One of the prevailing modes of local view performance is the display of organized and ritualized communal assemblage. Images of the community, and its friends and neighbors as they march down Main Street, play on the team, dance at the fair, don their new stiff bonnets, wave their proud pennants, and show off their fattened livestock all function to visibly reinforce the *Gemeinschaft* resulting from such collective cultural experiences. The anthropologist Clifford Geertz, refers to these types of formalized community gatherings as the "stories a people tell about themselves."[50] The films of these events work to represent and reaffirm a common social identity, and the narrativity of the live event is shaped and intensified through cinema's formal aspects of both production *and* exhibition.

Silveus's surviving footage evidences a dominant story of the Great War and its effect on Waynesburg's populace. He returned to the subject again and again over a three-year period from 1917 to 1919. As a main protagonist in his patriotic narrative, Silveus chose the men of Company K of the Tenth Infantry Regiment, a National Guard unit headquartered in Waynesburg. Shortly after President Wilson declared war on April 2, 1917, the company of 150 was activated by the federal government, and many of the town's young men began practicing maneuvers in the park in preparation for more extensive training at Camp Hancock, Georgia.[51] Filming one of these sessions, Silveus located his camera at the far end of the grassy park and as the soldiers (armed primarily only with broom poles) advanced in waves toward his lens, he provided his local viewers with a display most likely designed to foreground the men's military prowess and their use of modern war tactics.[52] In watching the footage, however, it is also difficult to ignore how the camera's perspective—"shot" from the "enemy position"— made visible to the Eclipse's audience how exposed and vulnerable Waynesburg's husbands, brothers, and sons would soon find themselves.

A few days prior to their initial departure from town, Silveus again filmed the men of Company K, this time being entertained at a reception and garden party held on the porch and lawn of Mrs. T. J. Wisecarver. Mrs. Wisecarver was the queen bee in the town's small hive of social elite because her husband, who owned major assets in the local gas and coal industries, was assumed to be the richest man in town. According to the local paper, an invitation to her exclusive home at the outskirts of town was considered a "rare and honored" privilege. Silveus's footage of the event includes images of the women of the local suffrage association dining al fresco in the garden, and a shot of Walter C. Montgomery, the captain of the unit, standing with Mrs. Wisecarver and Mrs. Robinson F. Downey, whose "French houseguest, Mlle. D'Aspe, greeted the soldiers on behalf of France" with a rousing version of "La Marseillaise."[53] The most significant image in the sequence, and one of the longest shots of all of Silveus's extant footage, is a procession of the entire company as they rather stiffly descend a set of garden steps with plates of food balanced carefully in their uniformed arms. The camera located at the bottom of the steps and angled slightly up is positioned in such a way that the men appear as one long continuous body while still allowing each soldier a moment of compositional dominance before moving out of the frame. The shot, over two minutes in length, would have provided those sitting and watching in the Eclipse a week later with a cinematic roll call and record of the town's communal patriotism—Mrs. Wisecarver's slices of cake marking the uniformed men's newfound status.

On the afternoon of September 7, 1917, Silveus set up his camera adjacent to the railroad station, framing the thousands of local well-wishers who came out to see this first group of soldiers off as they marched from their armory to the train. The shot is well composed and gives the viewer a good sense of both movement and depth within the frame and appears to follow the compositional advice of "The Camera" in regard to filming this type of event: "It should be borne in mind that people marching . . . should never be photographed directly in front of the camera at right angles . . . Processions in motion should be photographed coming towards the camera and passing off to the side of the view."[54] Silveus's footage of this event presents its viewers with a true parade—the mustering of a military body. The young men marching in crisp formation were not alone, however. Preceding them on this ritualized walk through town were additional "regiments" consisting of all the children from the local public schools who had been given the day off to participate in the event. The group of youngsters, each carrying a small American flag, moves down the street in a loose arrangement of two single-file rows.[55]

The parade, a particularly American ceremonial phenomenon, presents a form of cultural performance that, in its structure and type of participants, works to spell out a common social identity or purpose.[56] Here, the community, having come out into the streets to cheer on a procession of their flag-waving children and proud, if slightly more solemn, gun-toting soldiers, communicates public appreciation for the patriotic service by the town's young men. Silveus's images of this parade, shot from the top of a slight rise so as to look down on its participants and into the receding distance, also potentially presents the viewer with an overlapping or parallel narrative of sacrifice and impending loss. The children and their star-spangled banners at once reflect the youthful nature of those leaving to fight and signify a set of values—material and ideological—which the community deems worth exchanging for such potential risk. The following week, Silveus advertised in the town's newspaper the premiere of his resulting parade footage.[57]

Not all of Silveus's local films focus on such potentially dramatic events. Many of his films reveal the economic structures of the community, with local pictures of commerce, labor, and industry providing his audiences with images of the places where they bought their food, sold their goods, earned their pay. Unlike other local films, this footage was often subsidized or fully paid for by the owners whose businesses and factories were made the centers of attention. In essence, these were advertisements. To varying degrees, this subset of the local genre was an attempt by exhibitors to utilize their screens, and captive audiences, as a new, potentially lucrative, revenue stream. Exhibitors were not alone in this capital venture, as historian Janet Staiger has pointed out. Many of the large film manufacturers in this period actively sought to promote their medium to the consumer product industries as the newest and most effective promotional device for reaching a national customer base.[58] The local version of these promotions was aimed at a much narrower and more specific audience. At least some local newspapers expressed concern, however, that this modern promotional medium would seriously impact the revenue of their more traditional advertising avenues, as an editor from Chippewa Falls, Wisconsin, makes clear in his direct appeal to the town's businessmen: "[The exhibitor] hands you out a lot of strong talk and is positive that he can increase your business. Just how he can do this by throwing a moving picture on the screen in a local playhouse, the said picture showing a combination of letters making the man and his business and a few other frills, is hard to determine. He would show this picture at a night when your business is closed and by the next day the people who have seen have forgotten it."[59] Not all newspapers were apparently so threatened by what was ordinarily an infrequent practice by most movie theater exhibitors. The rhetoric of the *Waynesburg Republican* editors appears to support Silveus's production of local views —of course, Silveus advertised regularly in the newspaper. Moreover, until the early 1920s, Waynesburg's newspaper did not use any photography in its reporting of the week's events. For a small-town paper, this absence is not all that surprising; newspaper photography was a relatively new technology, first utilized by mass circulating dailies in New York City during the Spanish War, and did not become a regular feature of most newspapers in major cities until the early 1910s.[60] Because of this pictorial lack, Silveus's moving images of local happenings did not regularly compete with the paper's own. In at least some cases, in fact, these films provided the community with the primary visual record of an event. Even when the *Republican* began to publish photographs, Silveus's films were not exhibited on the kind of regular schedule that caused his local views to supplant the informational role of the newspaper.

If some exhibitors hoped that the production of local business views would allow them to steal advertising revenue away from the newspapers, they often found, to their disappointment, that their commercial work was unappreciated by their audiences. How, when, and why consumers are willing to have commercial messages inserted into their lives was, and remains, a conundrum for advertisers, and audiences in the 1910s and 1920s were no more appreciative of on-screen commercials than we are today. In *Picture Theatre Advertising*, Sargent warned exhibitors of the potential dangers involved in taking advantage of their patrons in just such a manner: "would you like it if your barber should suddenly leave you with your face unshaved while he stopped to tell you the price of Schmidt's meat, or sing the praises of Denton's shoes and Hummer's sugar? You rather expect to be asked to purchase a bottle of hair tonic and be told that your hair needs cutting, but that is about all you will permit. The two situations are precisely the same. You have patrons at your mercy and you take advantage of their helplessness. In time they are bound to resent it."[61]

With their power base shrinking within the industry and during a period of intense competition for people to regularly fill their theaters, exhibitors were extremely wary of displeasing their patrons; but the role of producer and the ensuing potential for profit (and associated power) proved too enticing for many. The result for this subgenre is that many local filmmakers attempted to hide or conceal the film's central commercial purpose by subtly (or not so subtly) integrating images of businesses and their wares into a type of early city symphony. These so-called "town pictures" included shots of the citizens of the community, their schools and children, their famous (or not so famous) landmarks, *and* the commercial districts and individual establishments of the town or neighborhood. E. A. Wheeler offered, in an interview with the *Pittsburgh Moving Picture Bulletin*, to produce these promotional local views for the city's theater owners who, according to the editors, could not help but find "the proposition interesting ... in the way of price, [as] veiled advertisements of local merchants will be inserted."[62] A theater owner in Marquette, Indiana, merited a short article in the *Moving Picture World* of 1915 when he came up with a pleasing way to blend this kind of promotion into a "novel" multimedia event for his theater called "Marquette in Pioneer Days and Today." The show integrated lantern slides representing the "historic past" and motion pictures of "the Progressive little city of the present," including prominent views of its businesses.[63] Most of the trade papers supported such commercial possibilities for the exhibitor if he was creative and clever in the ways he "inserted" paid images, and the *Bulletin* repeatedly provided examples of Pittsburgh-area businesses that were eager to participate in such cooperative enterprises: "Even the Chinese laundryman in the town [of Ambridge] grabbed the opportunity of securing an ad in this way, and was downhearted when he was told the pictures could not be made on the inside of his place of business. His ready wit was equal to the emergency, however, and he brought his tub on to the sidewalk and commenced washing for dear life while the photographer turned the crank taking it all in."[64]

In a city the size of Pittsburgh, some exhibitors did produce their own footage, but many instead turned to freelance cameramen. This group of professional cameramen included E. A. Wheeler as well as George Bates Jr., whose Pittsburgh Commercial Motion Picture Company was active in Western Pennsylvania at least through 1923. Bates had been professionally trained in New York City, and was successful in making his living shooting views for local theater owners, industry, and private citizens. He often photographed the city's society weddings for both private and public exhibition. The owners of the Colonial Theatre in nearby Wilkinsburg hired Bates to produce a "fine series of moving picture views," consisting of one thousand feet of footage of the town's schools, homes, and businesses, "making for a film of exceptional interest which will be viewed by practically everybody."[65]

In Waynesburg, Charlie Silveus produced and exhibited these local business-centric views. In one short film, from the mid-1910s, Silveus creates a multiple-shot sequence in which a group of townspeople erect an elaborate birdhouse on a high pole in front of the Waynesburg train station.[66] The birdhouse—as another shot makes clear via a sign painted on the side of a lumber truck—was built with wood donated from the town's paper mill and constructed by the Jacobs Bird-House Company. A local business owned by J. Warren Jacobs, the company held the distinction of the world's largest manufacturer of homes for purple martins. Silveus was also not above using local views, in a variety of ways, to promote his own place of business. In the summer of 1921, he engaged in a major remodeling project for the Eclipse, spending approximately twenty-five thousand dollars on construction to increase seating to 650 and enlarge the size of the theater's lobby. In early September, at the celebration of its completion, Silveus exhibited an extended sequence of workers mixing concrete and building the theater's new walls.[67] In another form of self-promotion, Silveus turned the camera on himself, or rather on his theater. The short section of surviving footage was taken directly outside the Eclipse at the end of a performance. As his patrons leave the theater they look and wave to the camera and to Silveus, its operator. From their knowing glances, it is apparent that the patrons knew that their exit was to be captured on film. A well-used form of cinematic ballyhoo, the stunt was designed to draw a crowd to the theater not once but twice, as Silveus would have heavily promoted the next day's show as a chance for the audience who had just left the Eclipse to see themselves on screen.

Less frivolous in their construction of community are the local views of disaster and misfortune that offered their audiences a visual record of things destroyed or taken from the community by nature or man. In the first week of January 1914, the manager of the Elite Theatre in Homestead, Pennsylvania, across the Monongahela River from Pittsburgh, was "drawing a big house" with a reel that George Bates had recently shot and which the local press had dubbed "The Terrible Murder Pictures." The murder referred to by the newspaper was actually a triple homicide committed by a local steelworker, Henry Rokoski. Rokoski's affections had recently been spurned by a young woman, Stella Yakabik, and he went into a murderous rage, killing his previous girlfriend, Ignatz Bankoski, a local constable, Martin Windt, who attempted to stop Henry on his way to Stella's home, and Stella's mother, Estella, whom Rokoski killed after "she had placed Stella and her sister, Josephine in the cellar and thus sacrificed her life in the protection of her children." The murders occurred in late December but they remained newsworthy because the killer was still at large and sending taunting postcards to the local police declaring, "You can't catch me." According to the local newspaper, the theater's manager exhibited footage that included: "Views of the two houses in which the tragedy took place . . . along with the pictures of the three victims and their youthful slayer. The point where officer Windt fell, the point where the young man's sweetheart fell, the spot where Mrs. Rokoski was killed by the train and other interesting views in connection with the murder will be shown."[68] Unable, and/or unwilling, to actually photograph images of these bloody corporeal acts, Bates instead produced a landscape of death, cinematically drawing a visual map of misfortune that could be best read by a local audience who lived their everyday lives within its now tainted geography. Murder was a rather extreme and rare topic for a local view, and can be seen as a marker of the ways in which the urban form of the local may have allowed for a more visceral and voyeuristic presentation. More typical footage displayed collapsed bridges, the results of industrial accidents, and the popular category of "wrecks," which encompassed post-collision images of all manner of vehicles, including the crashed remains of trolley cars and large livestock.[69]

The popular reception of this type of local disaster films is difficult to gauge. There is, beyond a recording of loss, an obvious potential for morbid spectacle, a kind of tabloid voyeurism that can be ahistorically attributed to such images. We might assume that these films, with their potential for melodramatic excess and shock, most clearly competed with studio-manufactured narratives for audiences' attention. But there is little evidence that local views of disaster and misfortune were promoted any differently than those of the summer fair or the big football game. Although Silveus's surviving footage does not contain images related to murder or even traffic accidents, the most formally dramatic of his views belong to this disconsolate subgenre.

Waynesburg, on a major tributary of the Monongahela River, was prone to flooding, particularly in the spring when ice melt and runoff in the higher elevations often caused the area's rivers to overflow their banks. Using long, slow pans of the camera, the footage shot by Silveus of one of these floods in the late 1910s incorporates individuals or groups of local people in the foreground, providing a human scale through which the viewers could more fully grasp the enormity of their community underwater. This conventional framing technique—the creation of a frame within the frame—emphasizes the spectacular nature of the event and is compositionally designed to drive the viewer's gaze "deeper" into the image. Silveus's frame uses the people of the community standing on embankments, bridges, or even in boats, watching the high water flow slowly past. The local view somewhat complicates the formal tendencies of such a framing device, because the people gazing out into the waters from within the frame were either known to, or the same as, the people later gazing at this image from their seats in the theater. The strong potential for visual recognition—

"Hey that's me standing on the railroad trestle!"—could cause viewers to oscillate between a more absorbed mode of reception, triggered by the framing device and the images' powerful illusionistic realism, and a more frenetic set of looks both toward and within the frame, but also inside the theater itself—"Hey that's George sitting on the bridge, and he's also sitting three rows in front of me!" As was not unusual with many of these local films, the audience viewing the flood from the confines of the Eclipse often found itself watching itself watching.

Silveus incorporated similarly wide-angled compositions, again framed by local citizenry, in his footage of the aftermath of the "greatest disaster which has ever occurred in the history of Greene County."[70] Specifically, the disaster was an explosion, in spring 1917, which killed six local men at a natural gas compressing station in the town of Brave, just outside of Waynesburg. Like the Homestead murder footage, Silveus's imagery of this catastrophe was designed for local consumption. For a viewer located outside of the community's boundaries, it would be difficult to grasp exactly what is being represented by the image of people looking out into the distance at a rural industrial landscape punctuated only by a gray wisp of smoke. The footage alone provides little contextual visual information regarding the catastrophe that warranted the making of the film. The fact that there is no shot or sequence that signifies the death and misfortune involved in this event was of little consequence for the local view's overall system of experiential meaning. Because the film was made specifically for those viewers whose body of (local) knowledge precedes this footage, such seemingly unreadable images allowed Silveus's audience in the Eclipse to clearly comprehend the tragic signification of this dark plume upon their landscape.

By this point in time, the apparent lack of need or desire on Silveus's part to produce a film that is diegetically self-enclosed is striking. Against the dominant backdrop of fictional studio cinema and its set of formal strategies and conventions that characterize classical filmmaking, Silveus's local views may appear outmoded and primitive. Silveus's seeming unwillingness to render his local views easily comprehensible to outsiders may partially be a function of the fragile nature of cinema's object. The fragments of footage that survive are from the original nitrate negative, which leaves questions regarding a number of ways in which he may have manipulated his films for wider comprehension and increased narrativity. Because there are no surviving prints, the final form in which Silveus actually presented his films is difficult to fully ascertain, particularly how much and what kinds of editing he might have done for each sequence he shot and presented. There remain, in the extant footage, a few "scenes" that appear to utilize "classical" editing patterns—typically a sequence of two or three shots that "match" continuous action from longer to closer shots. However, the vast majority of the footage is uncut and flash frames are visible at the start-up of almost every shot. Whether Silveus may have edited the print, rather than the negative, is unfortunately impossible to establish.[71]

The other viable cinematic device Silveus might have employed to increase diegetic clarity is expositional intertitles. According to Charlie Keil, titling used to summarize on-screen action began as early as 1903 and by the late 1910s had developed into a routine but sophisticated narrational aid for fiction filmmakers.[72] At least one trade manual author felt that titles were crucial because without them, even "[t]he most intelligent audience would fail to get the significance of an author's intention."[73] Nonfiction filmmakers, particularly newsreel manufacturers, also commonly incorporated expository titles into their footage, and most independent laboratories offered titling services to their customers. Because titling is ordinarily completed in the printing stage of the process, there are no titles attached to any of Silveus's surviving negatives. There is no way of knowing if, or how often, he felt the need to create titles for his local views. But unlike films made elsewhere in this period, this local genre had a distinct advantage that may have precluded the need for intertitles, in that direct authorial exposition could be introduced not just as written text on the screen but as words spoken in the theater.

The lecturing showman/exhibitor is a figure associated with cinema's earliest beginnings when movie exhibition, according to Hansen, "still claimed the singularity of a *live performance*." The exhibitor, as lecturer, provided his patrons with an interpretive aid, but, more importantly, his work within the space of the theater also maintained the traditional performative aspects of live entertainment. According to the standard historiography, the lecturer largely disappeared by the early 1910s because: "By definition the lecturer eluded the methods of mass distribution because his success depended upon interaction with local and particular audiences—upon rhetorical skills and personal involvement, upon professional experience and familiarity with the situation of reception."[74] This performative model, which relies on the lecturer's indigenous knowledge for its success, is perfectly matched in its needs by the local view genre. The local view provides strong cinematic evidence of the lasting "personal involvement" of the exhibitor. It is not hard to imagine that Silveus and other exhibitors continued to interact audibly with their audiences and their screens through the exhibition of their local views.

Not all of the local views related to the disaster subgenre required the interpretive or performative skills of the exhibitor. The most common calamity that Silveus found worthy of filming was fire—the bigger the better. Besides the men of Company K, the Waynesburg footage is most heavily weighted toward images of local buildings on fire and their sooty aftermath. In one particular day-after sequence, Silveus uses camera movement to create a visual surprise for his audience. Slowly panning along a facade of intact and apparently unharmed buildings, the frame remains continuously filled with local businesses until the camera comes to rest on a large gap consisting of sky and billowing black smoke, revealing through its absence the destruction of the town's bakery.[75] Scenes of huge conflagrations, flames jumping high into the sky, or shots of the smoldering husks of previously well-known structures provided moviegoers with an efficient late-model cinema of attractions through the footage's ability to "incite visual curiosity" and to "supply pleasure through an exciting spectacle."[76]

Films of fire and the men who fight them constitute a popular genre of early American cinema, one that includes both nonfiction and fictional examples. The genre provided its audience with aspects of both spectacle and melodrama and effectively tapped into the privileged position given to the firefighting occupation in American culture. Promotional material from the most well-known film belonging to this early genre, Edwin S. Porter's *Life of an American Fireman* (1903), highlighted the fireman's culture of risk and made the resulting heroism a feature of national identity: "The record work of the modern American fire department is known throughout the universe, and the fame of the American fireman is echoed around the entire world. He is known to be the most expert, as well as the bravest, of all fire fighters. This film faithfully and accurately depicts his thrilling and dangerous life, emphasizing the perils he subjects himself to when human life is at stake."[77] Although local view footage of firefighting may not have provided the melodramatic pleasures afforded by a film like *American Fireman*, neither did it need such hyperbolic discourse to promote its verisimilitude to the actual disaster. When an exhibitor like Silveus photographed such an event, the building was really on fire, and so these local views did not always have the luxury of the happy ending typically found in the fictional films of this genre.

One of the unhappiest endings for Silveus's films of local fires occurred in 1925 when the town's primary hotel, The Downey House, burned to the ground. In the ensuing blaze, which occurred late at night, six of the town's firemen died attempting to put out the flames and rescue the hotel's unknown number of paying guests. There is one short piece of surviving footage that is assumed to have been taken the night of this fire; it shows the silhouette of a large building engulfed in flames. Most of Silveus's footage of this tragedy, though, was taken the next day, as the town's citizens came out in force to see the damage and mourn their collective losses. These deaths had a major impact on the town, not just because firemen were culturally marked as "heroic," but because these men in many ways represented the community, at least in its public and masculine manifestations. The Waynesburg firefighters, who were largely untrained volunteers belonged to a fraternal and occupational institution with a long American tradition of mutual interest and civil obligation.[78] The firemen and their firehouse, here as elsewhere, functioned (and often still function) for the small town as a central institution for its social and political life.

Not a Newsreel

From the standpoint of the trade journals, the local view of the early twentieth century was a kind of provincially circumscribed newsreel. In its general aesthetics of display, its lack of concern or apparent need for diegetic closure, and its degree of revealed self-awareness on the part of its participants, manifested most commonly by the subjects' direct look at the camera and cameraman, however, Silveus's films share an overriding mode of recognition with another indigenously defined genre, the home movie. Amateur filmmaking was possible in the early 1900s but became a wider cultural and discursive presence in the late 1920s, (perhaps not coincidentally) just as Silveus's career as a cameraman was winding down. These two genres share characteristics of both form and function, both production and reception, by concerning themselves with a purposeful limited array of participants who each have the capacity to be cameraman and exhibitor, actor and audience.

Silveus's camerawork is, overall, technically informed; almost without exception, the surviving films show consistent exposure and sharp focus. But in their everyday images filtered through a stylistic vocabulary of flash frames, sequences edited within camera, rough or jerky camera moves, repeated panning motifs, and the occasional unbalanced compositions, these films present a strong visual affinity with the home movie and its "amateur" aesthetic. This lack of adherence to classically-derived stylistic norms and conventions should not immediately be dismissed for what Patricia Zimmerman has described in another context as "naiveté regarding visual coding and literacy."[79] Silveus, a man who spent his life at the movies and whose economic existence largely depended on it, was aware of the aesthetic paradigms of the studio-manufactured film that daily appeared on his theater's screen. Yet his own images consistently refuse this more formal agenda. In the production of the Waynesburg films, Silveus mounted his camera on a geared-tripod head that, when panned left or right, produced a distinct ratcheting effect, a kind of ongoing visual stutter. Although one might expect Silveus to limit such awkward movement, or purchase a new, smoother-acting mechanism, he instead frequently incorporated lengthy pans into his local sequences and remained faithful to the hiccupping device for his entire career as a cameraman.

Although Silveus was clearly not attempting to replicate studio-manufactured films in either mode or method, he typically programmed his work in tandem with the much more seamless narrative offerings of the industry's fiction filmmakers. Sometimes his films were presented as the "feature" offering of the program (typically with a comedy short playing before the local view), and sometimes in the secondary, lead-in position, with a longer studio feature to follow. Silveus's local audiences were apparently willing to put up with, or perhaps even to take pleasure in, the formal differences visible between his singular style and the systemic orderliness of the studios' products. In part, local views, like home movies, escaped the stylistic evolution required of studio-manufactured films because the cooperative framework of the local view produced an aesthetic hierarchy in which *how* something is shown is secondary to what and why something is shown.

Obviously, the differences between these more homespun genres and the studio-based narratives go beyond temperamental equipment. The self-contained analysis so common to our readings of fiction film cannot begin to acknowledge the full experience of either the local film or the home movie, as these are defined by their social situations and depend upon a high level of viewer recognition for a pleasurable effect. In most cases, elaborate foreknowledge is required for the richest viewing experience, and sometimes simply for basic comprehension. This is because the local view, like the home movie, provides its audience with an extremely open text. The structure shaped by the community and its history, not simply by the images on the screen.

Silveus's local views established parallel relationships, bonding filmmaker to participant and exhibitor to audience. These films, in both their production and exhibition, worked to produce localness by establishing, reestablishing, and reifying the relationships between the people, places, and things of a community. There is currently little sense of the range of reception practices available for audiences watching local views in a period in which the feature film emerged as the classical paradigm. According to Shelley Stamp, as the "prolonged story became the single focus ... patrons were encouraged to sit through an entire show without talking or disturbing others ... [and] interaction among patrons within the theater space was discouraged in favor of viewers' solitary, voyeuristic engagement with illusory cinematic space."[80] If we were to attempt to imagine an approximate model of reception for the local view by borrowing from our own experiences with home movies, it is difficult to imagine the possibility or desire, on the part of exhibitor or audience, for such singular, silent absorption. Instead, using the home movie as a beau ideal for the local view's performative potential—in its tendency to provoke exhibitor commentary ("Here we are at Mt. Rushmore last summer, remember how scared you were of Teddy Roosevelt?") and its power to trigger voiced recall and response on the part of the audience ("Hey look at Mom's funny hair!")—we find a theater atmosphere much more vocal and "alive" than the normative model or the discursive construction of a behavioral ideal in this period assumes.[81]

As much as local views and home movies are related, what ultimately makes the local view matter to a history of cinema is their differences. Home movies are and almost always have been culturally, discursively, and ideologically marginalized by their amateur status and by their location within the private, limited (and feminized) sphere of family and home. As Patricia Zimmerman has stated, "amateur film functions as a form of social control ... harnessing subjectivity, imagination, and spontaneity within the privatized contexts of leisure and family life."[82] Local views, however, announce themselves from within a shared public space and commercial arena and little or no rhetoric of the dilettante is attached to these films or their makers. One significant technological reason for this, at least in Silveus's particular case, is that he photographed and exhibited in 35mm, which not only availed the genre of large-gauge film's aesthetic potential, but also allowed it to remain squarely within the industrial structures of commercial production and exhibition.

Silveus's local views make visible a set of exhibition practices and communal behaviors that are primarily associated with the heterogeneity of cinema's early years, but that remained, and even thrived, in the 1910s, 1920s, and beyond. The local view provided exhibitors and audiences with a nonfiction cinema locally produced and socially specific, whose meanings were always dependent on local conditions and contingencies. The desire for this type of cinematic autonomy usually is visible to historians only as discursive traces of attempts to suppress or assimilate such alternative conditions.[83] By most theoretical accounts, the industrialization of cinema closed off or eliminated the necessary conditions for participation, interaction, and self-representation. Silveus's local views, however, required and produced a matrix of conditions in opposition to these assumptions.

Whether the local view genre became useful to exhibitors and audiences because of its differences to studio cinema, or in spite of them, the very fact that these films were regularly programmed alongside the studios' raises serious questions about how we should imagine the moviegoing experience in this era, whether in Waynesburg, Pittsburgh, or elsewhere. While the authors of "The Camera" felt that "local pictures have absolutely no value except in the town where they are taken," they represent for us a collective history of local cinema—histories of communities both real and imagined.

EPILOGUE

CHARLIE SILVEUS DIED IN 1957. His local films, however, remained—saved by his son, Charles Jr., who continued to run the family's restaurant in Waynesburg after his father's death. Charlie Jr. eventually grew old, retired, and, unlike his father, moved away from the town where he had been born and raised. In preparation for his departure, the son divided his possessions into those he would take and those he would discard. His father's reels of film would be left behind. Although Charlie Jr. had not followed his father into the movie business, he knew enough about the incendiary dangers of nitrate-based film not to simply throw the cans in the trash. Instead, on his way out of town, Charlie brought the film to the town's fire department to be safely destroyed. Perhaps because fireman are less afraid of spontaneous combustion than most of us, or perhaps because they are as curious as the rest of us, they decided to first look in the cans.

What they found, as we now know, were fifty-year old images of their own community, including those scenes of an earlier generation of local firefighters fighting local fires. Their pleasure in seeing this past meant that the films, rather than becoming smoke and fire, became history.[1]

This moment of history making, in both its smallness and its accidental beauty, is in many ways a symbol for the multiple histories of the men and women whose stories populate this book. Moving through time and space, traveling through circuits of exchange, the ephemeral traces of evidence that help us trace these lives can rapidly shift in value from meaningful to meaningless, from trash to history. Although some of these resulting histories, which collectively reveal Pittsburgh's relationship to the movies in this era, are more comprehensive than others, even the most detailed are necessarily incomplete: partial histories from a brief moment in time and place. Some, like Miss A. of the Independent Exchange or Harry Mintz of the Evaline, simply disappear from our collective purview and their role in film's historiography remains quite small. Others mentioned here, however, continued to make their mark in the movies both beyond Pittsburgh and beyond the chronological end of this book.

Richard A. Rowland, who at the young age of eighteen was forced by the death of his father to take over the family-run theatrical supply shop, is one such figure whose interest in and influence on the movies goes well beyond the scope of this purposefully local project. In 1910, when the Trust's General Film Corporation purchased his and James B. Clark's regional exchanges for millions of dollars, they found themselves wealthy and, briefly, out of the movie business. They subsequently used their considerable profits to open a small chain of theaters in Pittsburgh, including the Regent. Rowland also turned to making movies, starting Metro Pictures in late 1915. One of the early figures involved in the formation of the Hollywood studio system, Rowland soon departed Pittsburgh for New York and Los Angeles, leaving the management of the theaters to his older business partner, Clark. As the studio head of Metro, Rowland produced, among other films, the World War I drama *The Four Horses of the Apocalypse* (1921), best remembered today for the highly exoticized performance of a then largely unknown young actor, Rudolph Valentino. Movie mythology and later comments from Valentino himself directly attribute this casting decision and his subsequent stardom to Metro's powerful head screenwriter, June Mathis, who supposedly saw Valentino in a bit part in a film and, recognizing his potential, demanded that he be cast in the new feature she was writing. While this may be true, it is doubtful that Mathis had to do very much to convince Rowland to give Valentino a role, as two years prior Rowland had been the best man at Valentino's wedding to actress Jean Acker. Although this bit of Hollywood trivia is relatively unknown, Rowland *is* well remembered for a single line he is supposed to have spoken on hearing about the formation of United Artists in spring 1919. United Artists was organized as a joint venture that year by four of the leading figures in early Hollywood: Charles Chaplin, Douglas Fairbanks, Mary Pickford, and D. W. Griffith. Already hardened veterans of Hollywood, the four stars came together to form their own distribution company in order to better control their own work as well as their profits. Rowland's reaction to this piece of news was the unforgettable words, "The inmates are taking over the asylum." In 1920, after the success of *The Four Horses*, Rowland sold Metro, along with the previously purchased Goldwyn Picture Corporation, to another early exhibitor, Marcus Loew, who, like Rowland, had expanded his involvement in films into production. Four years later, Loew merged with Louis B. Mayer to form Metro-Goldwyn-Mayer, MGM, which became one of the dominant studios of Hollywood's golden age. Rowland also sold his share in the Pittsburgh theaters soon after leaving Metro, and continued for the next two decades to work as a producer for a number of studios, including Paramount and Fox. His last film, produced independently, was the melodrama *Cheers For Miss Bishop* (1941), distributed by United Artists. Rowland died in New York in 1947.

Not all of Pittsburgh's "big four" entertainment entrepreneurs left the steel city. Rowland's partner, Clark, stayed closer to home for much of his career, although he too broadened his motion picture interests to encompass production, both as the vice president of Rowland's Metro and as president of the Educational Film Corporation, a smaller independent studio that made and distributed short subjects and cartoons. Clark's primary business remained exhibition, and by the early 1920s, he owned almost two dozen movie theaters in Pittsburgh and across western Pennsylvania. In 1925, he sold them all to Harry Davis and became president of Davis Enterprises. The following year, Davis passed control of all of his moving picture and vaudeville theaters to the Stanley Company of America in return for three million dollars and places on the Stanley board for both Clark and himself. These theater mergers and consolidations were part of a rapidly transforming industry structured around fewer, more powerful companies, each vertically integrated with nationwide exhibition outlets. With the purchase of Davis Enterprises, Stanley Company operated 233 theaters across the Midwest and East Coast. The following year, Clark took his considerable profits and built a luxurious, twenty-three-story office building on prime real estate at the downtown corner of Liberty and Seventh avenues. With marble hallways, brass elevators, and a screening room, the building attracted filmmen from Pittsburgh and beyond, including Warner Brothers. whose regional offices occupied the skyscraper's penthouse suite. Clark died in 1942, but the "Clark Building," as it is still known, stands today, and recently sold to a real estate investor for more than twenty-two million dollars.

Harry Davis eloped in 1906, at the age of forty-five, to Edith Pichel, a Jewish-German immigrant who was, depending on the source, either seventeen or nineteen years old at the time of their unannounced wedding. According to national newspaper reports of the unexpected event, the Pittsburgh impresario had met Edith in nearby Crafton, where she "had lived a stone's throw from the home of Mr. Davis," who had "for many years" lived there in a house with his mother.[2] The couple eventually moved to an apartment in the Schenley Hotel in downtown Pittsburgh. In December 1926, less than a month after successfully arranging for the sale of his business to the Stanley chain, Davis suffered a massive stroke, which paralyzed most of his body. Largely immobile and unable to speak for the next thirteen years, he remained essentially confined to his hotel apartment, isolated from the swirl of city life that he helped create over the last three decades.

When Davis died in 1940, his widow received the bulk of his then considerable estate. The only other close family Davis had at the time of his death was his sister Eleanor, widow of his former protégé and partner, Senator John P. Harris.

Harris, was vice president of Harry Davis Enterprises and director of his own Harris Amusements when he was nominated in 1922 to fill an unexpired two-year term for the Forty-fifth District of the Pennsylvania State Senate.[3] Harris, a Republican, won the election easily and was reelected in 1924 for a full four-year term, having campaigned largely on strengthening election laws, which were (correctly) seen as favoring political bosses such as Penrose and his successor in the state senate, Max Leslie. Harris had by this time, much like his brother-in-law Davis, expanded his theatrical empire well beyond the city and established an independent chain of movie theaters and vaudeville houses throughout Michigan, Ohio, West Virginia, and Delaware. Harris and his wife had five children, three daughters, and two sons, and when Harris, at the age of fifty-five, unexpectedly died of a heart attack on the floor of the state senate in January 1926, his family continued to run and develop his entertainment company. In particular, John H. Harris, his twenty-eight-year-old son, "who had spent his vacation in the theatrical business ever since he was a young boy," succeeded his father as president and general manager of Harris Amusements.[4] But by 1930, following the general trend of industry consolidation, John H. had sold most of the family's Pittsburgh theaters to Warner Brothers and disposed of the affiliated Harris companies in Ohio and Michigan to another growing movie conglomerate, Radio-Keith-Orpheum, RKO. John H. Harris worked for a number years as Warner Brothers' regional manager, but he continued to personally invest and operate other local entertainment opportunities, including the Pittsburgh Hornets, an early team in the American Hockey League. In 1936, while running the team and managing the Duquesne Gardens where the team played, Harris hired Sonja Henie to skate for the Hornets' fans between periods. Like his father before him, John H. was a showman who recognized potential. He took the attractive Olympic skating champion and organized and promoted an entire show around her called the Ice Capades. Entertainment on ice became a multimillion dollar business for the Harrises, operating tours around the world for the next twenty years.

The son of John P. Harris and his extended family did not want to forget their father and his nickel beginnings in their home city, nor did they want the rest of Pittsburgh to forget. In August 1936, Harris wrote a letter to the editor of the city's largest daily paper, the *Pittsburgh Press*: "I wonder if you couldn't run a picture of my Father . . . sometime in September. I would like to have a nice photograph of my Father with some line about the creator of the Moving Picture Theatre here in Pittsburgh, etc. . . . I'm sure it would be appreciated by my family."[5] In the following month, a large photo of John P. Harris appeared in the *Press*, with text naming him the "creator" of the Nickelodeon. Harry Davis was not mentioned in the newspaper or on the bronze plaque placed on Smithfield Street by the local Historical Society, which bore a portrait of the late Senator Harris above the words: "This Tablet Marks the Site on Which the Hon. John P. Harris in June 1905 Opened The World's First Motion Picture Theatre The Nickelodeon This Was the Beginning Of The Motion Picture Theatre Industry."[6] What survives—a newspaper, a film, or a family—often determines what is remembered and what is forgotten. In only a few decades, the entwined histories of Harris and Davis had been divided.

If their stories eventually became separated, the two men belong to a much larger group of men that remains tied together by their inked existence in the pages of the *Pittsburgh Moving Picture Bulletin*. The *Bulletin*'s historical survival into the present day was much more purposeful than Charlie Silveus's films, and, like John Harris's place in history, was a result at some level of the desire for familial legacy. Sometime in the 1960s, twelve bound volumes of the *Bulletin* were donated to the library of the Western Pennsylvania Historical Society by Stanley D. Mayer, a relative of the two Mayer brothers. But even this record is incomplete, for the last volume to be found on the shelves of the history center's library ends in December 1924, more than four years before the Mayers ceased all publication of the *Bulletin* in 1929. According to William Mayer, the journal's run ended in early 1929 because by that time the "gold mine [had] petered out, resulting from the big combinations of film producers and theaters. Sad to say, there was no more need for the *Bulletin*. The field was gone, there wasn't any field any more. Just one phase of 'big business.'"[7] Why the remaining five years of the *Bulletin* are absent from the archive remains unknown; perhaps the Mayers got tired of annually binding the journal's thinning pages, or maybe in the shadowy gloom of the print shop's basement, Stanley simply missed the boxes containing those additional years when he went to gather them for donation. We know, however, that those issues existed, because sitting on my desk is a single copy of the *Bulletin* from August 1928, eleven brittle pages found in a pile of old *Life* magazines some years ago by a friend in a local junk shop. Half the length of its well-archived predecessors, its dwindling content largely reveals the truth of William Mayer's assertion: the movies had become big business, and most of that business was run by people and corporations headquartered far from Pittsburgh. The 1928 advertisements promote the new "trend" in "synchronized pictures . . . movies with music, sound effects and dialogue," and its articles mention names mostly unfamiliar to readers of the first decade of the *Bulletin*. But not everyone we know had disappeared. George Callahan, Jack's grandfather, with whose story this book began, merits one last mention in the *Bulletin's* thinning pages. Callahan it seems, had recently "augmented his fleet of automobile trucks by the edition of four Sterlings . . . bringing his total fleet in service to thirty-seven which [collectively] travel 3,000 miles seven days a week." The Mayers were already nostalgic for the recent past—a simpler, perhaps more local past—when all of Pittsburgh's movies were delivered by George himself with "a single horse and wagon hauling the films to and from the theatres and exchanges."[8] That past was gone. A history, however, remains.

NOTES

Chapter 1: Nickels and Steel

1. "New Photoplay" advertisement in *Gettysburg Times,* May 12, 1914, 12.

2. The story of the Theatorium comes from e-mail correspondence (July 10, 2005; Feburary 18, 2006; March 27, 2006) and letters (March 28, 2006; October 15, 2006) between the author and John G. Arch, grandson of the Gorseks, the theater's original owners, and son of their youngest daughter, Isabelle Clementine.

3. Charles Musser, *The Emergence of Cinema: The American Screen to 1907* (Los Angeles: University of California Press, 1990), 523. Musser does not list the *Pittsburgh Moving Picture Bulletin* in the book's bibliography of trade journals.

4. David Robinson, *From Peep Show to Palace: The Birth of American Film* (New York: Columbia University Press, 1996), 89.

5. In addition to a number of articles focusing on exhibition in major East Coast population centers, particularly New York and Boston, a few book-length local studies have previously been written, including: Greg Waller, *Main Street Amusements: Movies and Commercial Entertainment in a Southern City, 1896–1930* (Washington DC: Smithsonian Institution Press, 1995), a seminal work on Lexington, Kentucky; Lauren Rabinovitz, *For the Love of Pleasure: Women, Movies, and Culture in Turn-of-the-Century Chicago* (New Brunswick: Rutgers University Press, 1998); Jacqueline Najuma Stewart, *Migrating to the Movies: Cinema and Black Urban Modernity* (Berkeley: University of California Press, 2005), which concentrates on Chicago's African American exhibitors and audiences; Kathryn H. Fuller, *At the Picture Show: Small-Town Audiences and the Creation of Movie Fan Culture* (Washington DC: Smithsonian Institution Press, 1996); and Charlie Musser, *High Class Moving Pictures: Lyman H. Howe and the Forgotten Era of Traveling Exhibition, 1880–1920* (Princeton: Princeton University Press, 1991), which, like the Fuller, explores the exhibition history of itinerant showmen.

6. Paul U. Kellogg, "The Pittsburgh Survey," *Charities and the Commons: A Journal of Constructive Philanthropy* 21, no. 14 (January 1909): 517–26.

7. Roy Lubove, *Twentieth Century Pittsburgh,* vol. 1, *Government, Business, and Environmental Change* (Pittsburgh: University of Pittsburgh Press, 1996), 2.

8. Francis G. Couvares, *The Remaking of Pittsburgh Class and Culture in an Industrializing City, 1877–1919* (Albany: State University of New York Press, 1984), 82. For a good, easy-to-read description of how these mills operated see John A. Fitch, *The Steel Workers,* vol. 3 of *The Pittsburgh Survey,* ed. Paul Kellogg (1910; repr., Pittsburgh: University of Pittsburgh Press, 1989).

9. Quoted in Frank C. Harper, *Pittsburgh: Forge of the Universe* (New York: Comet Press Books, 1957), 6.

10. See Margaret Byington, *Homestead: The Households of a Mill Town*, vol. 4 of *The Pittsburgh Survey*, ed. Paul Kellogg (1910; repr., Pittsburgh: University of Pittsburgh Press, 1996); 40; and Paul U. Kellogg, ed., *Wage Earning Pittsburgh*, vol. 6 of *The Pittsburgh Survey* (1914; repr., New York: Arno Press, 1974).

11. Hilda Becker, "A Statistical Analysis of the Census Reports on the Distribution of the Foreign-born White Population of Pittsburgh, Pennsylvania, 1890–1930" (master's thesis, University of Pittsburgh, 1932), table 2.1; and George T. Fleming, *Pittsburgh: How to See It: A Complete, Reliable Guidebook* (Pittsburgh: William G. Johnston Co., 1916), 11. The larger cities were (in descending order): New York, Chicago, Philadelphia, St. Louis, Boston, Cleveland, and Baltimore.

12. Couvares, *Remaking of Pittsburgh*, 88–92.

13. In the wage-earning sector overall, wages were increasing and average hours of work were decreasing. Although the Amalgamated Union successfully fought in the mid-1880s to end the seven-day workweek, the violent response to the Homestead strike of 1892 led to employers reinstating Sunday work—a policy that existed into the early teens. See *Recent Trends in the United States* (New York: McGraw-Hill Book Co., 1933), 828, cited in S. J. Kleinberg, "Technology's Stepdaughters: The Impact of Industrialization upon Working Class Women, Pittsburgh, 1865–1890" (PhD diss., University of Pittsburgh, 1973), 10.

14. David Brody, *Steelworkers in America: The Nonunion Era* (New York: Harper Torchbook, 1969), 37–40.

15. Kleinberg, "Technology's Stepdaughters," 44. The complications attendant with any critical analysis that involves the intersection of ethnicity and labor history are numerous —issues of shifting national formations, purposeful and incidental erasure, and assimilation of ethnic identity and history to name some of the more salient. Yet despite the potential oversimplifications and overqualifications when ethnicity is thrown in the historical mix, it is crucial to recognize that ethnicity informs much of this country's labor and social history and its critical inclusion ultimately produces a much richer version of our cultural and social formations.

16. Fleming, *Pittsburgh*, 35.

17. John H. Ingham, *The Iron Barons: A Social Analysis of an American Urban Elite, 1874–1965* (Westport, Conn.: Greenfield Publishing Co., 1978), 108.

18. Fleming, *Pittsburgh*, 18.

19. Ileen Devault, *Sons and Daughters of Labor Class and Clerical Work in Turn-of-the-Century Pittsburgh* (Ithaca: Cornell University Press, 1990), 12. By 1920, this office staff accounted for close to 15 percent of the working population in Pittsburgh.

20. DeVault, *Sons and Daughters*, 170.

21. Robert C. Allen, "Manhattan Myopia; or Oh! Iowa!" *Cinema Journal* 35, no. 3 (Spring 1996): 94.

22. Edward K. Muller, "Metropolis and Region: A Framework for Enquiry into Western Pennsylvania," in *City at the Point: Essays on the Social History of Pittsburgh*, ed. Samuel P. Hays, 181–212 (Pittsburgh: University of Pittsburgh Press, 1991).

23. For the definitive work on the region's industrial history, see Roy Lubove, *Twentieth-Century Pittsburgh*, vol. 1, *Government, Business, and Environmental Change*, and vol. 2, *The Post-Steel Era* (Pittsburgh: University of Pittsburgh Press, 1996).

24. Lubove, *Twentieth-Century Pittsburgh*, 1:1.

25. Daniel L. Marsh, *The Challenge of Pittsburgh* (New York: Missionary Education Movement of the United States and Canada, 1917), 91.

26. Of the six bound volumes of the survey, four were designed as monographs and two were collections of articles and research that were not long enough to merit their own title. The monographs are: Elizabeth Beardsley Butler, *Women and the Trades, Pittsburgh 1907–1908*, vol. 1 of *The Pittsburgh Survey*, ed. Paul Kellogg (1909; reprint, Pittsburgh: University of Pittsburgh Press, 1984); Crystal Eastman, *Work-Accidents and the Law*, vol. 2 of *The Pittsburgh Survey*, ed. Paul Kellogg (1910; repr., New York: Arno Press, 1969); Fitch, *Steel Workers*; and Byington, *Homestead*. The anthologies were first published as volume 5 and 6: Paul U. Kellogg, ed. *The Pittsburgh District: Civic Frontage*, vol. 5 of *The Pittsburgh Survey* (1914; repr., New York: Arno Press, 1974); and Kellogg, *Wage Earning Pittsburgh*.

27. See Maurine W. Greenwald and Margo Anderson, eds. *Pittsburgh Surveyed: Social Science and Social Reform in the Early Twentieth Century* (Pittsburgh: University of Pittsburgh Press, 1996) for an extended analysis of the historical meaning/use of the survey.

28. Byington, *Homestead*, 111. Progressive discourse makes the distinction between commercial leisure and recreation or "play," the latter being an important aspect of urban reform groups including the Playground and Recreation Association of America. *The Pittsburgh Survey* spends considerable time discussing the city's lack of purposefully-designed areas for children to play.

29. R. Earl Boyd, *"The Strip": A Socio-Religious Survey of a Typical Problem Section of Pittsburgh, Pa.* (Pittsburgh: Christian Social Service Union, 1915), 37.

30. Boyd, *"The Strip*," 11.

31. Boyd, *"The Strip*," 35. Chartered clubs were provisionally private organizations which were created to allow local residents access to liquor on Sundays when state and local "blue" laws required regular saloons to remain closed. Such "private" clubs continue to exist in a number of the city's neighborhoods.

32. Marsh, *Challenge of Pittsburgh*, 91.

33. Fleming, *Pittsburgh*, 114, 115, 116.

34. Marsh gives the number 130 in the city proper with another 65 in the metropolitan area (*Challenge of Pittsburgh*, 197). See also Michael G. Aronson, "The Wrong Kind of Nickel Madness," *Cinema Journal* 42, no. 1 (2002): 71–96, for a map describing the location of known theaters in 1914.

35. Fleming, *Pittsburgh*, 119.

Chapter 2: The Eponymous Nickelodeon

1. "Nickelodeons Overcrowded," *Pittsburgh Leader*, November 26, 1905, 4.
2. "Amusement Is Turned to Horror" *Pittsburgh Post*, November 19, 1905, 1.
3. "Nickelodeons Overcrowded," *Pittsburgh Leader*, 4.
4. "Nickelodeons Overcrowded," *Pittsburgh Leader*, 4.
5. "Nickelodeons Overcrowded," *Pittsburgh Leader*, 4.
6. See Hayden White, *Metahistory: The Historical Imagination in Nineteenth-Century Europe* (Baltimore: John Hopkins Press, 1973).
7. See, among others, Sally Dixon, "In Pittsburgh the Silent Years Roared," *Carnegie Magazine*, November 1972, 381.
8. In part this narrative has resulted because a number of Hollywood's eventual moguls began their careers as nickelodeon operators, men like Adolph Zukor and Marcus Loew in New York and Lewis Selznick and the Warner brothers in Pittsburgh. See Neil Gabler, *An Empire of Their Own: How The Jews Invented Hollywood* (New York: Anchor Books, 1988).
9. Ben Singer, "Manhattan Nickelodeons: New Data on Audiences and Exhibitors," *Cinema Journal* 34, no. 3 (Spring 1995): 5–35.
10. Tom Gunning, *D. W. Griffith and the Origins of American Narrative Film* (Urbana: University of Illinois Press, 1991), 31.
11. Tom Gunning, "Introduction," in Laurent Mannoni, *The Great Art of Light and Shadow: Archaeology of the Cinema* (Exeter: University of Exeter, 2000), xxi. Gunning's introduction to Mannoni's work provides a sound theoretical model for producing histories which neither ignore nor heroize the role individual historical figures/living-breathing people play in the development of the cinema.
12. Douglas Gomery, *Shared Pleasures: A History of Movie Presentation in the United States* (Madison: University of Wisconsin Press, 1991), 18.
13. Kenneth Macgowan, *Behind the Screen: The History and Techniques of the Motion Picture* (New York: Dell, 1965), 22–27.
14. Musser, *Emergence of Cinema*, 125. Musser has researched numerous other accounts of these storefront theaters and has written in *Emergence* what amounts to the best and most thorough documentation of the pre-nickelodeon storefront motion picture show.
15. Musser, *Emergence of Cinema*, 125. Newspaper advertisements from various newspapers across Texas, Arizona, and New Mexico show that Rock took the Vitascope show on the road. "Woodmen of the World," *Dallas Morning News* October 18, 1896, 13.
16. Classified advertisement, *Los Angeles Times*, June 1, 1902, A12.
17. According to Musser, Tally ran his show fitfully from April 1902 to sometime early in 1903, eventually switching the Electric to a ten-cent vaudeville house called the Lyric. See Musser, *Emergence of Cinema*, 299. Lewis Jacobs, however, claims that Tally, after initially hitting a rough patch, added the phrase "A Vaudeville of Motion Pictures" to his theater's name and was then "an auspicious success" which led Tally to open a second theater and to act as a catalyst for the storefront theater boom. See Lewis Jacobs, *The Rise of The American*

Film (New York: Harcourt, Brace and Co., 1939), 7. The Electric has also been called "a success from the start." See Benjamin B. Hampton, *History of the American Film Industry: From Its Beginnings to 1931* (New York: Dover Publications, 1970), 120.

18. Display advertisement, *Los Angeles Times*, February 22, 1903, 1.

19. Eugene Lemoyne Connelly, "The First Motion Picture Theater," *Western Pennsylvania Historical Magazine*, March 1940, 1–12.

20. "The Life Story of Harry Davis," *Sunday Telegraph*, January 3, 1940.

21. Musser, *Emergence of Cinema*, 417.

22. There may be evidence, somewhere, of one of these early exhibition sites charging five-cent admission, but almost every account I have been able to locate lists regular admission costs at a dime or higher.

23. Robert Sklar, *Movie-made America: A Cultural History of American Movies*, 2nd ed. (New York: Vintage Books, 1994), 18

24. See David Nasaw, *Going Out: The Rise and Fall of Public Amusement* (New York: Basic Books, 1993), 10–33.

25. W. Stephen Bush, "The Coming Ten and Twenty Cent Moving Picture Theater," *Moving Picture World* [hereafter *MPW*], August 29, 1908, 152.

26. *Pittsburgh Moving Picture Bulletin* [hereafter *PMPB*], April 30, 1914, 4.

27. "In the Curio Halls," *Boston Daily Globe*, September 16, 1888, 12.

28. British Film Institute, *Who's Who of Victorian Cinema*, s.v. "Benjamin Franklin Keith," Deac Rossell, accessed October 21, 2006, http://www.victorian-cinema.net/keith.htm.

29. "In the Curio Halls," *Boston Daily Globe*, October 2, 1888, 3.

30. Andrea Stulman Dennett, *Weird & Wonderful: The Dime Museum in America* (New York: New York University Press, 1997), 5.

31. Exhibition scholar Richard Abel has found that by 1896, at least one small vaudeville theater in a Los Angeles amusement park was named "nickelodeon." Richard Abel to author, personal correspondence.

32. "Amusements," *Trenton Evening Times*, October 12, 1897, 8.

33. Advertisement, *Fitchburg Daily Sentinel*, January 1, 1904, 12.

34. This assertion is based on a keyword search and analysis of the web-based newspaper archive, newspaperarchive.com, for the period June 1905 through June 1906.

35. "High Sounding Appellations," *New York Herald*, reprinted in *Dallas Weekly Times Herald*, June 14, 1890, 2. Interestingly, the New York paper blames this trend on the airs of Bostonians, giving some credence to the idea that the word "nickelodeon" began there.

36. Lee Grieveson, *Policing the Cinema* (Berkeley: University of California Press, 2004), 2.

37. Davis and Harris are often wrongly given "joint" credit for first bringing the movies to Pittsburgh, a myth that seems to have begun during the twenty-fifth anniversary of the nickelodeon. See "The Marvelous Vitascope," *Pittsburgh Press*, May 8, 1927, 1.

38. "The Marvelous Vitascope: Pictures of People, Life Size, Produced in Action," *Pittsburgh Dispatch*, September 5, 1896, 1. The first films shown to the American public occurred in New York City on April 23, 1896, at Koster and Bial's Music Hall.

39. "Marvelous Vitascope," 1.

40. Musser, *Emergence of Cinema*, 418.

41. Laurie Anne Stepanian, "Harry Davis Entrepreneur, 1893–1927" (PhD diss., University of Missouri, Columbia, 1988). In the late nineteenth and early twentieth centuries, the term "fakir" was slang for a street hustler, schemer, or peddler of cheap goods.

42. "The Life Story of Harry Davis," *Pittsburgh Sun Telegraph*, January 3, 1940, 12.

43. See "Billiard Cue Tips," *Los Angeles Times*, August 9, 1890, 5; and "For the Pittsburg Billiard Tourney," *Chicago Daily Tribune*, January 29, 1897, 9.

44. "The Walking Match," *Hartford Courant*, April 9, 1889, 1.

45. "The Man Who Didn't Stand Still," *Pittsburgh Leader*, January 16, 1910, 12.

46. See for example: William Fell Smith, ed. *The Greater Pittsburgh Real Estate Reference Book* (Pittsburgh: Davis and Wade Press, 1903), 8.

47. "Avenue Joins Davis Syndicate," *New York Dramatic Mirror*, August 6, 1898, 6.

48. "Dispute over Theaters," *Washington Post*, August 23, 1899, 2.

49. See for example: "A Theatrical Row in Pittsburg. Theatre Manager Refuses to Be Discharged by the Lessee," *New York Times*, August 22, 1899, 7.

50. "Blaze in the Pittsburgh Musee," *Washington Post*, January 8, 1897, 1. Although Davis attempted to keep the museum going, in part by displaying Old Rube's charred remains, the damage was too severe and eventually forced closure later that winter.

51. Arthur Gordon Burgoyne, *All Sorts of Pittsburgers* (Pittsburgh: Leader All Sorts Company, 1914), 66–67.

52. John Harris Jr., quoted in John M. Kelly, *J. M. Kelly's Handbook of Greater Pittsburg* (Pittsburgh: n.p., 1895), A088. See also "World's First Movie House, Nickelodeon, Founded in Pittsburgh by Senator Harris," *Pittsburgh Press*, May 8, 1927, *Pittsburgh Post-Gazette* archive, "Harris."

53. "John Harris Dies in Home," *Pittsburgh Sun Telegraph*, September 2, 1927, *Pittsburgh Post-Gazette* archive, "Harris."

54. Frank Harper, "Hon. John H. Harris," *Pittsburgh of Today* (New York: American Historical Society, 1931), 511.

55. Avenue and Grand Opera House playbills, circa 1903, Curtis Theatre Collection, University of Pittsburgh Special Collections Archive.

56. "Amusements," *Pittsburgh Post*, September 4, 1904, 6b, quoted in Musser, *Emergence of Cinema*, 418.

57. See Stepanian, "Harry Davis Entrepreneur," 134–35, and Musser, *Emergence of Cinema*, 420–21.

58. See Allegheny County, *Deeds Direct*, vols. 1243, 1264–65 (1903).

59. Allegheny County, *Deeds Direct*, "John Kearns to Davis," vol. 1317 (December 16, 1903), 43.

60. "Davis Holds Good Values," *Pittsburgh Press*, June 4, 1905, 4. Leasing properties was made profitable by either subleasing the storefront and office spaces within the larger property and/or by "selling" back the lease.

61. George T. Fleming, *Pittsburgh: How to See It: A Complete, Reliable Guidebook* (Pittsburgh: William G. Johnston Co., 1916), 132–33.

62. *Pittsburgh Leader*, January 19, 1905, 2.

63. "The First Neckolodeon [*sic*] in the United States," *MPW*, November 30, 1907, 629.

64. "To Improve Property," *Pittsburgh Press*, 12.

65. "Davis Holds Good Values," *Pittsburgh Press*, 4.

66. "The Life Story of Harry," *Sunday Telegraph*, January 3, 1940, *Pittsburgh Post-Gazette* archive, "Harry Davis."

67. Advertisement for the Link Piano Company of Binghamton, New York, circa 1900. Generously shared with me by David Q. Bowers.

68. "The Price of Admission," *Nickelodeon*, January 15, 1910, 30. Bread price: *1907 Bureau of Labor Report*, cited in Margaret Byington, *Homestead: The Households of a Mill Town*, vol. 2, The Pittsburgh Survey (New York: The Russell Sage Foundation, 1910; reprint, Pittsburgh: University of Pittsburgh Press, 1996), appendix 1, table 9. Intriguingly, in a list of sixteen food staples, and their corresponding prices in ten American cities, only bread remains the same price regardless of locale, a potential indication that a one-pound loaf of bread had its economic and psychological value bound in a similar fashion to the nickelodeon. Trolley fare: Fleming, *Pittsburgh*, 38. Beer: Kellogg, *Wage Earning Pittsburgh*, 132.

69. "Mill Reports of the Week. The Outlook for Busy Plants Still Continues Bright and Rosy" *Pittsburg Leader*, July 2, 1905, 12.

70. "Price of Admission," *Nickelodeon*, 30.

71. David Nasaw, *Going Out: The Rise and Fall of Public Amusements* (New York: Basic Books, 1993), 159.

72. Stepanian, "Harry Davis Entrepreneur," 131–34. The three Davis penny arcades opened in 1904 were located at 431 Smithfield Street, 305 Fifth Avenue, and 326 Fifth Avenue.

73. *PMPB*, April 30, 1914, 4. Although Charles Musser notes Royer's claim for introducing the "first nickelodeon," there are at least two other competing claims: J. G. Foley, see *PMPB*, November 25, 1914, 12; and John P. Harris, see, for example, "Harris Firm Started Nickelodeon Trade," *Pittsburgh Post*, April 20, 1930, E5.

74. *PMPB*, April 30, 1914, 4

75. "Theater Burns While Audience Escapes," *Pittsburgh Press*, June 3, 1905, 1.

76. "Looking for a New Site," *McKeesport Daily News*, June 7, 1905, 1.

77. "The Festive Nickelodeon," *Pittsburgh Sun*, May 18, 1906, 16.

78. Ibid.

79. See "First Neckelodeon," *MPW*, 629; and Connelly, "First Motion Picture Theater," 7.

80. "The Nickelodeons," *MPW*, January 11, 1908, 21.

81. Connelly, "First Motion Picture Theater," 3. Connelly, a lifelong press agent and ballyhoo man by nature, unfortunately provides many of the few details that exist about the nickelodeon. Possibly these seats came from one of his two legitimate theaters that were closed at the time because of the fire. The Alvin remained closed for the entire season.

82. "First Neckelodeon," *MPW*, 629. The two best known images, of the exterior and interior of the nickelodeon, were first published in *MPW* in 1907 and reprinted in Musser's *Emergence of the Cinema*, 419, were most likely taken sometime after a seven-thousand-dollar makeover to the theater's decorative plaster front, which occurred a few months after the nickelodeon first opened.

83. "The Nickelodeon" *MPW,* April 5, 1907, 140.

84. "Harris Firm Started Nickelodeon Trade," *Pittsburgh Press*, April 20, 1930, E5.

85. See Abel, *Red Rooster Scare*, 48–80.

86. Sally F. Dixon, "In Pittsburgh the Silent Years Roared," *Carnegie Magazine*, November 1977.

87. *Variety*, March 31, 1906, 13.

88. "First Neckelodeon," *MPW,* 629.

89. See, for example, Harry Davis Enterprises advertisement, *MPW.* April 27, 1907, 122.

90. "Nickelodeons Overcrowded," *Pittsburgh Leader*, 4.

91. "The Year Ahead," *Nickelodeon*, January 1909, 2. This is the very first issue of the journal.

Chapter 3: The Wrong Kind of Nickel Madness

1. *Pittsburgh Moving Picture Bulletin* [hereafter *PMPB*], April 15, 1914, 3.

2. For identification of "Miss A." as a booking clerk at the Independent Film Exchange, see *PMPB*, April 15, 1914, 3.

3. *PMPB*, May 12, 1915, 2.

4. *PMPB*, May 12, 1915, 2.

5. *Mayer Press: Fifty Years of Printing Service* (Pittsburgh: Mayer Press, 1937).

6. Stanley Mayer, "Of My Father and Remarques—A Memoir," *Western Pennsylvania Historical Magazine*, January 1980, 83.

7. Unfortunately, currently there are no known archival holdings of the *Pittsburgh Herald*.

8. Mayer, "Of My Father," 2–3.

9. *PMPB*, April 15, 1914, 1.

10. Circulation numbers for magazines and journals were and often still are inflated by their publishers to promote advertising sales. Still, it is worth comparing the *Bulletin's* 1,500 to the 15,000 circulation put forth by the editors of *Moving Picture World*, which was, at that time, the largest national trade in publication.

11. *PMPB*, April 15, 1914, 3.

12. *Moving Picture World* began publication in 1907, and *Motion Picture News* in 1908.

13. The Minneapolis *Amusement* appears to have begun publication as early as 1914, but did not focus its content on moving pictures until sometime in 1916. There are no known

archival holdings of the journal prior to 1938. Known archival holdings of the *Exhibiter* begin in 1923 and 1920 for the *Weekly Film Review*.

14. The *Bulletin* delineates between "filmmen" as owners or workers of an exchange and "picture men" as exhibiters. *PMPB*, March 12, 1915, 10.

15. *Mayer Press*, 3.

16. See Richard Abel, *Americanizing the Movies and "Movie Mad" Audiences, 1910–1914* (Berkeley: University of California Press, 2006), in particular, chapter 1.

17. See Richard Abel, ed., *The Encyclopedia of Early Cinema* (New York: Routledge, 2005), which does not bother to include the term "exchange" in either its entries or index, although it is briefly discussed in the section on "distribution." See Musser, *Emergence of Cinema*, for one of the few histories that includes a brief discussion of the role of the exchange in the nickelodeon era.

18. Musser, *Emergence of Cinema*, 360–67.

19. *PMPB*, April 22, 1914, 4.

20. From Stieren Company letterhead, dated July 21, 1881, author's collection.

21. Actual calcium light is colloquially better known as "limelight," the chemical compound used in theatrical lighting prior to arc lights, which produced its characteristic greenish glow.

22. *PMPB*, August 22, 1917, 1.

23. "Pittsburgh, Pa., Has a Record Date for 'Store Shows,'" *Moving Picture World* [hereafter *MPW*], July 15, 1916, 405.

24. This material comes from correspondence between Selig and exchanges located in Pittsburgh, dated variously from February 1907–August 1903. Selig Collection, "Correspondence" folders 458–60, 571–72, Margaret Herrick Library, Academy of Arts and Sciences, Los Angeles.

25. Movie theaters were not open in Pittsburgh on Sundays until the late 1930s.

26. See Richard Abel, *The Red Rooster Scare: Making Cinema American, 1900–1910* (Berkeley: University of California Press, 1999), 20–37.

27. J. G. Foley business card, author's collection.

28. Eugene LeMoyne Connelly, "The First Motion Picture Theater," *Western Pennsylvania Historical Magazine*, March 1940, 1–12.

29. David Kiehn, *Broncho Billy and the Essanay Film Company* (Berkeley: Farwell Books, 2003), 7.

30. Connelly, "First Motion Picture Theater," 8.

31. Duquesne Amusement Supply Company to Selig Polyscope, April 22, 1907, Selig Collection. The correct title of the film is *The Bandit King*.

32. Selig Collection, "Correspondence," folder 458.

33. See Eileen Bowser, *The Transformation of Cinema, 1907–1915* (Los Angeles: University of California Press, 1990), 81–82.

34. Bowser, *Transformation*, 83.

35. *PMPB*, April 30, 1914, 1.

36. In August 1914, the *Bulletin* announced a fourth film schedule was about to begin to be produced by the Popular Photoplays Corporation. The service, according to its president, Charles Bauman, planned to issue twenty-eight reels weekly produced from fourteen different "brands," made up of one-, two-, and three-reel films (or basically, four reels each day). This service appears to have never started, at least in Pittsburgh. *PMPB*, August 26, 1914, 6.

37. Paul H. Davis, "Investing in the Movies," part 7, *Photoplay Magazine*, February 1916, 71.

38. William Mayer, *PMPB*, June 23, 1915, 24.

39. Western Film Company advertisement, *PMPB*, June 17, 1914, 11.

40. *PMPB*, May 13, 1914, 5.

41. Western Film Company advertisement, *PMPB*, March 20, 1914, 21.

42. *PMPB*, March 13, 1914, 5.

43. Charlie Keil and Ben Singer, "USA," *Encyclopedia of Early Cinema* (New York: Routledge, 2005), 657.

44. *The Price Woman Pays* (six reels, 1919), produced by J. Frank Hatch, California Motion Picture Company. See *The American Institute Film (AFI) Catalog: Feature Films, 1911–1920* (Los Angeles: University of California Press, 1988), 735.

45. Michael Quinn, "Distribution, the Transient Audience, and the Transition to the Feature Film," *Cinema Journal* 40, no. 2 (Winter 2001): 35–56; Abel, *Americanizing*, 23–25.

46. Michaels and Freeman advertisement, *PMPB*, June 30, 1915, 23.

47. *Neptune's Daughter* (seven reels, 1914), *AFI Catalog*, 656.

48. *PMPB*, May 13, 1914, 5.

49. *PMPB*, May 13, 1914, 2.

50. According to at least one source, the film was not released until 1911. BFI online Film and TV Database, http://ftvdb.bfi.org.uk/sift/title/320530.

51. *PMPB*, May 13, 1914, 2.

52. "Use Your Brain," Apex Film Co. ad in *MPW*, February 1914, 542.

53. *PMPB*, October 21, 1914, 1.

54. Western Film Company advertisement, *PMPB*, April 15, 1914, 1–2.

55. *PMPB*, October 28, 1914, 8.

56. *PMPB*, April 15, 1914, 12.

57. *PMPB*, March 20, 1914, 10.

58. *PMPB*, March 15, 1914, 11; Abel, *Americanizing the Movies*, 37.

59. *PMPB*, April 14, 1915, 2.

60. *PMPB*, October 21, 1914, 1. A number of movie-only theaters in the downtown entertainment district held 1,000 or more, including the 2,500-seat Olympic on Fifth Avenue.

61. *PMPB*, September 23, 1914, 8. According to the article, the 309 raised "bleacher" seats in the back of the theater could be reserved by phone at an admission of twenty cents.

62. *PMPB*, March 5, 1915, 1–2. The term "jitney" was slang for a nickel.

63. To name a few: Ben Singer, "Manhattan Nickelodeons: New Data on Audiences and Exhibiters," *Cinema Journal* (*CJ*) 34, no. 3 (Spring 1995): 5–35; Julie Ann Lindstrom, "Getting a Hold Deeper in the Life of the City: Chicago Nickelodeons, 1905–1914" (Ph.D. dissertation, Northwestern University, 1998). One of the few exceptions would be Abel's *Americanizing the Movies*, which describes a broad range of picture theaters in the mid-1910s, some of which, he rightly notes, were still described as nickelodeons.

64. W. Stephen Bush, "The Coming of the Ten and Twenty Cent Moving Picture Theatre," *MPW*, April 29, 1908, 152, in Robert C. Allen, "Manhattan Myopia; or Oh! Iowa!" *Cinema Journal* 35, no. 3 (Spring 1996): 87. What Allen doesn't bother to quote from the very same article is Bush bemoaning the continued strength of the nickel theater, and its "abomination of a name."

65. *PMPB*, October 31, 1914, 12; *PMPB*, September 6, 1916, 4. According to the article, another East Liberty house, the Rex, was the last theater to begin charging a dime, but the Regent was only a month or two ahead in this increase. The Cameraphone was one of the last Downtown theaters to change to a dime admission at the end of April 1917. *PMPB*, March 2, 1917, 14.

66. *PMPB*, September 25, 1916, 1.

67. "What Is a Picture Theatre?" *Motion Picture News* [hereafter *MPN*], August 5, 1916, 1.

68. "The Motion Picture Theatre," *MPN*, November 4, 1916, 1.

69. "What is a Picture Theatre?" *MPN*, 1.

70. *PMPB*, March 5, 1915, 1–2.

71. Mayer Publishing & Printing Company advertisement, *PMPB*, March 13, 1914, 17.

72. *PMPB*, April 15, 1914, 3.

73. *PMPB*, April 30, 1914, 3.

74. Allen, "Manhattan Myopia," 83.

75. *PMPB*, March 6, 1914, 1.

76. "Raising Prices in Philadelphia," *MPN*, March 21, 1914, 33; "Is the 'Nickel Show' Passing?" *MPN*, April 4, 1914, 27.

77. See, for example: *PMPB*, April 22, 1914; *PMPB*, July 15, 1914, 5.

78. "Quality Films at Quantity Prices," *MPN*, April 18, 1914, 25.

79. "Observations by Our Man about Town," *MPW*, March 5, 1910, 334, reprinted in Allen, "Manhattan Myopia," 83.

80. *PMPB*, June 23, 1915, 13. The North Side was, until 1907, the autonomous Allegheny City. It was incorporated into the city of Pittsburgh against the will of the residents.

81. *PMPB*, July 22, 1914, 6.

82. Bill Urichio and Roberta Pearson, "Dialogue: Manhattan's Nickelodeons: New York? New York?" *Cinema Journal* 36, no. 4 (Summer 1997): 99.

83. *PMPB*, May 12, 1914, 12.

84. Allen, "Manhattan Myopia," 79.

85. Unlike New York, Pittsburgh's "floating clientele" would have been mostly derived from its residents, as well as some business travelers and a few day visitors from surrounding towns.

86. Ileen Devault, *Sons and Daughters of Labor Class and Clerical Work in Turn-of-the-Century Pittsburgh* (Ithaca: Cornell University Press, 1990).

87. Epes Winthrop Sargent, "Advertising for Exhibitors," *MPW,* February 7, 1914, 668; "Masses of Pictures" *MPN,* December 11, 1915, 41.

88. *PMPB,* May 12, 1915, 1. The next issue of the *Bulletin* informs its readership that the live rooster was replaced the following week with a ham!

89. One question this potentially addresses is why there are, in a time of transition when the lowly penny still carried productive economic power, very few documented instances of theatres charging six, seven, or eight cents a show. My thinking about the psychological value of the nickel was initially stimulated by a related question Donald Crafton raised when I gave a version of this paper at the annual Society of Cinema Studies conference in 1999.

90. See Moya Luckett, "Advertising and Femininity: The Case of *Our Mutual Girl,*" *Screen* (December 1999): 363–83, for a persuasive example of the role of the bargain in attracting a middle-class audience to the movies.

91. At least one of the reasons for the historiographic absence around this issue is that we have so few existing psychological values available in our present economy to compare with the nickelodeon. The one example, and it is not nearly as culturally pervasive, is the "Super Value Menu" at the fast-food chain, Wendy's. Items are all priced at 99 cents, the same price they have been for approximately the last decade, regardless of inflation or other increases in costs. Once this menu began to function as an expected and popular feature of the chain the price became "sacred," with the sign "Super Value Menu" signifying 99 cents. Wendy's, which wants to be associated with "value," cannot change the price without disrupting its associational meaning. I would also argue, that this works regardless of the class of people visiting the chain—although I can afford a "Classic Bacon Double Cheese Burger" for $2.49, I almost always order the 99-cent "Jr. Bacon Cheese Burger"—part of its pleasure being its low price. A similar psychological binding of price and object contemporary with early cinema, and pointed out to me by Lucy Fischer, would be the dime novel.

92. This is not unique to Pittsburgh if the rhetoric of *MPW* is any indication. There are almost weekly articles during the period in question about attempts/successes/failures by exhibitors in various cities and towns to "breaking 'em [patrons] in to dimes" and to show less film for more money. See "Dime or Jitney," *MPW,* July 31, 1915, 846.

93. "The Box Office Revolution," *MPN,* March 28, 1914, 19.

94. "Three Big Problems," *MPN,* January 31, 1914, 13; "Box Office Revolution," *MPN,* 19.

95. *PMPB,* September 8, 1915, 1.

96. "Report of the Pennsylvania Board of Censors, 1916," Pennsylvania State Archives, Harrisburg, RG:22, C4. From December 1, 1915, to November 30, 1916 (the fiscal year for the state at that time), the state board, which had to approve every film commercially

shown in the state, examined 17,020 reels, or approx. 17 million, feet of film. The board included this statistic in its annual report because it wanted more money from the governor for its operating budget.

97. *PMPB*, January 5, 1916, 10.

98. *PMPB*, April 14, 1915, 1.

99. Michael J. Quinn, "Early Feature Distribution and Development of the Motion Picture Industry: Famous Players and Paramount, 1912–1921" (Ph.D. dissertation, University of Wisconsin–Madison, 1998), iii.

100. "Do Features Pay?" *MPN*, March 21, 1914, 20.

101. "Motion Picture Theatre," *MPN*, 1.

102. "What Is a Picture Theatre?" *MPN*, 1.

103. "On the Outside Looking In," *Motography*, May 2, 1914, 303–4.

104. "The Price of Admission," *Nickelodeon*, January 15, 1910, 30.

105. "Pittsburg [*sic*]," *MPW*, December 13, 1913, 1295. From the date of this article, it appears that the failed attempt to raise prices, at least downtown, started sometime prior to the Regent's "revolutionary" announcement in the spring of 1914.

106. "El Paso the Ideal," *MPW*, April 10, 1915, 211; "Higher Prices Evenings," *MPW*, September 18, 1915, 2025; and "Raising Prices in Philadelphia," *MPN*, March 21, 1914, 33.

107. *PMPB*, May 12, 1915, 11.

108. Singer, "Manhattan Nickelodeons," 26–27.

109. Admittedly, this ethnographic study is less than empirical. Pittsburgh's city directories from the period do not list owners' names next to theater names, and there are no complete ownership records for the period. As a result, I am relying on reports of events listed in the *Bulletin*, particularly exhibitor parties and the local film industry baseball league, as a way of gauging the ethnicity of those locally involved in the moving picture show. From the hundreds of names listed in the *Bulletin* in this period, there appears to be no dominant ethnicity in terms of exhibition ownership or local involvement in the movie business.

110. "Pittsburgh Theaters Raise Admission Prices," *MPN*, September 30, 1916, 2013.

111. *PMPB*, 25 October 25, 1916, 1.

112. *PMPB*, December 18, 1914, 1. This passage is from a speech given by H. B. Kester, the newly inaugurated president of the Screen Club.

113. *PMPB*, April 30, 1914, 3.

114. *PMPB*, December 12, 1919, 1.

Chapter 4: Swatting Flies and Winning Chickens

1. *PMPB*, 30 June 30, 1915, 21.

2. See Candice Jacobson Fuhrman, *Publicity Stunt Great Staged Events That Made the News* (San Francisco: Chronicle Books, 1989).

3. *Motion Picture News* advertisement, *MPN*, November 15, 1924, 203.

4. Epes Winthrop Sargent, *Picture Theatre Advertising* (New York: Chalmers Publishing Company, 1915). Today Sargent is best known for his columns in *Moving Picture World* on both photoplay writing and exhibitor promotion, including "Selling the Picture to the Public," which began in 1911. See Robert Grau, *The Theatre of Science: A Volume of Progress and Achievement in the Motion Picture Art* (New York: Broadway Publishing Company, 1914), 306–9.

5. Sargent, *Picture Theatre Advertising*, 231–33. Sargent says that although "Catch the Rat" is a newer "crusade" run along similar lines, but for obvious reasons "it is well to keep away from this . . . [as] women will not want to come to the theatre if small boys with their pockets full of dead rats are apt to be hanging around" (233).

6. "Time to Swat the Fly," *Edwardsville (IL) Intelligencer*, August 8, 1915, 2.

7. Spectatoritis was a "disease" that caused excessive absorption in the movies, and "Serialitis" was a related disease that caused the "sick" person to suffer from an over-identification and compulsive addiction to the serial. See Shelley Stamp, *Movie-Struck Girls: Women and Motion Picture Culture after the Nickelodeon* (Princeton: Princeton University Press, 2000), 102–3.

8. Jane Gaines, "From Elephants to Lux Soap: The Programming and 'Flow' of Early Motion Picture Exploitation," *Velvet Light Trap* 25 (Spring 1990): 30–43.

9. Janet Staiger, "Announcing Wares, Winning Patrons, Voicing Ideals: Thinking about the History and Theory of Advertising," *Cinema Journal* 29, no. 3 (Fall 1990): 6.

10. See Moya Luckett, "Cities and Spectators: A Historical Analysis of Film Audiences in Chicago, 1910–1915" (PhD diss., University of Wisconsin, 1995).

11. Eileen Bowser, *The Transformation of Cinema, 1907–1915* (Los Angeles: University of California Press, 1990), 21.

12. "Convention of Manufacturers and Film Renters," *MPW*, November 16, 1907, 592.

13. Petitioner's Exhibit No. 9, Edison license agreement of February 15, 1908, *U.S. v. MPPC* 1:350–56, cited in Bowser, *Transformation of Cinema*, 27.

14. O. T. Crawford, quoted in "The Pittsburg Conference" *MPW*, November 23, 1907, 608.

15. In 1908, the United Film Services Protective Association, now under Edison's control became the Film Service Association, better known as the FSA.

16. Typically in the 1910s, features that actually were feature-length were described as "super" features or "special" features.

17. There were, of course, exceptions to this rule. See Roberta Pearson and William Urrichio, *Reframing Culture: The Case of the Vitagraph Quality Films* (Princeton: Princeton University Press, 1993), 17–64.

18. The price per foot ran from eight to twelve cents a foot during the life of the MPPC. See Michael J. Quinn, "Early Feature Distribution and the Development of the Motion Picture Industry: Famous Players and Paramount, 1912–1921" (Ph.D. dissertation, University of Wisconsin–Madison, 1998), 55.

19. "The Backbone of the Business," *Motography*, September 20, 1913, 191–92. In many ways, this earlier model of film reflects our understanding of television and its program "flow."

20. See "Motion Picture News Chart of National Film Trade Conditions," *MPN*, May 22, 1915, 40–41. The *Motion Picture News* ran "snapshot" polls occasionally throughout 1914–1915. Set up as a comparison grid with cities ranging from Phoenix, Arizona, to Trenton, New Jersey, each poll gave city by city answers to questions like "Are Stage Stars on the Screen Regarded as a Success?" and "What Is the Demand for Feature Films if Any?" Unfortunately, *MPN* gives no sense of who in those cities answered the actual questions.

21. According to Michael Quinn, theaters showing only first-run films were exceedingly rare, and "full first-run service" was eliminated by the GFC in 1913. Michael Quinn, "Distribution, the Transient Audience, and the Transition to the Feature Film," *Cinema Journal* 40, no. 2 (Winter 2001): 37.

22. Bowser, *Transformation of Cinema*, 33.

23. *PMPB*, April 30, 1914, 1.

24. Those who continued to supply programs based on short films include General Film (which remained intact after the court-ordered dissolution of the MPPC), Mutual and Universal (which were the result of a series of divisions of the independent Sales Company), and two smaller services, United and Kriterion (of which little is currently known).

25. "The Pittsburgh Bulletin," *Motography*, May 2, 1914, 308.

26. "Pittsburgh Bulletin," *Motography*, 308.

27. *PMPB*, May 30, 1915, 14.

28. *PMPB*, May 20, 1914, cover, 8.

29. In the nine-year extant run of the *Bulletin*, there is only a single passing reference to a black-only theater.

30. *PMPB*, April 15, 1914, 1.

31. *PMPB*, December 23, 1914, 1.

32. Denol Chemical Company advertisement, *PMPB*, May 13, 1914, 3.

33. *PMPB*, November 11, 1914, 1.

34. See Richard Abel, *Americanizing the Movies and "Movie Mad" Audiences, 1910–1914* (Berkeley: University of California Press, 2006), 13–42.

35. Susan Strasser, *Satisfaction Guaranteed* (New York: Random House, 1989), 31.

36. William W. Hodkinson, editorial, "Why National Advertising Is Necessary," *MPN*, December 25, 1915, 58.

37. *PMPB*, July 22, 1914, 1.

38. Western Film Company advertisement, *PMPB*, May 20, 1914, 1.

39. Michael Quinn, "Distribution, the Transient Audience, and the Transition to the Feature Film," *Cinema Journal* 40, no. 2 (Winter 2001): 37.

40. *PMPB*, December 23, 1916, 2.

41. *Saturday Evening Post,* December 1, 1918, 39. Kathy Fuller-Seeley brought this ad to my attention during her presentation of "Panacea for the Ills of Modern Life: The Movie-Going Consumption Ideal in Paramount's National Magazine Advertising, 1917–1927" (paper, Society for Cinema Studies Conference, Denver, Colorado, May 2002).

42. ALCO Film Service advertisement, *PMPB,* December 9, 1914, 5. Although the action in *The Three of Us* is supposed to take place at an unprofitable Colorado gold mine, the film was actually shot on location in Wilkes-Barre, Pennsylvania. *The American Film Institute (AFI) Catalog: Feature Films, 1911–1920.* (Berkeley: University of California Press, 1988), 929.

43. See Colette Lindroth and James Lindroth, *Rachel Crothers: A Research and Production Sourcebook* (Westport, Conn.: Greenwood Press, 1995).

44. *Three of Us* advertisement, *PMPB,* December 9, 1914, 6; Famous Players Film Service advertisement, *PMPB,* December 9, 1914, 8. Famous Players Film Service did not actually last any longer than ALCO, and its organization became the primary basis for Paramount. See Quinn, "Distribution, the Transient Audience," 37.

45. *PMPB,* July 22, 1914, 1.

46. Kathryn H. Fuller, *At The Picture Show: Small-town Audiences and the Creation of Movie Fan Culture* (Washington DC: Smithsonian Institution Press, 1996), 137.

47. *PMPB,* April 28, 1915, 4.

48. See Sally Dumaux's *King Baggot: A Biography and Filmography of the First King of the Movies* (New York: McFarland and Company, 2002).

49. Mayer Publishing and Printing advertisement, *PMPB,* June 16, 1915, inside cover. These kinds of "cuts" must have been fairly popular and common because the last page of *Building Theater Patronage* gives theater owners detailed plans for building a jigsaw, designed specifically to make these kinds of self-standing ads. John Barry and Epes Sargent, *Building Theater Patronage* (New York: Chalmers Publishing, 1927), appendix.

50. Liberty Film Renting Company advertisement, *PMPB,* October 20, 1915, inside cover.

51. "An Exhibitor Has His Say," *MPN,* December 16, 1916, 1.

52. Richard A. Rowland, "If I Were an Exhibitor," *MPN,* December 25, 1916, 57. As a partner in Rowland and Clark Theaters, Rowland was, obviously, an exhibitor himself.

53. Charles Musser references Pittsburgh's advertising history in "Reading Local Histories of Early Film Exhibition: Sylvester Quin Breard's 'A History of the Motion Pictures in New Orleans, 1896–1908,'" *Historical Journal of Film, Radio, and Television* 15, no. 4 (October 1995): 581.

54. *PMPB,* April 14, 1914, 1.

55. Note the rhetorical shift here from moving pictures to "photoplay" as the attempts at legitimizing the movies begins to take effect. This paper, and its readership, could be broadly construed as middle-class.

56. "Anthony and Cleopatra," *Pittsburgh Index,* October 14, 1914, 16.

57. "Feature Photoplays to Be Seen in Pittsburg This Week," *Pittsburgh Press,* August 12, 1914, 32.

58. See Sargent's *Picture Theatre Advertising* section on "Newspaper Advertising," 82–93, for an explanation of the relationship between "paid" and "free" newspaper advertising. The two local exhibition companies to begin advertising with any regularity are Harris Amusements and Clark and Rowland.

59. *PMPB*, May 12, 1915, 1.

60. Rowland, "If I Were," 57.

61. Stamp, *Movie-Struck Girls*, 104.

62. I. G. Edmonds, *Big U: Universal in the Silent Days*. (London: Thomas Yoseloff, 1977), 36.

63. Stamp, *Movie-Struck Girls*, 105.

64. See for example: *The Shielding Shadow* serial advertisement, *Pittsburgh Press*, October 8, 1916, 6. Because of their fleeting nature, and their single-reel length, very few of these serials still exist in anywhere near complete form.

65. "Pathe Will Blanket Whole Country with Publicity," *MPN*, September 30, 1916, 2007.

66. Stamp, *Movie-Struck Girls*, 107–8.

67. Luckett, "Cities and Spectators," 41.

68. Sargent, *Picture Theatre Advertising*, 1, 3.

69. It appears that the local exchange that rented the serial had three to five copies of each week's episode, which were then booked into different regional theatres on a regular scheduled day. The result was that twenty to thirty different theaters in the region could show a serial each week.

70. L. C. Moen, "Statistics of the Motion Picture Industry," *MPN*, December 16, 1922, 3024, 2772. The prevalence of six-day-a-week changes began to decline by 1922, by which time 10 percent kept a film for an entire week.

71. "Small House and Short Film," *MPN*, October 21, 1916, 1.

72. Gaines, "From Elephants to Lux Soap," 31.

73. *PMPB*, October 17, 1915, 6. Albert Cook was a salesman for Ludwig Hommel and Company, which sold theater supplies such as lighting, seats, projectors, and so forth.

74. Leslie Midkiff DeBauche, "Advertising and the Movies: 1908–1915," *Film Reader* 6 (1985): 118.

75. Epes Winthrop Sargent, "Advertising," *MPW*, May 5, 1912, 753.

76. Sargent, *Picture Theatre Advertising*, v.

77. Sargent, *Picture Theatre Advertising*, 50. Surprisingly, little mention is made of advertising via magic lantern slides in the pages of the *Bulletin*, although there are occasionally ads for companies that would custom make slides for theaters and business. The Cleveland Public Library has an online collection of lantern slides advertising films from the 1910s and 1920s available at W. Ward Marsh Lantern Slide collection, http://cplorg.cdmhost.com/cdm4/browse.php?CISOROOT=%2Fp4014coll16.

78. Fort Pitt Film Company advertisement, *PMPB*, May 5, 1915, 11.

79. *PMPB*, May 20, 1914, 3.

80. *PMPB*, August 5, 1914, 3. This predates by almost two years the use of this advertising device by Famous Players, who Janet Staiger notes as the "earliest exploiters of the trailer." See Staiger, "Announcing Wares," 9. Staiger derides the innovation of the trailer as "hardly the act of a genius."

81. *PMPB*, April 7, 1915, 4. Photoplay Entertainment also promised stock Film announcements such as "Ladies please remove your hats," and "Don't spit on the floor," for its other interested customers.

82. "Masses of Pictures," *MPN*, December 11, 1915, 1.

83. Advertisement, *PMPB*, June 24, 1914, 1.

84. *PMPB*, October 28, 1914, 1.

85. *PMPB*, December 30, 1914, 4.

86. *PMPB*, June 23, 1915, 6. A 3-sheet measures 41 × 81 inches, a 28-sheet is an odd size, more typically a 24-sheet was billboard in size.

87. Information on the poster business was given by Kathy H. Fuller, "Antecedents of the Movie Poster: Lithography, Circus Advertising, and the Story of the Hennegan Brothers" (paper, Society for Cinema Studies Conference, West Palm Beach, Florida, 1999).

88. DeBauche, "Advertising," 120.

89. *PMPB*, August 25, 1928, 11.

90. Sargent, *Picture Theatre Advertising*, 60.

91. Pennsylvania Law for Censorship of Moving Pictures, standard 24, quoted in Ellis Paxson Oberholtzer, *The Morals of the Movie* (Philadelphia: The Penn Publishing Company, 1922), 215.

92. *PMPB*, July 29, 1914, 2.

93. Staiger, "Announcing Wares," 7.

94. Van Lewen advertisement, *PMPB*, June 23, 1915, 6.

95. These include the Penn Poster Mounting Company, which offered the "Right Kind of Re-inforcing." Before 1915, the companies seemed to have contracts with either General Film or the independents—Exhibitors' Display featured "mounted 3 and 6-sheets on all multiple-reel licensed releases" and the Independent Display Company, "renters of mounted paper," requested orders for Metro serials and all Pathé Gold Rooster films.

96. *AFI Catalog*, 785.

97. Sargent, *Picture Theatre Advertising*, 63.

98. Sargent, *Picture Theatre Advertising*, 16.

99. *PMPB*, September 23, 1914, 13.

100. *PMPB*, August 9, 1916, 19.

101. *PMPB*, May 6, 1914, 30.

102. *PMPB*, November 18, 1922, 16.

103. "Pittsburg" [sic], *MPW*, August 19, 1911, 470.

104. Sargent, *Picture Theatre Advertising*, 213–15.

105. *PMPB*, September 26, 1916, 1.

106. Sargent, *Picture Theatre Advertising*, 264, 69.

107. *PMPB*, August 16, 1916, 8.

108. Epes Winthrop Sargent, "Development of Exploitation," *Variety*, December 29, 1931, 12, 178.

109. *PMPB*, July 28, 1915, 8.

110. Gaines, "From Elephants to Lux Soap," 32.

111. *PMPB*, August 9, 1916, 12.

112. *PMPB*, December 3, 1919, 10. In the same issue, Robson pens a poem entitled "The Film Man's Christmas Prayer."

113. Sargent, "Development of Exploitation," 12.

114. *PMPB*, June 12, 1920, 24.

115. Universal Film Company, "The Wonderful Universal Moviegame" advertisements, *PMPB*, September 29, 1915, 4, 19.

116. *PMPB*, September 29, 1915, 7.

Chapter 5: The Morals of the Movies

1. "Vim Comedies Lynch Mr. Censorship at Garden Exposition," *MPN*, June 11, 1916, 3384.

2. Lee Grieveson, *Policing Cinema: Movies and Censorship in Early-Twentieth-Century* (Berkeley: University of California Press, 2004). See also Richard S. Randall, *Censorship of the Movies: The Social and Political Control of a Mass Medium* (Madison: University of Wisconsin Press, 1968); and Ira Carmen, *Movies, Censorship and the Law* (Ann Arbor: University of Michigan Press, 1966). Newer studies tends to break down into three categories. For an example of PCA work based on the code's files, see Lea Jacob, *The Wages of Sin: Censorship and the Fallen Woman Film 1928–1942* (Madison: University of Wisconsin Press, 1991). For an example of studies of the National Board of Censorship and reviews based on materials available at the Edison archives see Nancy J. Rosenbloom, "Between Reform and Regulation: The Struggle over Film Censorship in Progressive America, 1909–1922," *Film History* 1 (1987): 307–25. For an example of the growing number of local case studies, see George Potanmianos, "Movie Mad: Audiences and Censorship in a California Town, 1916–1926," *Velvet Light Trap* 42 (Fall 1998): 62–75. For an important non-American work, see Annette Kuhn, *Cinema, Censorship, and Sexuality, 1909–1925* (London: Routledge, 1988).

3. Grieveson, *Policing Cinema*, 3. Although Grieveson's Foucauldian approach to describing these early years of movie censorship as part of broad generative practices delimiting the cinema and its culture is highly productive, I continue in this chapter, as in the rest of the book, to purposefully trace out a more narrow and peopled path.

4. The dates listed are for the passing of the legislation; in more than one case it took a year or two for the boards to be adequately funded and begin their work. According to

Nancy Rosenbloom, at least seventeen states threatened to legislate their own boards in 1917. See Rosenbloom, "Between Reform and Regulation," 319.

5. Paul Salley, "Censorship of Motion Pictures in Kansas," *Classic Theaters of Kansas: Movie House History*, http://www.reeldiaries.com/moviehouse/articles/censorship.htm.

6. Ernest Morris, *Censored: The Private Life of the Movies* (New York: Cape and Smith, 1930).

7. *Mutual v. Industrial Commission of Ohio*, 236 U.S. 230 (1915).

8. Francis G. Couvares primarily attributes the development of self-censorship to the industry's "encounter[s]" with the Protestant and Catholic church. See Francis G. Couvares, "Hollywood, Main Street, and the Church: Trying to Censor the Movies before the Production Code," in *Movie Censorship in American Culture* (Washington DC: Smithsonian Institute Press, 1996), 129–58.

9. See Robert A. Armour, "Effects of Censorship Pressure on the New York Nickelodeon Market, 1907–1909," *Film History* 4 (1990): 113–21, for an extended telling of this particular narrative.

10. See David Hammack, *Power and Society: Greater New York at the Turn of the Century*. (New York: Russell Sage Foundation, 1982).

11. Mary Gray Peck (member, Board of Programs of Motion Picture Shows; member, Motion Picture Committee of the General Federation of Women's Clubs), quoted in Channing Pollock, "Swinging the Censor," *Photoplay*, February 1917, 66.

12. Charles Matthew Feldman, *The National Board of Censorship of Motion Pictures, 1909–1922* (New York: Arno Press, 1977), 121.

13. French films seem to have received a disproportionate share of the few rejections. See Richard Abel, *The Red Rooster Scare: Making Cinema American, 1900–1910* (Berkeley: University of California Press, 1999), 101. Also see Robert J. Fisher, "Film Censorship and Progressive Reform: The National Board of Censorship of Motion Pictures, 1909–1922," *Journal of Popular Film* 4 (1975): 147.

14. Report of the Board of Censorship to the Gentlemen of the Motion Picture Patents Company, July 24, 1909, as well as May 10, 1912. Document File, Edison Archives, West Orange, New Jersey. Clearly, the fear over media effects did not originate with the invention of television.

15. Eileen Bowser, *The Transformation of Cinema, 1907–1915* (Los Angeles: University of California Press, 1990), 49.

16. *Mutual v. Industrial Commission of Ohio*, 236 U.S. 230 (1915).

17. *New York Dramatic Mirror*, December 4, 1915 (no title or page number provided), in Kevin Brownlow, *Behind the Mask of Innocence: Sex, Violence, Prejudice, Crime: Films of Social Conscience in the Silent Era* (Los Angeles: University of California Press), 7; Robert Fisher, "Film Censorship and Progressive Reform," *Journal of Popular Film* 4 (1975): 149.

18. Moya Luckett, "Cities and Spectators: A Historical Analysis of Film Audiences in Chicago, 1910–1915" (PhD diss., University of Wisconsin, 1995), 2–3.

19. Initially, the superintendent of police in Chicago was granted to power to censor and ban movies from the city limits, but in 1912 these duties were turned over to a deputy and a set of examiners. See Ellis Paxson Oberholtzer, *The Morals of the Movie* (Philadelphia: The Penn Publishing Co., 1922), 116–17.

20. Luckett, "Cities and Spectators," 2–3.

21. Mary Erickson, "'In the Interest of the Moral Life of Our City': The Beginning of Motion Picture Censorship in Portland, Oregon" (unpublished manuscript, University of Oregon, 2007).

22. Morals Efficiency Commission, *Report* (City of Pittsburgh, 1913), 8.

23. Morals Efficiency Commission, *Report*, 20. According to the report, up to 80 percent of all local men had been infected with the disease at least once, and 30 percent of all the patients at the Western Pennsylvania Institute for the Blind had lost their sight due to the disease.

24. Shelley Stamp, *Movie Struck Girls* (Princeton: Princeton University Press, 1999), 43. Also see Roy Lubove, "The Progressive and the Prostitute," *Historian* 24, no. 3 (1962): 312–33.

25. Morals Efficiency Commission, *Report* (1913), 23–24.

26. Department of Public Health and Safety Records, University of Pittsburgh Archives and Collections. Although the existing archive for the department is too incomplete to draw a very accurate picture, it seems that only movies that had attracted attention in some negative way were viewed by the city officials for potential banning or censorship. Unlike the state board, the city's public safety department did not view every film to be exhibited in the city.

27. Stamp, *Movie Struck Girls*, 41.

28. "Shun the Slavers," *MPW,* October 14, 1916, 227. As early as March 1914, the Pittsburgh Cameraphone Theater, located downtown, was showing *Traffickers On Soles* which was advertised as "A Burlesque in 3 Reels Ridiculing White Slave Films," *Pittsburgh Sunday Post*, March 22, 1914, sec. 2, p. 4.

29. "Pittsburgh Clamps the Lid on Immoral Movie Films," *Variety*, February 27, 1914, 22.

30. *PMPB*, May 22, 1914, 10.

31. Pennsylvania State Board of Censors, *Eliminations 1915*, State Board of Censors collection, Department of Education, RG22, Pennsylvania Bureau of Archives and History, Harrisburg (hereafter cited as Censors, PA Archives).

32. Oberholtzer, *Morals of the Movie*, 119.

33. Additionally, the board was legislated "to banish posters or hand bills or other advertising matter concerning motion pictures where the same are sensational and misleading." Pennsylvania State Board of Censors, *Rules and Standards, Act Passed June 19, 1911* (Harrisburg: Wm. Stanley Ray, 1914), sec. 2, p. 3.

34. Pennsylvania State Board of Censors, *Rules and Standards, Act Passed June 19, 1911*, sec. 2, p. 3. Also see Oberholtzer, *Morals of the Movie*, 118. Although five other states eventually

had their own censor boards, almost all of which included at least one woman participant, Pennsylvania's was the only one that actually legislated the gender of its members.

35. See Lucy Fischer, *Cinematernity: Film, Motherhood Genre* (Princeton: Princeton University Press, 1996).

36. For a productive analysis of American class structure in this time period, see Richard Ohmann, *Selling Culture: Magazines, Markets, and Class at the Turn of the Century* (New York: Verso, 1996).

37. Christine Stansell, *City of Women: Sex and Class in New York, 1789–1860* (Chicago: University of Illinois Press, 1987), 63–75.

38. Harriet McClintock, Editorial, *Charleroi Mail*, January 28, 1914, 1.

39. See Miriam Hansen, "Chameleon and Catalyst: The Cinema as an Alternative Public Sphere," in *Babel and Babylon: Spectatorship in American Silent Film* (Cambridge: Harvard University Press, 1991).

40. Pennsylvania State Board of Censors, 15. "Pictures Will Be Judged as a Whole," *Rules and Standards, Act Passed June 19, 1911*, 9.

41. *PMPB*, May 27, 1914, 10. The lobbyists included former Pennsylvania senator J. Thompson.

42. "Herrington Plans to Unite Pennsylvania," *MPN*, November 28, 1914, 23. Previously, Pittsburgh exhibitors had belonged to the Motion Picture Exhibitors' Association of Pennsylvania while Philadelphia exhibitors pledged allegiance to the Exhibitors' League of Pennsylvania. Another Pittsburgh-based organization, the Moving Picture Protective Association, had a membership open to other branches of the state industry, particularly exchange owners.

43. Although film histories typically invoke the Fourteenth Amendment when discussing this case and the Pennsylvania Supreme Court's refusal to grant the movies the same freedoms of speech granted to the press and other traditional communication mediums, in 1914, the U.S. Supreme Court had yet to include those guarantees among the fundamental rights and liberties protected by the due process clause of the Fourteenth Amendment. Accordingly, only the Ohio Constitution protected the right of free speech from abridgement by the Ohio state government. Note that the arguments in this case were similar to those that motion picture produces would use in the 1915 suit, *Mutual Film Corporation v. Industrial Commission of Ohio* (1915).

44. "Keystone Censor Law Case up on Review," *MPN*, April 10, 1915, 35.

45. Although the court eventually ruled that this particular argument had no legal standing, it remains somewhat of a mystery how three people watched all these movies, day after day, week after a week. Although we can assume that additional assistant censors were hired, there is no indication of this in the available annual reports (1914–1918) by the board, either by name or budget line.

46. *PMPB*, June 23, 1915, 10. Although the actual trial did not occur until December 1915, a deal six months prior to the ruling between the various producers and the state said that any fees paid to the state for board approval (at $2.50 a reel) would be held by a

financial trust until the outcome of the trial—and the legality of the bill—was concluded. It appears that the industry's initial test case was *Equitable Motion Picture Corporation vs. Pennsylvania State Board of Censors,* sur appeal from the decision of the board on final disapproval of motion picture entitled *Sealed Life,* December 1915. There is no record of this film in *The American Film Institute (AFI) Catalog: Feature Films, 1911–1920* (Berkeley: University of California Press, 1988).

47. Oberholtzer, *Morals of the Movie,* 118.

48. Eventually, the Pennsylvania Supreme Court actually ruled in favor of the original 1911 censorship code. A letter from Oberholtzer in May 1917 to the state's attorney general asks if he has the legal power to prosecute an exhibitor who was in accordance with the 1915 code but not the original 1911 code. It appears the general attorney gave the go-ahead to do so, even though the Act of 1915 specifically repealed the previous act. Ellis P. Oberholtzer to Francis S. Brown, May 12, 1917, Censors, PA Archives, RG22.

49. Oberholtzer, *Morals of the Movie,* 214–15.

50. Oberholtzer, *Morals of the Movie,* 204.

51. Although the previous governor, John Tener, had appointed Breitinger and Nivers to the Board three years before there is no indication that they actually ever began the process of censoring the movies until the new bill was later passed and Oberholtzer was added.

52. Robert Douglas Bowden, *Boise Penrose, Symbol of an Era* (New York: Greenburg Publisher, 1937), 250.

53. J. Louis Breitinger to Hon. Boise Penrose, Senate Chamber, September 3, 1915, Censors, PA Archives, RG22. Of course, the attorney general was not officially a Penrose appointment, since his position legally would have involved the governor and then approval by the state senate, but the reality was that the Penrose machine was in charge of deciding virtually every major (and minor) position in state government, as well as many municipalities, particularly Philadelphia.

54. "Pennsylvania Censors Appointed for Movies," *Variety,* January 23, 1914, 19, and "Penn State Movie Men Take Protest to Governor," *Variety* January 28, 1914, 23. Breitinger's work as counsel for the Exhibitor's League is confirmed by its mention in "State Censors Named," *Gettysburg Times,* January 12, 1914, 2.

55. Couvares, "Hollywood, Main Street," 138.

56. See Frederick Marshall Wirt, "State Film Censorship with Particular Reference to Ohio" (PhD diss., Ohio State University, 1956), 58–64; and "A Year of Censorship," *MPN,* June 13, 1914, 96.

57. "Editor Edward C. Nivers Dies at Brockwayville," *Charleroi Daily Mail,* July 13, 1914, 1. Charleroi's economic base came from the surrounding coalfields and its glass-blowing factories.

58. "Strong Plea Is Made for Boys and Girls," *Charleroi Daily Mail,* February 3, 1912, 1; "To Hold Meeting Friday," *Charleroi Daily Mail,* October 3, 1912, 1; "Marketing Club Becomes Reality," *Charleroi Daily Mail,* August 15, 1912, 1, 2.

59. Oberholtzer, *Morals of the Movie,* 6–7.

60. Ellis Paxson Oberholtzer, *The Literary History of Philadelphia* (Philadelphia: The Penn Publishing Co., 1906); and Ellis Paxson Oberholtzer, *History of the United States since the Civil War* (New York: MacMillan, 1928). In 1922, after fulfilling his secretarial role for six years, Oberholtzer was ousted from the censorship board for political reasons and subsequently published *The Morals of the Movie*, a memoir and treatise on the important role of state censorship.

61. *AFI Catalog*, 475. By 1916, London was dead, suicide by poison, which according to his friend, Upton Sinclair, he took "to escape the claws of John Barleycorn."

62. Brownlow, *Behind the Mask*, 122.

63. Research on this issue is scarce, but see Anna McCarthy, "The Front Row Is Reserved for Scotch Drinkers: Early Television's Tavern Audience," *Cinema Journal* 31, no. 4 (Summer 1995): 31–49.

64. *PMPB*, May 6, 1914, 2.

65. *AFI Catalog*, 475. Quote is from "Pennsylvania and Ohio Censors Attack 'John Barleycorn' Film," *MPN*, August 1, 1914.

66. Although the film is listed as being distributed via state rights in the *AFI Catalog*, my impression from the trade journals is that Bosworth, Inc., paid a percentage of the profits to the exchange branch of Famous Players to distribute and promote the film. However, to further confuse the situation, an ad placed in *Motion Picture News* (August 1, 1914) states that "after September 1 all Bosworth Releases Handled through Paramount Program." More work needs to be done on early distribution patterns and structures to further understand the growing power of this branch of the industry as the studio system developed.

67. *PMPB*, July 29, 1914, 2.

68. *PMPB*, July 29, 1914, 2. The proviso reads, "this act shall not apply to any exhibition or use of moving pictures and stereopticon views, given for purely educational, charitable, fraternal or religious purposes, by any religious association, fraternal society, library, museum, public or private school, or any institution of learning, or any organization duly chartered under the laws of the Commonwealth as a corporation of the first class" (P.L. 534, Censors, PA Archives, RG22). These broad exceptions were, in fact, what successfully allowed the state to argue that the board was not infringing upon First Amendment rights.

69. "Pennsylvania and Ohio Censors Attack," *MPN*, 19; *PMPB*, July 29, 1914, 2.

70. The endorsement of the film by the WCTU was a relatively unusual move. According to Alison M. Parker, the WCTU had a long history of generally opposing the medium, which it saw as a major influence on the corruption of America's youth, and actively pursued an agenda that called for federal censorship of the industry. See Alison M. Parker, "Mothering the Movies: Women Reformers and Popular Culture," in *Movie Censorship and American Culture*, ed. Francis G. Couvares (Washington DC: Smithsonian Institution Press, 1996), 73–96.

71. "Pennsylvania and Ohio Censors Attack," *MPN*, 20. The "local option" was a popular, if ultimately failed, regulation structure that would have left the option of legal prohibition up to individual municipality and county governments.

72. Legal Briefs, 1915–1940, 6–0151 Box 10 (end), Censors, PA Archives, RG22.

73. "Pennsylvania and Ohio Censors Attack," *MPN*, 20.

74. "State Movie Censor Stops Jack London's Film upon Rum Evils," *Pittsburgh Post*, August 5, 1914, 12.

75. In fact, when Bosworth did begin spending money on traditional advertising, the ads consisted of a montage of newspaper clippings, all with headlines announcing the film's censorship controversy. See Bosworth Film advertisement for *John Barleycorn*, *MPN*, August 8, 1914, 164.

76. *PMPB*, August 5, 1914, 10.

77. Epes Winthrop Sargent, *Picture Theatre Advertising* (New York: Chalmers Publishing Company, 1915), 70.

78. Sargent, *Picture Theatre Advertising*, 74.

79. "Producers Engage Philadelphia Theatre to Show 'John Barleycorn' as Censor Weakens," *MPN*, August 8, 1914, 17.

80. "Censors Balk at Stopping 'John Barleycorn,'" *MPN*, August 15, 1914, 17.

81. "Censors Balk," *MPN*, 18.

82. "Censor, in Compromise, Passes 'Barleycorn,'" *MPN*, August 22, 1914, 19. See also *AFI Catalog*, 475.

83. Famous Players Film Service advertisement for *John Barleycorn*, *MPN*, August 1, 1914, 65.

84. *Mutual Film Corporation v. Industrial Commission of Ohio*, 236 U.S. 230 (1915).

85. *Buffalo Branch v. Breitinger*, 250 Pa., 225, affirming 23 Pa. District Reports, 837 Censors, PA Archives, RG22. The test case was brought by the Buffalo branch of Mutual Film Corporation; the Mutual Film Corporation of Pennsylvania and Interstate Film Company by Albert E. Brown, William Sachsenmaier, and Vernon R. Carrick (representing the Overbrook Theatre), and by the Pittsburgh Photoplay Company. The law was tested not just on its First Amendment merits but also on the contention that it was an unlawful interference with interstate commerce.

86. "*Nixon Theatre Company v. Joseph G. Armstrong, Mayor of the City of Pittsburgh*, Court of Common Pleas of Allegheny County, No. 1247, October Term, 1915," 3. See also Nickieann Fleener-Marzec, *D. W. Griffith's The Birth of a Nation: Controversy, Suppression, and the First Amendment as it Applies to Filmic Expression, 1915–1973* (New York: Arno Press, 1980).

87. *PMPB*, June 12, 1915, 1–2. Also see Pennsylvania State Board of Censors, *Report of the Pennsylvania State Board of Censors, June 1, 1915–December 1, 1915* (Harrisburg: Wm. Stanley Ray State Printer, 1916). The board hired Samuel Johnson as projector operator at twenty-five dollars a week and George Locker as the assistant censor at a dollar more a week. The General Film Corporation was reimbursed on a monthly basis for these expenses by

various other major film producers. As the Trust had done, General Film passed on a portion of the expenses to the other major producers and distributors who operated in the state.

88. Pennsylvania State Board of Censors, *Report of the Pennsylvania Board of Censors, 1916* (Harrisburg: Wm. Stanley Ray State Printer, 1916), 4. The board included this statistic in its annual report because it wanted more money from the governor.

89. Pennsylvania State Board of Censors, *Report of the State Board of Censors, 1916*, 5.

90. The application fee was lowered in 1917 by legislation that the film industry helped push through the state governing body, to a dollar, but then subsequently raised to two dollars when the country entered World War I. The November 1917 release of *The Sex Lure* garnered a "POOR" in each of the categories: "Educational Value, Artistic Value, Entertainment Value and Moral Effect." Censor Slip for *The Sex Lure*, November 3, 1917, Censors, PA Archives, RG22.

91. After the first year, this logo was imprinted with the title of the film that had been approved; this practice was instituted in order to keep distributors from cutting up or duping the approval strip and affixing it to non-approved films.

92. Pennsylvania State Board of Censors, *Report, 1916*, 5.

93. Chief Inspector to Mr. Edgar Moss, Manager, Fox Film Company, July 5, 1927, Censors, PA Archives, RG22, C4.

94. Fox Exchange to Pennsylvania State Board of Censors, July 11, 1923, Censors, PA Archives, RG22, C4. It is highly likely that this *Slaves of Beauty* is a board-required replacement for the film's original title, *Slaves of Desire* (1923).

95. "Pennsylvania Makes 600 Police Chiefs New Film Spies," *MPN*, January 22, 1916, 347. Unfortunately, there is no record of this list of titles in the Pennsylvania Bureau of Archives and History.

96. Pennsylvania State Board of Censors, *Report of Pennsylvania State Board of Censors, for the Year Ending November 30, 1917* (Harrisburg: J. L. L. Kuhn, 1917), 9.

97. James M. Farr to J. Louis Breitinger, May 12, 1915, Censors, PA Archives, RG22, 6–0150, C6.

98. Savoy Theater advertisement for *Three Weeks*, clipping, Censors, PA Archives, RG22, 6–0150, C6; *AFI Catalog*, 929. Another adaptation was made in 1923, which caused a very similar outcry, and which helped lead to the MPPDA's first regulation of motion picture content in June, 1924. Richard Maltby, "To Prevent the Prevalent Type of Book," in *Movie Censorship and American Culture*, 104.

99. Glyn provided her readers with plenty of rolling around, kissing, and moaning but no actual descriptions of sexual intercourse. A typical passage: "Then a madness of tender caressing seized her. She purred as a tiger might have done while she undulated like a snake. She touched him with her finger-tips, she kissed his throat, his wrists, the palms of his hands, his eyelids, his hair. Strange subtle kisses, unlike the kisses of women. And often, between her purrings she murmured love words in some fierce language of her

own, brushing his ears and his eyes with her lips the while." Elinor Glyn, *Three Weeks* (New York: Duffield and Co, 1907), 126.

100. Circa 1908, quoted in Lori Landay, *Madcaps, Screwballs, and Con Women: The Female Trickster in American Culture* (Philadelphia: University of Pennsylvania Press, 1998), 76.

101. George Potamianos, in writing about the Sacramento Better Film Board's response to the 1924 remake of this film, assumes that "the board most likely objected because the film condones the queen's adultery." Most likely, however, they too were worried about Glynn's extratextual relationship to the material. See George Potamianos, "Movie Mad: Audiences and Censorship in a California Town, 1916–1926," *Velvet Light Trap* 42 (Fall 1998): 69, 74.

102. Louis J. Breitinger to Electric Theatre Supply Company, March 8, 1915, Censors, PA Archives, RG22, 6–0150, C6. An unsent draft copy of this letter shows that initially, Breitinger was going to require that the title *Three Weeks* also be eliminated, based on the wide popular knowledge of the title and the sexual signifiers already attached to it. Louis J. Breitinger to Electric Theatre Supply Company, draft, December 23, 1914, State Archives RG22, 6–0150, C6, Censors, PA Archives, Harrisburg.

103. John M. Cooper Jr., *Pivotal Decades: The United States: 1900–1920* (New York: W. W. Norton, 1990), 227.

104. Leslie Midkiff DeBauche, *Reel Patriotism: The Movies and World War I* (Madison: The University of Wisconsin Press, 1997), 5.

105. DeBauche, *Reel Patriotism*, 196; and Kevin Brownlow, *Behind the Mask of Innocence* (Los Angeles: University of California Press, 1990), 15.

106. *War Brides* Intertitles, Censors, PA Archives, Harrisburg, RG22, C4. This film remains among the missing.

107. Pennsylvania State Board of Censors, *War Brides* Eliminations, December 16, 1916, Censors, PA Archives, RG22, C4.

108. Pennsylvania State Board of Censors, *Report, 1917*, 6.

109. Most of the eliminations were of subtitles that referred to Joan's unborn child such as "You shall be held in prison until the birth of your child, then shot." *War Brides* Eliminations, November 28, 1916, and December 4, 1916.

110. *War Brides* Telegrams, Censors, PA Archives, Harrisburg, RG22, C4.

111. Francis Shunk Brown to Frank R. Shattuck, June 23, 1917, *War Brides* Correspondence, Censors, PA Archives, Harrisburg, RG22, C4. See also *PMPB*, February 7, 1917, 4.

112. *War Brides* Eliminations, October 23, 1917.

113. "War Brides," *MPN*, December 9, 1916, 3654.

114. See "Revenue and Budgets," in *Annual Reports for the State Board of Censors, 1915–1917*, Censors, PA Archives, Harrisburg. Self-sustaining government institutions are by their nature difficult to eliminate, since there is little economic incentive to do so. The Pennsylvania State Board of Censors lasted until the late 1950s, and was one of the last two film censorship boards in the country to disband.

115. *PMPB*, November 15, 1916, 1.

116. Although there is no particular evidence that explains the predisposition for "going underground" with comedy shorts, I would hypothesize that it was because these films, which were very popular with audiences, included the types of antisocial and/or sexually risqué images and actions that the state board refused to allow exhibitors to show. Also, because they were shorts, if the board eliminated one or two significant sequences, the film became virtually useless—under such conditions Pennsylvania's exhibitors and distributors must have felt they had little choice but to show the films unexamined by the board.

117. Pennsylvania State Board of Censors, *Annual Report of the State Censors, 1915*, Censors, PA Archives, Harrisburg. A brief article from March 1917 notes that in one week, all but four of the city's exchangemen (approximately twenty) were cited and forced to pay fines for neglecting to make ordered eliminations. *PMPB*, March 14, 1917, 1.

118. "Censors Impose Fines," *MPW*, August 7, 1915, 1029.

119. "Pennsylvania Censors Find Films Exhibited with 'Cuts' Retained Following Investigation," *MPN*, July 31, 1915, 67.

120. Pittsburgh Moving Picture Protective Association advertisement, *PMPB*, June 28, 1914, 1, 3.

121. *PMPB*, April 22, 1914.

122. *PMPB*, June 9, 1914, 2.

123. *PMPB*, November 15, 1916, 1.

124. "Liberty Bell Slides," *MPW*, April 17, 1915, 420.

125. *PMPB*, November 15, 1916, 1.

126. *PMPB*, July 4, 1917, 1. The article notes that the amendment was most likely specifically directed at Pittsburgh's exhibitors.

127. *PMPB*, October 18, 1916, 10.

128. Pennsylvania State Board of Censors, *Report, 1917*, 11.

129. William A. Nealey, "Motion Picture Censorship and Organized Labor," quoted in J. R. Rutland, ed., *State Censorship of Motion Pictures* (New York: H. W. Wilson Co., 1923), 107.

130. "President Wilson Consents to Be the Guest of the Motion Picture Board of Trade," *MPN*, January 29, 1916, 504.

131. See David Yallop, *The Day the Laughter Stopped* (New York: St. Martin's Press, 1976) for a full accounting of the Arbuckle debacle; and Bruce Long, *Taylorology*, http://www.silent-movies.com/Taylorology, for a fascinating (and obsessive) look at every possible aspect of the murder of William Desmond Taylor.

132. *PMPB*, September 24, 1921, 1.

133. Motion Picture Producers and Distributors of America, *The Open Door* (New York: MPPDA, 1927).

134. Ernst Morris and Pare Lorentz, *Censored—the Private Life of the Movie* (New York: Cape and Smith, 1930), 52.

135. The major cases that overturned *Mutual Film Corp v. Industrial Commission of Ohio* (1915) include: *Burstyn v. Wilson* (1952), better known as the *Miracle* decision, and *Freedman v. Maryland* (1965). See Randall, *Censorship of the Movies*, 77–112.

136. Pennsylvania State Board of Censors, *Act and Rules, Passed May 15, 1915*, P.L. 534 (Harrisburg: The Telegraph Press, 1926).

Chapter 6: The Local View

1. *PMPB*, October 29, 1919, 16; November 19, 1919, 16.

2. *PMPB*, December 24, 1919, 16.

3. See, for example: Daan Hertogs and Nico de Klerk, eds., *Uncharted Territory: Essays on Early Nonfiction Film* (Amsterdam: Stichting Nederlands Filmmuseum, 1997); Alison Griffith, *Wondrous Difference: Cinema, Anthropology, and Turn-of-the-Century Visual Culture* (New York: Columbia University Press, 2002); and Vanessa Toulmin, Patrick Russell, and Tim Neal, "The Mitchell and Kenyon Collection: Rewriting Film History," *Moving Image* 3 (Fall 2003): 1–18.

4. Miriam Hansen, *Babel and Babylon: Spectatorship in American Silent Film* (Cambridge: Harvard University Press, 1991), 91.

5. "Premiere Report," *Waynesburg Republican*, December 3, 1914, 1.

6. Charles Musser, *Before the Nickelodeon: Edwin S. Porter and the Edison Manufacturing Company* (Los Angeles: University of California Press, 1991); see also Richard Abel, *The Red Rooster Scare: Making Cinema American, 1900–1910* (Los Angeles: University of California Press, 199), 131–32.

7. Dwight Swanson and Caroline Frick, "See Yourself on the Screen: Local Stars, Itinerant Films and Complicating History" (unpublished paper, presented at Orphans 4 Conference, University of South Carolina, March 2004).

8. Filmmakers Edwin S. Porter, William K. L. Dickson, and G. W. "Billy" Bitzer, for example, embodied all things cinematic. See Charles Musser, "Pre-Classical American Cinema: Its Changing Modes of Film Production," in *Silent Film*, ed. Richard Abel, 85–107 (New Brunswick: Rutgers University Press, 1999).

9. Tom Gunning, "The Cinema of Attractions: Early Film, Its Spectators and the Avant-Garde," in *Early Cinema: Space, Frame, Narrative*, ed. Thomas Elsaesser (London: BFI Publishing, 1990), 58.

10. See Kathryn Helgesen Fuller, "Viewing the Viewers: Representations of the Audience in Early Cinema Advertising" in *American Movie Audiences*, ed. Melvyn Stokes and Richard Maltby, 112–28 (London: BFI Publishing, 1999).

11. Musser, "Pre-Classical American Cinema," 154. Biograph in particular, however, continued to produce local views for specific theaters. According to Musser (266), Billy Bitzer (D. W. Griffith's eventual cameraman) spent most of 1899 in the Boston area photographing local views that "were intended primarily for Keith's Boston House."

12. Musser, "Pre-Classical American Cinema," 159.

13. Obituary for Charles Silveus, *Waynesburg Republican*, May 1, 1957, 12. Silveus was born October 30, 1878, in the nearby town of Kirby, where his parents also owned a restaurant.

14. Epes Winthrop Sargent, *Picture Theatre Advertising* (New York: Chalmers Publishing Company, 1915), 2.

15. Sargent, *Picture Theatre Advertising*, 2.

16. "Theatres and Their Admission Prices," *MPN*, October 28, 1916, 1. The survey was sent by the trade to more than 12,000 theaters and answered by 2,528 exhibitors.

17. "Eclipse to Open," *Waynesburg Republican*, April 2, 1912, 1.

18. G. Wayne Smith, *The History of Greene County, Pennsylvania*, vol. II (Cornerstone Genealogical Society, 1996). The Opera House had a main seating area and two upper galleries. Although there is no current record of when nickelodeons first appeared in Waynesburg, by 1907 the Edisonia Theater was operating in the business district. Another nickel theater, the Lyric, was operating downtown as late as 1912, the year that Silveus opened the Eclipse. The *Republican* records that in 1912 Jesse Fordyce sold the Edisonia to J. B. McIntosh, a retired magician from Pittsburgh, and mentions in passing, on January 21, 1915, a show at the "Old Lyric Theater Room," *Waynesburg Republican*, March 6, 1912, 1, and January 21, 1915, 4.

19. Opera House advertisement, *Waynesburg Republican*, December 2, 1914.

20. In December 1912, the *Republican* reported that the Opera House had installed a second projector so that "features with more than one reel could be shown continuously." This is a good indication that the Opera House was moving toward feature-focused exhibitions. "Opera House," *Waynesburg Republican*, December 10, 1912, 2.

21. "At the Opera House," *Waynesburg Republican*, January 21, 1911, 1. This film does not appear to have survived.

22. Sargent, *Picture Theatre Advertising*, 4.

23. "At the Eclipse," *Waynesburg Republican*, December 12, 1912, 1.

24. Ellis Paxson Oberholtzer, *The Morals of the Movie* (Philadelphia: The Penn Publishing Co., 1922), 83.

25. "Benefit Show," *Waynesburg Republican*, October 23, 1914, 2.

26. *PMPB*, September 23, 1914, 5.

27. Because the Cinématographe utilized a single perforation for each frame, it was not compatible with the majority of systems that utilized Edison's double-perforated format, which became standard, eventually dooming Lumière's elegant machine.

28. We know that Silveus owned a camera and shot his own film rather than employed an outside freelancer because his camera was available for sale in a Waynesburg antique/junk store for a period of time in the late 1970s. It has since disappeared.

29. Barry Salt, *Film Style & Technology: History & Analysis*, 2nd ed. (London: Starwood 1992), 80–81.

30. Bass Camera Company advertisement, *MPW*, July 6, 1918, 117.

31. Obituary for Charles Silveus, *Waynesburg Republican*, May 1, 1957.

32. "The Camera," *MPN*, March 25, 1916, 1808–9.

33. For a contemporary description of the division of labor in Hollywood, see Austin C. Lescarboura, *Behind the Motion Picture Screen* (New York: Scientific American Publishing 1919).

34. David S. Hulfish, *Motion Picture Work: A General Treatise on Picture Taking, Picture Making, Photo-Plays, and Theater Management and Operation* (Chicago: American Technical Society, 1915), Section II, 76.

35. "The Camera," *MPN*, April 8, 1916, 2106.

36. Although there was nowhere near the trepidation associated with many of the toxic chemicals that are needed for processing that there is today, solutions requiring sulfuric acid and caustic potash would have put many exhibitors off from the idea.

37. Carl Louis Gregory, ed., *Condensed Course in Motion Picture Photography* (New York: New York Institute of Photography, 1920), 134–35. During this period, Kodak produced a single negative and single printing stock, both of which were orthochromatic—insensitive to the red end of the light spectrum. Although from a photographic standpoint this was a pretty serious limitation for the developer, a person could see his work in process by using a red safety light and could "judge" the negative by eye during its development.

38. See, for example, Gregory, *Condensed Course*, 133–64.

39. "How Can Negative Film Be Effectively Reversed into Positive Film?" *MPN*, March 21, 1914, 27.

40. "The Camera," *MPN*, March 25, 1916, 1808.

41. Dan Streible, "Itinerant Filmmakers and Amateur Casts: A Homemade 'Our Gang,' 1926," *Film History* 15, no. 2 (2003): 177–92.

42. "The Camera," *MPN*, March 21, 1914, 27.

43. "The Camera," *MPN*, April 9, 1916, 2590.

44. "Rules for Exhibitors Planning Films for Weeklies," *MPN*, April 29, 1916, 2590.

45. Miles Davin (amateur local historian of Waynesburg), personal lecture notes on Waynesburg history, 1973–2001. Provided to author at interview with Miles Davin, May 27, 2001.

46. "The Camera," *MPN*, April 29, 1916, 2590.

47. Gunning "Cinema of Attractions," 60.

48. Tom Gunning, "Before Documentary: Early Nonfiction Films and the 'View' Aesthetic," in *Uncharted Territory: Essays on Early Nonfiction Film*, ed. Daan Hertogs and Nico de Klerk (Amsterdam: Stichting Nederlands Filmmuseum, 1997), 14.

49. Gunning, "Before Documentary," 18.

50. Clifford Geertz, *Interpretations of Culture* (New York: Basic Books, 1973), 24.

51. The unit, which began with only 65 members, reached its authorized wartime strength of 150 in May and was drafted into federal service in August of that year. See Smith, *History*, 2:606. According to the local newspaper, Silveus later sent four thousand

feet (ten rolls) of these practice sessions, some of which survives, to Camp Hancock, where it was shown to the men of Company K preparing to leave for Europe. *Waynesburg Republican*, February 16, 1918, 1.

52. In the surviving footage, the men move forward over the park's slight hills in groups of ten vs. en masse—a relatively new strategy aimed at lowering casualties in advancing from trench to trench.

53. "Wisecarvers Entertain Company K," *Waynesburg Republican*, August 28, 1917, 1.

54. "The Camera," *MPN*, April 8, 1916, 2106.

55. Miles Davin (amateur local historian of Waynesburg), interview by the author, May 22, 2001.

56. For an excellent account of the role of parades in American culture, see Susan G. Davis, *Parades and Power: Street Theatre in Nineteenth Century Philadelphia* (Philadelphia: Temple Press, 1986).

57. Eclipse Theatre advertisement, *Waynesburg Republican*, September 12, 1917, 4. Missing from this discussion/description is the role of African Americans in the town and in the war. There is no indication of whether or not the Eclipse was in any way segregated, or whether local black patrons were even allowed admission to the theater to see Silveus's local views or any other film. However, at least once, Silveus acknowledged the town's black population on film. In one very brief medium shot, four young black men, dressed in suits and each bearing a ribbon on his chest, look straight at the camera and respectfully remove their hats. This image is believed to represent the first four black men from the county to be drafted into service in the fall of 1917. If true, the *Republican* notes that two of this group of four includes "Homer Jackson and William Turner of Waynesburg," *Waynesburg Republican*, October 5, 1917, 4.

58. See Janet Staiger, "Announcing Wares, Winning Patrons, Voicing Ideals: Thinking about the History and Theory of Advertising," *Cinema Journal* 29, no. 3 (Fall 1990): 11–13.

59. "Do Local Pictures Pay?" *MPN*, July 31, 1915, 846.

60. See Frank Luther Mott, *American Journalism: A History: 1690–1960*, 3rd ed. (New York: The Macmillan Company, 1962), 539.

61. Sargent, *Picture Theatre Advertising*, 50.

62. *PMPB*, April 30, 1914, 4.

63. "Do Local Pictures Pay?" *MPN*, 846.

64. *PMPB*, May 20, 1914, 3.

65. *PMPB*, May 27, 1914, 4.

66. Smith, *History*, 524. According to Smith, Jacobs's birdhouses could be found in the yards of Henry Ford, William Rockefeller, and Thomas Edison.

67. The workers also expanded theater seating to 650, installed a heating and cooling system, and constructing a fireproof projection room. *Waynesburg Republican*, July 18, 1921, 4.

68. "Showing the Murder Pictures," *Homestead Daily Messenger*, January 9, 1914, 1; "The Murder Pictures," *Homestead Daily Messenger*, January 10, 1914, 2; "Rukoski Writes a Postal,"

Homestead Daily Messenger, January 7, 1914, 1. Apparently Henry's mother killed herself by throwing herself in front of a train upon hearing what her son had done.

69. *PMPB*, April 30, 1914, 4.

70. "Five Killed by Explosion," *Waynesburg Republican*, April 3, 1917, 1. The station owned by Peoples Natural Gas Co. was the world's largest at the time.

71. If, in fact, Silveus relied on an outside lab to process his negatives and make his prints, it would have saved him the time/expense of resending to the lab the conformed negative.

72. Charlie Keil and Shelley Stamp, eds., *American Cinema's Transitional Era: Audiences, Institutions, Practices* (Berkeley: University of California Press), 60–65.

73. Carl Louis Gregory, *Motion Picture Photography* (New York: Falk Publishing Company, 1927), 200.

74. Hansen, *Babel and Babylon*, 43, 98.

75. Davin, interview.

76. Gunning, "Cinema of Attractions," 58.

77. Edison Manufacturing Company, *Edison Films Supplement 168* (Orange, NJ: Edison Manufacturing Company, 1903), 2–3, in George C. Pratt, *Spellbound in Darkness* (New York: University of Rochester Press, 1966), 29–30.

78. See Francis G. Couvares, "Plebian Culture," in *The Remaking of Pittsburgh Class and Culture in an Industrializing City, 1877–1919* (Albany: State University of New York Press, 1984), 31–50, for the role of the firehouse and fireman in nineteenth-century Pittsburgh.

79. Patricia Zimmerman, *Reel Families: A Social History of Amateur Film* (Bloomington: University of Indiana Press, 1995), 66–71.

80. Shelly Stamp, *Movie-Struck Girls: Women and Motion Picture Culture after the Nickelodeon* (Princeton: Princeton University Press, 2000), 5.

81. Moya Luckett, "Filming the Family: Home Movie Systems and the Domestication of Spectatorship," *Velvet Light Trap* 36 (Fall 1995): 30.

82. Zimmerman, *Reel Families*, 4.

83. See, for example, Hansen, *Babel and Babylon*, 22.

Epilogue

1. In the 1970s, one of the firemen, Miles Davin Sr., an amateur local historian, had a 16mm print struck from some of the original negatives, particularly of footage of the local men training for World War I and the same reserve company later heading to fight Pancho Villa in 1917. Davin, in fact, traded at least some of this negative to a lab somewhere in Chicago in exchange for the print. In the early 1980s, a local videographer, Bill Molzon, who works for Waynesburg College, became interested in the footage after going to one of the local functions at which Davin exhibited the footage. Davin had amassed

a considerable amount of information about the events and the people in the films ("Hey, I'd recognize that nose anywhere, that's my great uncle Harry marching in the front!"). It is Davin's local expertise that allowed me to date and specify many of the events and people that occur in Silveus's footage. Molzon, on finding the deteriorating condition of the remaining nitrate negatives in the basement of the firehouse, was eventually able to get a grant from the American Film Institute to have the Library of Congress produce a 35mm safety negative and print from the cobbled-together pieces of original film that survived. Unfortunately, the remaining nitrate negatives were subsequently lost or destroyed by the library.

2. "Millionaire Eloped," *Syracuse Herald*, October 13, 1906, 5.

3. The Forty-fifth District was composed of the cities of Duquesne and Clairton, the Twentieth and Twenty-eighth Wards of the city of Pittsburgh, and all the boroughs and townships in Allegheny County south of the Ohio and Monongahela Rivers, which included Crafton, where Harris lived with his family.

4. Frank C. Harper, *Pittsburgh of Today, Its Resources and People* (New York: The American Historical Society, 1931), 512.

5. John H. Harris to Wally Forrester, editor of the *Pittsburgh Press*, August 31, 1936. "Harris Family" file, *Pittsburgh Post-Gazette Archives*, Pittsburgh.

6. This plaque was eventually replaced in the 1950s by a state historical marker that continued to give Harris sole ownership of the nickelodeon.

7. *Mayer Press: Fifty Years of Printing Service* (Pittsburgh: Mayer Press, 1937).

8. *PMPB*, August 25, 1928, 8.

INDEX

Note: Page numbers in italic type indicate illustrations.

Abbott, Lyman, 159
Abel, Richard, 46, 63, 72, 77–78, 118, 263n17
Acker, Jean, 250
Acktenheil, Fanny, 80
advance promotion, 73
The Adventure of Kathlyn (Selig-Polyscope), 132
advertisements: Bass Camera Company, *224*; Calcium Light and Film Company, *61*; "Chaplin Cuts," *127*; Eclipse Moving Picture Theater, Waynesburg, *219*; Famous Players Film Service, *125*; *The Lure of New York*, *75*; Pincus, *129*; Pittsburgh Commercial Motion Picture Company, *219*; S. Van Lewen, *143*; "Stars, Stars, Nothing But Stars," *126*; *The Three of Us*, *123*; *Three Weeks*, *188*, *189*; Universal Moviegame, *152*; Western Film Company, *71*. *See also* advertising
advertising: advance, 73; branding in, 119–22, 124–25; censorship of, 275n33; cut-outs for, 128, 270n49; by exhibitors, 130–36; of feature films, 120–21; by film exchanges, 54, 118–20, 122–24; film historiography and, 110; film stars in, 124–29, 131; film-specific, 121–22, 132, 144; illustration/photography in, 124, 131, 235; local films as, 139, 234–36; mechanical devices in, 145; in newspapers, 130–33, 234–35, 271n58; *Pittsburgh Moving Picture Bulletin* and, 54, 116, 118–20, 122, 124, 129–30, 141–42; posters for, 141–45; and quid pro quo, 70, 131, 141; of serials, 132–35; *The Shielding Shadow*, *134*; theater fronts and, 145–46; theater program schedule and, 113; in theaters, 138–39, 234–36. *See also* advertisements; promotions
African Americans, 116, 267n29, 286n57
A. G. Fontana Productions, 73
airdomes, 70–71
ALCO Film Service, 122
alcohol consumption, 173–76
Allegheny Film Exchange, 66
Allen, Robert, 10, 85, 88–89, 93, 215
All-Star, 123
Altoona, 49, 209

Alvin Theater, 15, 36, 42
Amalgamated Association, 7, 256n13
Ambrosia Studio, 77
American Feature Company, 120
American Federation of Labor (AFL), 202
American Film Co., 73
American Film Exchange, 62
American Theater, 141
Amusements (journal), 56
Anderson, Gilbert M. "Broncho Billy," 63–64
Anthony and Cleopatra, 131
Anti-saloon League, 175–76
Antonopolis, Pete, 5, 100, 136
Apex Film Company, 76
Applegarth, George S., *84*, *101*
Arbuckle, Fatty, 203
arcades, penny, 41, 43
Arthur, Tex, 146, *147*
Astra Film Corporation, 133
Athene Club, 172
Atlantis, 145
audiences: attendance of, 155; children as, 105–6, 109; class of, 92–95, 97–98; composition of, 91–92, 93, 114, 226n85; demographics of, 91–92; floating clientele, 93, 266n85; programs designed for specific, 98; strategies for attracting, 110–11, 113–14, 135, 217–18 (*see also* advertising; promotions); theater-going experience of, 114, 136, 146, 245–47; travel by, 92–93; youthful, 221
Austin, William, 26–27
Avenue Theater, 28–29, 33, 36, 37

Baggot, King, 125, 127
Bailey Circus, 142
Bair, Harry S., 80
ballyhoo artists, 146
The Bandit King (Selig), 64–65
Bankoski, Ignatz, 238
bargain exchanges, 68–72
Barnum Circus, 142
Barrymore, John, 78
bars. *See* saloons

289

Bass Camera Company, 223, 224
Bates, George, Jr., 139, 222, 237, 238
Bauman, Charles, 264n36
Beechwood Theater, 137
Bell and Howell 2709 camera, 223
Belmar Theater, 149
Bernardi, W. J., 92, 100
Beware of Strangers, 74
Bijou Dream theaters, 46, 47
Bijou Theatre, 28, 30, 36
billboards, 133
Biograph Company, 75, 112, 173, 215, 283n11
Bioskop, 76
The Birth of a Nation (Griffith), 181
Bitzer, Billy, 283n11
blue laws, 62, 221, 257n31, 263n25
Board of Programs of Motion Picture Shows, 159
Bochert, Charles, 26
Boston, Massachusetts, 26, 46, 255n5, 283n11
Bosworth Film, 78, 178, 278n66, 279n75
Bosworth, Hobart, 174, 177
Bowser, Ellen, 111, 114
Boyd, R. Earl, 13
branding, 119–22, 124–25
Breitinger and Breitinger, 176
Breitinger, Louis J., 155, 166, 170–71, 173, 175–78, 189, 194, 277n51, 281n102
Brenon, Herbert, 191
Britain, 213
Broadway Theatre, 5
Broski, Mary, 17
Brown, Francis S., 170, 194
Brumbaugh, Martin G., 170, 172
Bryan, William Jennings, 220
Building Theatre Patronage (Sargent and Barry), 138
Bulletin. See *Pittsburgh Moving Picture Bulletin* (journal)
Bureau of Building Inspection, 156
Burgun, A. J., 209, *210*
burlesque, 162
Burstyn v. Wilson (*Miracle* decision), 283n135
Bush, W. Stephen, 26, 85
Byington, Margaret, *Homestead: The Households of a Mill Town*, 12

Café Royal, 34
Calcium Light and Film Company, 61, 61–62, 65, 66, 226
Calcium Light Company, 60
Callahan, George, xii, *xiii*, xiv, 254
Callahan, Jack, xi–xii

"The Camera" column in *Motion Picture News*, 223–29, 233, 247
Cameraphone Theater, 265n65
cameras, 215–17, 222–25, 284n27
camerawork, 229–31, 239–40, 244–45
Carmen, Ira, *Movies, Censorship, and the Law*, 156
Carnegie, Andrew, 159
carnivals, 20, 109, 136, 142
Carr, E. H., 212
Carrie Nation Smashing a Saloon (Biograph), 173
Casino Theater, 31, 33, 149
Castroni, Professor, 26
Censoring Committee, of National Board of Censorship, 159
censorship: application forms concerning, 182, 183; and children, 160; comedies and, 282n116; controversies over, 160; exhibitors and, 168–71, 196–99, 201; federal control of, 203; film exchanges and, 199, 201; film industry and, 157–61, 167–69, 173–81, 202–3, 274n8; gender and, 165–66; local attempts at, 161, 164, 180–81; opposition to, 154–55, 198–99, 200, 201–2; in Pittsburgh, 155–56, 161–64, 181, 197–99, 275n26; *Pittsburgh Moving Picture Bulletin* and, 143–44, 198–99, 201; poster, 143–44; process of, 182, 184; social and film industry contexts of, 156; social support for, 158; standards for, 166–67, 169–70; state control of, 157–58, 164, 180–81, 201–2, 273n4; Supreme Court rulings on, 157, 180, 201, 204; and women, 193–96. See also morality; Pennsylvania State Board of Censors
Censorship of the Movies (Randall), 156
Chaplin, Charlie, 69, 127, *127*–28, 250
Charities Publication Committee of New York, 11
Charleroi Daily Mail (newspaper), 171
Charleroi Marketing Club, 172
chartered clubs, 13, 257n31
Chautauqua Lake Ice House, 16
Cheers for Miss Bishop, 250
Chicago, 129, 161, 255n5, 275n19
Chicago Tribune (newspaper), 132
children: censorship and, 160; as target of theater promotions, 105–6, 109
Cinématographe, 28–29, 222, 284n27
circus, 109, 136, 142, 146, 149
Civilization (Ince), 190–91, 193–95
Clark and Rowland, 80, 83, 86, 136, 271n58
Clark Building, 251
Clark, Gertrude, 61

Clark, James B., 55, 61–62, 65, 66, 80, 93, 249–51
class: of audiences, 92–95, 97–98; local films and, 221–22; middle, 95, 166, 174, 222; nickelodeons and, 25–26, 28; in Pittsburgh, 9–10; terminology and, 270n55; theater districts and, 92
clerical workers, 9–10, 93
Coffee, Rabbi Rudolph I., 163
Cohn, Harry, 19
Colonial Theatre, 237
comedies, censorship and, 282n116
commercial entertainment. *See* popular entertainment
community, local films and, 231–35, 238–43, 245–47
Company K of Tenth Infantry Regiment, 232–33, 285n51, 287n1
Connelly, Eugene, 19, 23, 26, 41
Cook, Albert, 137, 271n73
course tickets, 149
Court Theatre, 141
Couvares, Francis, 171, 274n8
Crawford, O. T., 112
Crimson Stain Mystery, 149
Croatians, 9
Crothers, Rachel, 122
Cunard, Grace, 149
curio halls, 26–27
cut-outs, for advertising, 127, 128, 270n49

Darkfeather, Mona, 146
D'Aspe, Mlle., 233
Davin, Miles, Sr., 287n1
Davis, "Ab," 52
Davis Company, 39
Davis, Harry, 16, 18–21, 23, 25–26, 28–31, 33–37, 39–44, 49, 57, 63, 93, 116, 181, 251–53, 259n37
Davis, John, 29
Davis Theater, 15
DeBauche, Leslie Midkiff, 137–38, 142, 144, 190
Demas, G. D., 141
Demas, P. J., 100, *101*
Democratic Party, 190
demonstration banquets, 76, 77, 121
Dennett, Andrea, 27
Denol Chemical Company, 118
Department of Public Safety and Military Authority, 194
department stores, 37
Deutschland, 145
DeVault, Ileen, 9, 93

Diamond Alley, 31
Diamond Street amusement arcade, 42
Dies, Samuel, 17–18
dime museums, 20, 26–27, 33–34, 36, 109, 136
disaster films, local, 238–43
distribution. *See* film distribution; film exchanges
Downey House, Waynesburg, 243
Downey, Mrs. Robinson F., 233
Downs, George, Jr., 131
Dreamland theaters, 46
The Drug Terror, 139, 164
Duquesne Amusement Supply Company, 62, 64–65
Duquesne Gardens, 252
Duquesne Garden Theater, 36
Duquesne Theater, 15

Eagle Theater, 92, 197
"early" cinema, 211, 213
East Carson Street, 91, 92
East End Journal, 53
East Liberty, 9, 91, 93, 100
East Liverpool, Ohio, 209
Eastman Kodak, 67. *See also* Kodak
Eclectic Film Company, 95
Eclipse Moving Picture Theater, Waynesburg, 208, 217–18, *219*, 220–21, 237–38, 284n18
Eden Musee, 33–35
Edison Manufacturing Company, 144, 173, 215
Edison, Thomas, 21–22, 36, 217, 284n27, 286n66
Edison Trust. *See* Motion Picture Patents Company (MPPC)
Educational Film Corporation, 250–51
educational role of movies, 159, 163
Electric Theatre, Los Angeles, 22–23, 258n17
Elite Theatre, 145, 238
The Emergence of Cinema (Musser), 4
Emmel, Mrs. C. C., 5
Empire Theater, 36
The Encyclopedia of Early Cinema (Abel), 263n17
entertainment. *See* popular entertainment
Equitable Motion Picture Corporation vs. Pennsylvania State Board of Censors, 277n46
Erie, 209
Essanay Studios, 63, 69
ethnicity: labor history and, 256n15; settlement patterns based on, 8–10, 91–92
Evaline Theater, 100, 104
exchangemen, xii, 52, 56, 102–3. *See also* film exchanges
Exhibitor (journal), 56

exhibitors: advertising by, 130–36; alternative practices of, 70–71; association of, 102–3, 168, 198, 276n42; audience-attracting strategies of, 110–11, 113–14, 135, 217–18 (*see also* promotions); bureaucratic regulation of, 155–56; and censorship, 168–71, 196–99, 201; community role of, 220–22; diversity of, 100; film industry role of, 171; as filmmakers, 213, 224–28; lectures by, 241–42; *Pittsburgh Moving Picture Bulletin* and, 56; posters used by, 144; and programs, 59, 65, 67, 68–70, 94, 113–15, 171, 217; promotional activities of, 136–41, 145–53; significance of, for film history, 52. *See also* nickelodeons; theaters

Exhibitors' Display Company, 144, 272n95

Exhibitors' League of Pennsylvania, 276n42

Exhibitors' Service Company, xii

exploitation, 109, 149–51

The Exposure of the White Slave Traffic, 163

Fairbanks, Douglas, 250

Famous Players Film Service, 77–78, 123–24, *125*, 175, 180, 270n44, 272n80

Farnum, Dustin, 78

Farr, James M., 186–87

feature films: advertising of, 144; character of, 97–98; costs of, 121; definition of, 113, 121; distribution of, 72–78, 115; film exchanges and, 72, 75–78, 115, 121; promotion of, 97, 120–21; rise of, 1, 75–76, 96–98, 112–13, 115, 227; states' rights distribution system for, 72–74; super/special, 268n16; and World War I, 190

Feature Play, 78

federal government, and censorship, 203

Federal Street, 91, 145

Federation of Women's Clubs, 202

Ferdinand, Archduke, 190

fiction films, 216, 245

Fifth Avenue, 33, 37

film development (chemical), 226, 285n36

film distribution, 57, 66–67, 78, 250. *See also* film exchanges

film exchanges: advertising by, 54, 118–20, 122–24; bargain, 68–72; and censorship, 182, *183*, 199, 201; circulation patterns of, 63; competition among, 62, 76; and feature films, 72, 75–78, 115, 121; film historiography and, 57, 59, 69–70, 263n17; local/non-licensed, 65–66; manufacturers and, 64–65; ownership of films by, 62, 63; in Pittsburgh, xii, 56–57, 59–62, 65–80; *Pittsburgh Moving Picture Bulletin* and, 54, 57, 70, 72, 118–20; programs compiled by, 59, 63, 113; regulation of, 111–12; rental charges by, 63, 69; role of, in film industry, 56–57, 59, 114–15; "the schedule" and, 68, 114–15; standardization of, 115; and states' rights contracts, 72–74. *See also* exchangemen

film historiography: and advertising, 110; and class, 95, 228; and exhibition, 52; and film exchanges, 57, 59, 69–70, 263n17; and film industry development, 112–13, 128; and film types, 210–11; and local history, 6, 52; and nickelodeons, 21, 85–86, 90–91

film industry: and censorship, 157–61, 167–69, 173–81, 202–3, 274n8; division of labor in, 224–25; exhibitors' place in, 171; and exploitation, 150–51; film exchanges' role in, 56–57, 59, 114–15; film historiography and, 112–13; and moral self-regulation, 158, 203–4, 274n8; political influence of, 202; public attitudes toward, 158; standardization of, 65, 78, 109–10, 112, 128, 151, 211; vertical integration of, 78, 110, 251

film manufacturers, 64–65

film production: by exhibitors, 213, 224–28; independent, 64, 67; local, 63–64, 210–48; manufacturers in, 64, 110; and morality, 203–4; pace of, 63, 96–97, 140, 182; regulation of, 66–67, 78, 110. *See also* producers

Film Renters Protective Association, 66

Film Row, 56–57, *58*, 78

film schedule, 66, 68, 115

Film Service Association (FSA), 268n15

film stars: advertisements featuring, 124–29, 131; and morality, 203; and star system, 78, 132

filmmen, 56

films: advertising of specific, 121–22, 132, 144; announcements preceding, 272n81; defining role and purpose of, 86–87, 97–98; differentiation of, 120–21; health concerns about, 107; introduction of, in Pittsburgh, 28–29, 259n37; physical condition of, 111–12; in *Pittsburgh Survey*, 12; popularity of, 87; purchase price of, 113; rental costs of, 63, 69; stage productions as basis for, 78, 97, 98, 122–23. *See also* local films

fire and firefighting, 242–43

First Amendment, 175, 278n68

first-run films, theaters showing only, 269n21

Fisher, Robert, 160

Fleming, George, *Pittsburgh, How to See It*, 14
floating clientele, 93, 266n85
flu, 107
fly-killing campaigns and promotions, 104–7, 108, 109
Foley, J. G., 41, 63, 261n73
The Folks from Way Down East, 76
Forbes Avenue, 56
Forbes Field, 15, 35
Ford, Francis, 149
Ford, Henry, 286n66
foreign films, 72, 77
Fort Pitt Film Company, 62, 66, 139
Fort Pitt Hotel, 112
The Four Horses of the Apocalypse (Metro), 249–50
Fourth Avenue, 57, 58
Fox Studio, 250
Fox Exchange, 186
Fox, William, 97
free speech rights, 168, 175
Freedman v. Maryland, 283n135
freelance cameramen, 139, 237
fronts, theater, 145–46, 149
Fuller-Seeley, Kathryn, 121, 142, 215

Gaines, Jane, 109–10, 150
Gales, Jane, 125
Garden of Allah (Selig), 73
Garrick Theatre, 178
Geertz, Clifford, 232
Gem Theatre, 222
gender: and morality, 165–66. *See also* women
General Film Corporation (GFC), 66–70, 78, 80, 112–13, 115, 181, 249, 269n24, 272n95, 279n87
geography, 8–9, 91–92
Gerwig, Hy, 16
GFC. *See* General Film Corporation
Glyn, Elinor, 186–89, 280n99
Golden Triangle, 9, 16, 37, 38
Goldwyn Picture Corporation, 250
Gomery, Douglas, 23, 24; *Shared Pleasures*, 21
Gompers, Samuel, 159
Gorsek family: Frank, 2; George, 1; Johanna, 2–3; Joseph, 2–3; Joseph, Jr., 2; Marian, 2; Oscar, 2; Stephanie, 1–2; William, 2
Grand Dime Museum, Boston, 26
Grand Moving Picture Theater, 17
Grand Opera House, 15, 31, 32, 33, 36, 42, 46
Graninger, C. A., 83, 84
Great Northern, 75
The Great Train Robbery (Porter), 23, 36, 46, 63

Grieveson, Lee, 28, 273n3; *Policing Cinema*, 156
Griffith (colonel), 194
Griffith, D. W., 250, 283n11; *The Birth of a Nation*, 181; *Intolerance*, 86
Gulick, R. M., 28–29, 30
Gunning, Tom, 20, 229–30, 258n10–11
gutter snipes. *See* snipes

Hansen, Miriam, 211, 241–42
Harris Amusements, 252, 271n58
Harris, Bridget (née Gaughan), 34
Harris, Eleanor (née Davis), 35, 252
Harris, Harry, 42
Harris, John H., 252–53
Harris, John P., 16, 18–21, 23, 25–26, 28–29, 34–36, 39, 41–43, 49, 93, 252–53, 259n37, 261n73, 288n6
Harris, John, Sr., 34–35
Harry Davis Eden Musee, 33–35
Harry Davis Enterprises, 35, 37, 39, 49, 62, 251–52
Harry Davis Exchange, 49
Harry Davis Stock Company, 36
Harry Davis Syndicate, 33
Harry Davis Theater, 99
Hatch, J. Frank, 70–71
Hays, Will, 203–4
Hazelwood, 63
Hearst, William, 25
Henie, Sonja, 252–53
Herring, Max, 116
Hickman, Howard, 191, 193
historiography, 3–6, 18. *See* film historiography
Hodkinson, William W., 120
Hollis-Smith, 57
home movies, 244–46
Homestead, 91
Homestead strike, 7, 256n13
Homestead: The Households of a Mill Town (Byington), 12
Homewood, 149
Homewood Street, 149
Howe, Lyman H., 220
Hubbard, M. L., 164
Hulfish, David, *Motion Picture Work*, 43
hygiene, 107

Ice Capades, 253
immigrants: as exhibitors, 100; in film industry, 19; in industry, 7–8; in Pittsburgh, 3, 7–8; and World War I, 190–95
In the Days of War (Pathé), 1

Ince, Thomas, *Civilization*, 190–91, 193–95
Independent Display Company, 272n95
Independent Film Exchange, 52, 76, 126
Independent Film Protective Organization, 66
Independent Moving Picture Company (IMP), 127
Indians, 146
The Inside of the White Slave Traffic, 163
inspectors, from Pennsylvania State Board of Censors, 184–85
intertitles, 241
Intolerance (Griffith), 86
It, 187
Italians, 9

J. Frank Hatch Film Company, 70–71
Jacobs Bird-House Company, 237, 286n66
Jacobs, J. Warren, 237, 286n66
Jacobs, Lewis, 258n17
John Barleycorn (film), 173–78, 179, 180, 188, 278n66
John Barleycorn (London), 173
Johnson, Ernie, 137
Johnson, Samuel, 279n87
Johnstown, 35, 49
Jones and Laughlin, 8
Jones, Mary, 80
Jones, R. A., 141
The Joseph Horne Company, 37

Kalem Film Company, 146
Kansas, 157
The Kansas Saloon Smashers (Edison), 173
Katz, Joseph, 74
Katzenjammer Kids, 160
Kaufmann's department store, 37, 39
Keil, Charlie, 241, 264n43, 287n72
Keith, Benjamin Franklin, 25, 26
Kellogg, Paul, 6
Kennywood amusement park, 14
Ketcham, W. H., 116
Keystone, 69
Kinetograph Company, 59, 60
Kleine, George, 59
Kodak, 285n37. *See also* Eastman Kodak
Ko-Ko Film Company, 128
Koster and Bial's Music Hall, New York City, 28
Kriterion, 269n24

Laemmle, Carl, 111, 127, 150
Lamont, May, 27
lantern slides. *See* magic lantern slides

Lasky, Jesse, 78, 123
Lawrence, Florence, 127
Lawrenceville, 2–3, 17
lectures connected with films, 241–42
Leight, Sol, 16–17, 19, 46
leisure: harmful, 13; *The Pittsburgh Survey* on, 257n28; varieties of, 13–14, 31; working-class, 17
Leslie, Max, 252
The Libertine, 74
"Liberty Bell" slides, 199
Liberty Film Renting Company, 5, 74–75, 128, 129, 201
The Life of an American Fireman (Porter), 243
limelight, 263n21
liquor industry, 174, 176
Lissman, Hilda, 80
Lithuanians, 9
local films, 63–64, 210–48; as advertising, 139, 234–36; as audience attraction, 217–18; "The Camera" column on, 223–29, 233, 247; camerawork of, 229–31, 239–40, 244–45; character of, 211–12, 214, 230–31; and community, 231–35, 238–43, 245–47; context for understanding, 228–31, 239–41, 245–47; Davis and, 63; of disaster and misfortune, 238–43; exhibitors as makers of, 213; feature-length, 214; film type used in, 246; filmmaker's role in, 230–31; free-lance cameramen and, 237; localness defined by, 231, 245; news and, 227–28; origins of, 215; producer-consumer roles in, 214; production companies and, 215; promotional value of, 22, 215–16, 237; Silveus and, 210, 212–14, 223, 228–35, 237–49, 284n28, 285n51, 286n57, 287n1, 287n71; technological changes and, 222–26; time frame of, 214; varieties of, 214
local history, 3–6, 248–49
Locker, George, 279n87
Loew, Marcus, 19, 250, 258n8
London, Jack, 174, 278n61; *John Barleycorn*, 173
Los Angeles Times (newspaper), 22
Lubin, 160, 173, 178
Luckett, Moya, 161, 266n90, 287n81
Ludwig Hommel Company, 271n73
Lumière Company, 28, 67, 215
Luna Studio, 77
The Lure of New York, 74, 75
Lusitania (ship), 190
Lyric Theater, 146

Macgowan, Kenneth, 21
magic lantern slides, 138–39, 199, 215, 271n77
Mama's Angel (Lubin), 160
Manhattan, movie business in, 92, 93, 100
manufacturers. *See* film manufacturers
Markey, Enid, 191
Marquette, Indiana, 236
Maryland, 157
Mason, "Smiling" Billy, 95
Massachusetts, 27, 202
Masterpiece Film Attractions, 73
Mathis, June, 250
Mayer, Charles, 53–54
Mayer, Louis B., 250
Mayer Publishing and Printing, 53, 87, 127, 128, 142
Mayer, Stanley, 57
Mayer, Stanley D., 253–54
Mayer, William, 53–54, 56, 67–70, 78, 80, 87–89, 94, 96, 99, 102–3, 118–19, 130–31, 198–99, 253–54
McCann, Frank, 33–34, 36–37, 39
McClellan, George B., 158
McClintock, Harriet, 166
McCloskey, William, 146, *148*
McKees Rocks, xi, 91
McKeesport, 35, 42
McKenna, Joseph, 160
mechanical devices in advertising, 145
Méliès Company, 62
Menjoy, Adolph, 34
Menjoy, Albert, 34
Metro Pictures, 144, 249–50, 272n95
Metro-Goldwyn-Mayer (MGM), 250
Michaels and Freeman, 72
middle classes, 95, 166, 174, 222
Millenori, Anita, 26
Minerva Theater, 100
Mintz, David, 100
Mintz, Harry, 100, 104, 109, 249
Miss A., 76, 85, 249; "The Nickel Show," 50–51
Mitchell and Kenyon, 213
Mittenthal Studio, 77
Molzon, Bill, 287n1
The Monte Carlo Girls, 220
Montgomery, Walter C., 233
morality: film industry self-regulation concerning, 158, 203–4, 274n8; gender and, 165–66; movies' influence on, 12–13, 156, 158–63, 165; public, 12–13, 161–62; uplift, 78, 96, 159–60. *See also* censorship

Morals Efficiency Commission, 156, 162–63
Morrisseey, Tom, 26
Motion Picture Board of Trade, 202
Motion Picture Exhibitors' Association of Pennsylvania, 276n42
Motion Picture Exhibitors League, 202
Motion Picture News (journal), 4, 54, 86–87, 89, 94, 96, 98, 105, 130, 135, 140, 155, 196, 197, 218, 223, 269n20. *See also* "The Camera" column in *Motion Picture News*
Motion Picture Patents Company (MPPC) (Edison Trust), 65–68, 75, 85, 112–13, 115, 159–60
Motion Picture Producers and Distributors of America (MPPDA), 158, 167, 203–4
Motion Picture Work (Hulfish), 43
Motography (journal), 4, 98, 115
movie-only theaters, 21–23, 102, 218
movies. *See* films
Movies, Censorship, and the Law (Carmen), 156
Moving Picture Protective Association, 180, 198, 276n42
Moving Picture World (journal), 4, 26, 43, 54, 90, 93, 94, 99, 102, 105, 116, 138, 146, 163, 197, 223, 236, 262n10
MPCC. *See* Motion Picture Patents Company (MPPC) (Edison Trust)
Mrs. Nation and Her Hatchet Brigade (Lubin), 173
Munsey's (magazine), 25
Munsterberg, Hugo, 73
murder, 238–39
Musser, Charles, 21–24, 29, 59, 130, 213, 215, 258n15, 258n17, 261n73, 283n11; *The Emergence of Cinema*, 4
Mutual Film Corporation, 68–69, 167, 269n24
Mutual Film Corporation v. Industrial Commission of Ohio, 180, 201, 279n85, 283n135

Nation, Carry A., 173–74
National Association of the Motion Picture Industry, 202
National Board of Censorship, 159–61, 164, 203
National Board of Review, 181, 202
The Navajo Blanket, 146
Nazimova, Ali, 191
Nealey, William A., 202
Neff, M. A., 171
neighborhood theaters, 12–13, 86, 91–92, 98, 153, 220–21
Neptune's Daughter (Universal), 73
Netter, Leon, 73

New Woman, 165–66
New World Theater, 34
New York, censorship in, 154–55, 157–61, 202. *See also* Manhattan, movie business in
newspapers: advertising in, 130–33, 234–35, 271n58; editorial coverage of movies in, 131; publicity from coverage in, 177–78, 279n75
newsreels, 227–28, 229, 244
Nickelodeon (journal), 16, 49, 98
Nickelodeon (Pittsburgh), 16, 18, 20–21, 25, 29, 36, 39, 41–44, *45*, 46, *48*, 253, 262n82
Nickelodeon (Fitchburg, Massachusetts), 27
nickelodeons: admission charge of, 24–26, 50–53, 83, 85–89, 92–96, 99–100, 102, 265n65, 266n89, 266n92; and class, 25–26, 28; competition among, 49, 62, 95–96, 99–100, 114, 144–45, 236; concept of, 89–90; dual attitude toward, 12–13; end of, 85–86, 89; exhibition culture of, 62; film historiography and, 21, 85–86, 90–91; and get-rich-quick mythology, 43–44; inspection of, 17–18; name of, 26–28; nationwide openings of, 46; Pittsburgh origins of, 4, 18–25, 27–29, 42–43, 253, 261n73, 288n6; *Pittsburgh Survey* description of, 12; popularity of, 18, 49, 88–89; precursors of, 21–23, 26–28, 41; prevalence of, 15; saloons vs., 174; social role of, 12–13. *See also* theaters
nickels: business model based on, 24–26, 39–41; psychological value of, 95, 266n91; purchasing power of, 40; significance of, 25, 40, 95
Niver, Edward Cyrus, 171
Niver, Katherine Anne (Mrs. E. C.), 166, 170–73, 277n51
Nixon Theater, 15, 181
Nordisk Company, 75, 145
North Side, 91
novelty fronts, 145

Oberholtzer, Ellis P., 170, 172–73, 193, *195*, 201, 202, 277n48, 277n51, 278n60
O'Brien, John W., 31
office staff, 9–10. *See also* clerical workers
Ohio, 157
Old Tivoli Garden, 31
Oliver Iron and Steel Mills, 8
Olympic Theater, 88, 100, 136, 264n60
open-air movie shows. *See* airdomes
openers, 74
Opera House, Waynesburg, 218, 220, 284n18, 284n20

pacifism, 190, 194–95
Panopolis, Frank, 146
parades, 233–34
Paramount Pictures Building, 78
Paramount Pictures Corporation, 78, 80, 115, 120–22, 150, 250
Parke, Alexander, 139, 163–64
Pathé Studio Model camera, 223
Pathé-Frères Company, 1, 5, 46, 62, 63, 95, 133, 160
Patria, 190, 194
Pearl Theater, 74
Pearson, Roberta, 92
Peck, Mary Gray, 159
Peg o' the Ring, 149
Penn Avenue, East Liberty, 9, *10*, 16, 93
Penn Poster Mounting Company, 272n95
Pennsylvania Exhibitors League, 170
Pennsylvania General Assembly, 164
Pennsylvania State Board of Censors, 5; application forms for, 182, *183*, 280n90; authority of, 180–81, 204, 275n33, 277n48, 278n68; bulletins published by, 184, 186; and censorship in other states, 201–2; and *Civilization*, 193–95; composition of, 165–66, 170–73, 275n34; disbanding of, 204, 281n114; enforcement operations of, 184–86; exhibitors and, 102, 168; finances of, 196, 201; fines levied by, 196–97; formation of, 143, 156–57, 164–65, 277n51; inspectors of, 184–85; and *John Barleycorn*, 175–78, 180; offices of, 181–82; operations of, 168, 182, 184, 276n45, 279n87; opposition to, 143–44, 155; and *Patria*, 194; seal of approval of, 184, *185*, 196, 280n91; standards of, 166–67, 169–70, 193, 205–7; and *Three Weeks*, 186–89, 281n102; violations of, 185–86; and *War Brides*, 193–95
Pennsylvania Supreme Court, 168, 180, 276n43, 277n48
penny arcades, 41, 43
penny presses, 25
Penrose, Boise, 170, 180, 252
People's Institute, 159
percentage fees, 78
Philadelphia, 168, 178, 181–82, 197, 276n42
Philadelphia Evening Bulletin (newspaper), 176
Photodrama Picture Company, 76
Photoplay Entertainment, 140, 272n81
photoplays, 28, 102, 131, 270n55
Pichel, Edith, 251
Pickford, Mary, 78, 123–24, 250

picture men, 56
Picture Theatre Advertising (Sargent), 105, 138, 177–78, 235, 271n58
Pierce, C. H., 178, 180
Pincus, 128–29, *129*
Pinkerton detectives, 33
Pitt Theater, 131, 200
Pittsburg Gazette (newspaper), 6
Pittsburgh: censorship in, 155–56, 161–64, 181, 197–99, 275n26; districts of, 91; downtown, 38, 91, 93 (*see also* Golden Triangle); geography of, 8–9, 91–92; immigrants in, 3, 7–9; incomes in, 11, 256n13; industry in, 6–8, 10–11; map of (c. 1914), *79*; movies introduced to, 28–29, 259n37; nickelodeon origins in, 4, 18–25, 27–29, 42–43, 253, 261n73, 288n6; population of, 8; public transportation in, 9, 91; real estate speculation and development in, 36–37, 39, 57; region surrounding, 208–9; settlement patterns in, 8–10, 91–92; social context of, 161; social research in, 11–12, 257n28; workforce in, 7
Pittsburgh Chronicle (newspaper), 133
Pittsburgh Commercial Motion Picture Company, *219*, 237
Pittsburgh Cut-Rate Exchange, 62, 66
Pittsburgh Dispatch (newspaper), 28–29, 131
Pittsburgh Herald (newspaper), 53
Pittsburgh Hornets (hockey team), 252
Pittsburgh, How to See It (Fleming), 14–15
Pittsburgh Index (newspaper), 131
Pittsburgh Leader (newspaper), 18
Pittsburgh Moving Picture Bulletin (journal), xiii, 4–5, 50–54, 80, 83, 104, 121, 124, 137, 177, 189, 223, 262n10; and admission prices, 50, 87–89, 96–97, 99–100, 102–3; and advertising, 54, 116, 118–20, 122, 124, 129–30, 141–42; advertising in theaters discussed in, 236–37; and censorship, 143–44, 198–99, 201; circulation of, 54; cover of inaugural, *55*; demise of, 253–54; editorial coverage of, 92, 116, 118, 267n29 (*see also* local emphasis of); establishment of, 53–54, *55*; and film exchanges, 54, 57, 67–70, 72, 74, 76–78, 115, 118–20; free distribution of, 54, 116, 118; goals of, 50, 54, 198; local emphasis of, 5, 50, 56, 116, 208–9; preservation of, 253–54; promotions discussed in, 104, 137–41, 145, 149–53; and temperance, 174
Pittsburgh Pirates (baseball team), 15, 35, 53–54
Pittsburgh Post (newspaper), 17, 39

Pittsburgh Press (newspaper), 37, 131, 133, 177, 253
Pittsburgh Screen Club, 102–3, 198–99
Pittsburgh Sun (newspaper), 43
The Pittsburgh Survey, 11–12, 257n26, 257n28
plays. *See* stage productions, as basis for films
Policing Cinema (Grieveson), 156
Polish Hill, 8, 92
pool halls, 13
popular entertainment, relation of nickelodeons to, 20, 25–27, 40–41, 43, 109, 136, 142
Popular Photoplays Corporation, 264n36
popular price amusements, 25
Porter, Edwin S.: *The Great Train Robbery*, 23, 36, 46, 63; *The Life of an American Fireman*, 243
poster-mounting companies, 144, 272n95
posters, 141–45, 272n86, 275n33
Premier Studio, 77
premiums, for theater admission, 140
The Price of Beauty, 75
A Prince of India, 95
prize days, 141
producers, 132. *See also* film production
Production Code, 158, 167, 204
programs: audience-designed, 98; balanced, 68–69, 114; categories of, 68; daily change of, 113–15, 135, 144; exhibitors and, 59, 65, 67, 68–70, 94, 171, 217; film exchanges' role in compiling, 59, 63, 113; length of, 94–96, 98–99; MMPC and regulation of, 64–67; nature of, 94, 114, 135; new vs. blended, 63, 65; older films in, 63, 94–95
Progressivism: and film industry, 65; and moral influence of movies, 12–13, 156, 158–63, 165–66, 173, 204, 221–22; and Pennsylvania State Board of Censors, 173; and public health, 106–7; and temperance, 173, 180; and women, 166, 172, 195–96
projectionists, 216
projectors, 215–17
promotions: advice on, 105, 138, 150, 220–21; by exhibitors, 136–41, 145–53; exploitation, 150–51; fly-killing, 104–7, 109; local films and, 22, 215–16, 237; local vs. national, 109–11; modern vs. old time, 151–53; newspaper coverage used for, 177–78, 279n75; premiums, 140; prize days, 141; for serials, 149; street-side performances, 146, 149. *See also* advertising
prostitution, 162–63
public health, 107
Pulitzer, Joseph, 25
Purity (American Film Co.), 73

INDEX

297

quid pro quo, advertising and, 70, 131, 141
Quinn, Michael, 72, 97, 121, 269n21
quotidian spectacles, 229

Radio-Keith-Orpheum (RKO), 252
Randall, Richard, *Censorship of the Movies*, 156
Randolph, Kitty, 26
Rappe, Virginia, 203
Rat Catching, 160
Ray, Mike, 116, *117*
real estate speculation and development, 33, 36–37, 39, 57, 251
Regal Amusement Company, 62
Regent Theater, 80, *81–83*, 82–83, 85–86, 90, 93–94, 102, 139, 197, 249
Reid, J., 180–81
Reiss, Jacob, 159
Reliable Feature Film Corporation, 186
Remarques (magazine), 53
Rex Theater, 265n65
Rhodes, Frederic, 163
Ringling Brothers Circus, 142
Robson, William N., 151
Rock, "Professor" William T. "Pop," 22, 258n15
Rockefeller, William, 286n66
Rokoski, Henry, 238
Rokoski, Mrs. (Henry's mother), 238, 287n68
Rolphe, B. A., *The Three of Us*, 122–23
Romeo and Juliet, 144
Rowland, Richard A., 60, 60–62, 65, 66, 80, 93, 249–50
Royal Theater, 92, 94
Royer, Howard, 26, 41–42, 261n73
Rules and Standards, 166–67
run-zone-clearance system, 78
Russell Sage Foundation, 11
Ruthven, H. J., *195*

Saint Paul Cathedral, 63
saloons, 13, 174, 257n31
Sargent, Epes Winthrop, 105–6, 135, 138–40, 142, 145–46, 149–50, 220–21, 268n4; *Building Theatre Patronage*, 138; *Picture Theatre Advertising*, 105, 138, 177–78, 235–36, 271n58
Saturday Evening Post (magazine), 43, 121, 173
Savoy Theater, 187
schemes, 105
Schenley Theater, 144
Sealed Life, 173, 277n46
Selig, William, 64–65, 73, 122
Selig-Polyscope, 132

Seltzer Building, 57, *58*, 67, 73, 78
Seltzer family, 57
Selznick, Lewis, 19, 191, 193, 194, 258n8
Selznick Productions, 57
Serial Film Company, 150
Serialitis, 107, 268n7
serials: advertising of, 132–35; distribution of, 271n69; origins of, 132; promotions for, 149
Shared Pleasures (Gomery), 21
Shattuck, Frank R., 194
The Shielding Shadow, 133, *134*, 135
short films, 97–98, 113, 115, 227, 269n24
Silverman, Mayer, 5, 74–76, *77*, 121, 128, 201, 210
Silveus, Charles, Jr., 248
Silveus, Charlie, 208, 210, 212–14, 217, 220–23, 228–35, 237–49, 284n13, 284n18, 284n28, 285n51, 286n57, 287n1, 287n71
Sinclair, Upton, 278n61
Singer, Ben, 19, 85, 100, 163, 265n63
single-reel films. *See* short films
Slovenes, 2–3
Smashing the Vice Trust, 139, 163–64
Smith, Russell, 80
Smith, William E., 175–78, 180
Smithfield Street, 16, 18, 29, 39, 43, 253
snipes, 149
South Side, 8, 91, 92
special features, 268n16
Specialty Film Company, 188–89
Spectatoritis, 107, 268n7
Square Deal Film Company, 57
stage productions, as basis for films, 78, 97, 98, 122–23
Staiger, Janet, 110, 121, 139, 144, 234, 272n80
Stamp, Shelley, 132–33, 162–63, 246
Stanley Company of America, 251
Stansell, Christine, 166
star system, 78, 132. *See also* film stars
"Stars, Stars, Nothing But Stars," 126
states' rights distribution system, 72–74, 123
steel mills and industry: economics of, 11; geographical location of, 8–9, 37; office staff of, 9–10; offices of, 9, 37; Pittsburgh dominated by, 10–11
Steele, Joseph, 80
Stepanian, Laurie, 36
Stieren Optical Company, 59
Stieren, William E., 59–60
stock posters, 141–44
storefront theaters, origins of, 21–23
Strasser, Susan, 119

street work, 137
street-side performances, 146, 149
Streible, Dan, 227
Strip District, 13, *14*
studio system, 109, 249–50
stunts. *See* promotions
Sullivan, Patrick, 17
Superba Studio, 77
Swat-the-Fly. *See* fly-killing campaigns and promotions
Sweitzer, Andy, 35

Taliaferro, Mabel, 122
Tally, Thomas L., 22, 24, 258n17
"The Tattler," 208–9
taverns. *See* saloons
Taylor, William Desmond, 203
temperance, 173–76
10–20–30 melodramas, 25
Tener, John K., 165, 166, 277n51
Tener, Mrs. J. K., 172
Tess, Gerard "John," 100
"The Nickel Show" (Miss. A.), 50–51
theater owners. *See* exhibitors
theaters: advertising in, 138–39, 234–36; attendance at, 155; audience experience of, 114, 136, 146, 245–47; commerce and shopping near, 93; defining role and purpose of, 86–87, 97–98; demographics of, 91–92; in districts, 91; downtown, 114; fronts of, 145–46, 149; health concerns about, 107; midsize, 218; movie-only, 21–23, 102, 218; neighborhood, 12–13, 86, 91–92, 98, 153, 220–21; patrons of, 9–10; personality of, 218, 220; seating capacity of, 218; size of, 80, 264n60; stock announcements for, 272n81; strictly first-run, 269n21; traveling to attend, 91–93. *See also* exhibitors; nickelodeons
Theatorium, Pittsburgh, 1–3, *2*
Thomas, H. F., 149
The Three of Us (Rolphe), 122–23, *123*
Three Weeks, 186–89, *188, 189,* 281n102
titles, in films, 241
town pictures, 236
trade journals: and admission prices, 96, 99; advertising in, 129; advertising in theaters discussed in, 236; cameras advertised in, 223; and local films, 244; promotion advice in, 138; regional, 56. *See also specific journals by title*
trailers, 139–40, 272n80
trolley system, 9, 91

Trust. *See* Motion Picture Patents Company (MPPC) (Edison Trust)
20,000 Leagues Under the Sea, 73–74

United Artists, 250
United Film Services Protective Association, 112, 268n15
United Kingdom, 213
United Program Service, 77–78
Universal Company, 68–69, 73, 74, 76, 124–25, 126, 150–52, 167, 269n24
Universal Exchange, 209, *210*
Universal Moviegame advertisement, *152*
uplift, moral, 78, 96, 159–60
Uricchio, Bill, 92
U.S. Court of Appeals, 67
U.S. Supreme Court, 157, 180, 201, 204

Valentino, Rudolph, 250
Van Lewen, S., 141, *143*
Variety (journal), 4, 46, 54, 105, 170
vaudeville: automatic, 41, 43; and censorship, 162; family, 25, 27, 36; "features" as originating in, 121; movies and, 27, 29, 59, 215, 216; in Pittsburgh, 91; as popular entertainment, 15, 25, 93; promotional methods of, 136
Vekroff, Perry, 186
venereal disease, 162, 275n23
vice, municipal concern with, 162
Villa, Pancho, 287n1
Vim Comedies, 154–55
Virginia, 157
Vitascope, 21–22, 28, 258n15

The Wages of Sin, 163
Wainwright, Walter, 22
walking matches, 31
War Brides, 190–91, *192,* 193–96
Warner, Albert, 62, 64
Warner Brothers, 77–78, 251, 252, 258n8
Warner, Harry, 19, 62, 64–65, 77–78
Wasburn, W. S., 60
Waynesburg, 208, 210, 212–13, 218, 220–22, 228, 232–35, 237–43, 284n18, 286n57
Waynesburg Republican (newspaper), 212, 235
Weekly Film Review (journal), 56
Weiland Film Company, 76
West View Park amusement park, 14
West Virginia, 174
Western Film Company, 69–71, *71,* 120
Western Pennsylvania Historical Society, 253

Wheeler, E. A., 236–37
Wheeling, West Virginia, 209
White House (saloon), 34
white slave pictures, 163, 205, 275n28
white-collar workers. *See* clerical workers
Wilson, Woodrow, 190, 202, 232
Windt, Martin, 238
Winning His First Case, 76
Wise, Stephen S., 159
Wisecarver, Mrs. T. J., 232–33
The Witching Hour, 73
women: censorship and, 193–96; as film audience, 174; and morality, 165–66; Progressivism and, 166, 172, 195–96
Women's Auxiliary of the County Juvenile Court Association, 172

Women's Christian Temperance Union (WCTU), 175–76, 278n70
World War I, 190–95, 232–33, 285n51, 286n52

Yakabik, Estella, 238
Yakabik, Stella, 238
The Yellow Menace, 150

Zerr, Ben H., 168
Zimmerman, Patricia, 244, 246
Zingo and the White Elephants, 78
Zingo in Africa, 78
Zingo of the Sea, 78
Zingo's War in the Clouds, 78
zone papers, 56
Zukor, Adolph, 19, 78, 80, 258n8